Pottery and Social Dynamics in the Mediterranean and Beyond in Medieval and Post-Medieval Times

Edited by

John Bintliff
Marta Caroscio

BAR International Series 2557
2013

Published in 2016 by
BAR Publishing, Oxford

BAR International Series 2557

Pottery and Social Dynamics in the Mediterranean and Beyond in Medieval and Post-Medieval Times

ISBN 978 1 4073 1178 4

© The editors and contributors severally and the Publisher 2013

The authors' moral rights under the 1988 UK Copyright,
Designs and Patents Act are hereby expressly asserted.

All rights reserved. No part of this work may be copied, reproduced, stored,
sold, distributed, scanned, saved in any form of digital format or transmitted
in any form digitally, without the written permission of the Publisher.

BAR Publishing is the trading name of British Archaeological Reports (Oxford) Ltd.
British Archaeological Reports was first incorporated in 1974 to publish the BAR
Series, International and British. In 1992 Hadrian Books Ltd became part of the BAR
group. This volume was originally published by Archaeopress in conjunction with
British Archaeological Reports (Oxford) Ltd / Hadrian Books Ltd, the Series principal
publisher, in 2013. This present volume is published by BAR Publishing, 2016.

Printed in England

BAR titles are available from:

          BAR Publishing
          122 Banbury Rd, Oxford, OX2 7BP, UK
EMAIL   info@barpublishing.com
PHONE +44 (0)1865 310431
FAX   +44 (0)1865 316916
          www.barpublishing.com

Contents

Introduction iii
John Bintliff and Marta Caroscio

Cooking pots and choices in the medieval Middle East 1
Alison L. Gascoigne

Rural Society in Al-Andalus during the Late Middle Ages. Ceramic Assemblages and Social Dynamics
in Eastern Andalusia 11
Alberto García Porras

Considering a Rural and Household Archaeology of the Byzantine Aegean: The Ceramic Spectrum 25
Athanasios K. Vionis

Poverty and resistance in the material culture of Early Modern rural households in the Aegean 41
John Bintliff

Town centre and minor settlements Cultural and social implications of tableware use during the
late Middle Ages in Florence and its environs 47
Marta Caroscio

Rubbish and the Creation of Urban Landscape. A case study from Medieval Southampton, UK 57
Ben Jervis

Gone Fishing! New dating evidence for the fish trade in the North Sea 73
Derek Hall

French Imported Pottery in Scotland 79
George R. Haggarty

Introduction

John Bintliff and Marta Caroscio

The papers collected here were originally given at a symposium during the European Archaeology Conference at Lake Garda, Italy in 2009. They have been revised and updated for this volume. Medieval and Post-Medieval ceramic studies have now for some decades been in the forefront of the archaeology of those periods, showing not only fascinating interactions with historical sources, in which both disciplines contribute novel information for each other, but also constantly exhibiting original methods and theories for the wider benefit of ceramology and archaeology in general. One thinks of key articles such as Hugo Blake's (1980) on the long-term study of the accessibility of rural populations to finewares of different value as an index of their relative wealth and the efficiency of marketing systems, or of David Gaimster's (1994) use of iconography and other sources to trace changing cultural behaviours such as forms of tableware and eating styles. Even more relevant is the pathfinding, broad examination of new approaches to ceramics in the wide chronological and thematic spread of the papers in Cumberpatch and Blinkhorn's edited volume *Not so much a pot, more a way of life* (1997).

This volume focuses more narrowly on the European Medieval and Post-Medieval eras, but through studies of ceramics it opens up original insights into issues of economic change, social and political relationships, ethnicity and identity, in all of which pottery offers much new information to accompany other kinds of evidence.

Alison Gascoigne opens up a cultural perspective to accompany and modify, but not displace basic economic considerations in our evaluation of the role of different materials from which household containers were made in the Medieval Middle East. Simple cost may have been countered by cultural associations or suitability for particular culinary forms when selecting vessels of ceramic, stone or metal. *Alberto García Porras* brings us a careful study of the ceramics from a Medieval village in Granada, utilizing the excavated architecture as context to subtly bring out differences between rooms, parts of individual farmhouses and between farms in the community, as well as contrasting contemporary urban assemblages with those at this rural site. Insights into functional areas, family size and integration into regional exchange systems are provided. *Athanasios Vionis* brings a new depth to the analysis of ceramic assemblages from Early to High Medieval rural and urban settlements in Greece and Turkey, revealing not only how careful restudy of older collections can alter our historical narrative for the post-Roman 'Dark Ages', but also how rich pottery can be for shedding light on cultural preferences, diet and exchange within rural society. *John Bintliff* uses ceramics, house architecture and dress to trace the variable effects of imperial incorporation and then global capitalism on the rural communities of the Greek Mainland and the Aegean Islands from the Medieval era up to the late 19th century AD. Here despite major influences in a political, economic and cultural sense on peasant life, rural villages find ways to create a sense of local identity and a creative expression of their own self-pride with whatever means they can afford.

Marta Caroscio covers the production and distribution of late Medieval ceramics within Florence and its rural region, comparing and contrasting city, major and minor rural centres as well as varied social contexts. The role of non-ceramic materials such as wooden tableware and metal vessels is raised by complementary research into monastic inventories, creating interpretative issues for archaeologists, comparable to those noted in Alison Gascoigne's Middle Eastern chapter. *Ben Jervis* with a fine-tuned study of ceramic contexts in Medieval Southampton, picks apart different consumption and disposal patterns, as well as social and economic contrasts, to challenge our normal assumptions that most archaeological deposits are undifferentiated 'rubbish'. He argues that different pathways of broken pot and their associated organic finds represent alternative means of creating order in the townscape.

Derek Hall shows how C^{14}, chemical analysis and detailed reanalysis of ceramic contexts can produce important new information on Medieval ceramic history, which in turn adds detail to our knowledge of international trade and fishing in the lands adjoining the North Sea. Finally *George Haggarty* summarizes an impressive project to record imported ceramics coming into Scotland from the Early Medieval up to Post-Medieval times, which not only complements but also corrects the variable documentary record for the history of economy and society in Scotland.

Bibliography

Blake, H. (1980). "Technology, supply or demand?" *Medieval Ceramics* 4: 3-12.
Cumberpatch, C. G. and P. W. Blinkhorn, Eds. (1997). *Not so much a pot, more a way of life*. Oxford, Oxbow.
Gaimster, D. (1994). The archaeology of Post-Medieval society, c. 1450-1750: material culture studies in Britain since the War. *Building on the Past*. B. Vyner. London, The Royal Archaeological Institute: 283-312.

Cooking pots and choices in the medieval Middle East

Alison L. Gascoigne
University of Southampton*

Abstract
Recent research into the form and functionality of pottery has considered ceramic transition as reflecting changes in cultural practice, in particular cooking and/or dining habits. This has raised questions of the choices and motivations behind the acquisition and use of new types of ceramic and associated technologies, which are bound up with issues of identity, lifestyle, acceptance or resistance to change, and so on. This paper considers these issues in relation to ceramic assemblages from the medieval Middle East. No significant changes can be discerned in such assemblages contemporary with the Arab conquests, but major innovation and transition came about through the 9th century, leading to the development of a largely new ceramic corpus. Other changes to the material culture associated with food preparation also occur, in particular the widespread trade of steatite cooking vessels, and the introduction of new foodstuffs. Certain forms of steatite vessel have been described as imitations of bronze cauldrons; additionally, ceramic wares have been described as imitations of steatite vessels. Such descriptions set up a questionable hierarchy of perceived value and quality. This paper will therefore address the relationships between different materials in terms of choices relating to food preparation, value and efficiency, in the light of archaeological and historical evidence for use and distribution.

Keywords: Cooking pots, cuisine, skeuomorphism, innovation, imitation, emulation.

The majority of archaeological pottery studies carried out to date have focussed on ceramics as a chronological indicator, and on the typological categorisation of assemblages. However, increasingly, research in the field has tried to reach the people behind the pots: their lifestyles, social and cultural interactions and responses to changing conditions around them. For example, Joanita Vroom's thought-provoking 2003 publication of the late antique to Ottoman pottery from the Boeotia survey examined formal and functional change in conditions of socio-cultural transition, analysing the ceramic corpus for evidence of different practices within the domestic sphere, in particular cooking and dining habits, rather than merely as a passive indicator of time passing. Such research raises questions of the choices and motivations behind the acquisition and use of innovative types of ceramic and associated technologies, which are bound up with issues of identity, lifestyle, subsistence, acceptance of or resistance to change, and so on. This paper aims to consider these ideas in relation to assemblages from the medieval Islamic world.

The Arab conquests of the Middle East in the mid-7th century resulted in no immediate, significant changes to the ceramic corpus, but widespread innovation and transition came about some 150 years later, leading to the development of a largely new ceramic corpus; as Alan Walmsley explains, 'towards the end of the 8th or early in the 9th century ceramic tastes underwent a sudden and significant transformation, a process recognisable [sic] a cultural 'punctuation point' due to the decisiveness of the stylistic changes involved' (2007, 54). Other changes to the material culture associated with food production also occurred, in particular the widespread trade of steatite cooking vessels northwards from the Hijaz, especially under the 'Abbasids during the 8th to 10th centuries; local industries using similar forms of stone also developed around this time (Walmsley 2007, 68-9; Harrell and Brown 2008; fragments of steatite bowls 'thought to be from Yemen' are recorded from 4th-century contexts at Ayla, becoming more common in the Islamic period: Tomber 2008, 80; Parker 1998, 389). Also perhaps of some significance, although in my view often over-stated, was the introduction of new crops and foodstuffs to the area, and changing traditions of cuisine (Watson 1983; Magness 2010).[1] The developments that took place within the ceramic corpus of the late 8th to early 9th century were thus just one aspect of a much wider cultural shift within Middle Eastern society at this time, which has been associated with the beginnings of widespread conversion to Islam; or more specifically, with social changes resulting from Umayyad cultural and economic reforms, and the diffusion of influences from the 'Abbasid court culture of Iraq, leading to 'growing community involvement in the cultural traditions of a wider Islamic World' (Walmsley 2007, 54, 57, quote on p. 58; see also Bulliet 1979).

It can be seen, then, that the early Islamic period was one of dynamic transition in multiple spheres of activity, and that the development and alteration of the ceramic corpus during this period might tell us a great deal about economic, social, cultural and religious matters, if only we can find a way to interrogate it to this end.

Innovation and imitation in the early Islamic period: cooking pots

Perhaps it is because the 8th to 9th century was such a period of innovation and diversification in Middle Eastern

---
* I would like to thank Matthew Johnson for his ever-helpful comments on a draft of this paper. Needless to say, all errors remain my responsibility.
[1] Andrew Watson's proposed 'Islamic agricultural revolution', has been much critiqued (and much mis-used) since its original publication; it has long needed revisiting in light of more recent archaeological data (see for example Rowley-Conwy 1989; Decker 2009), but there is much of value in it nonetheless.

material culture, that scholars have felt the need to find relationships between new types of artefact, manufactured from various materials. On occasion, this has had the effect of facilitating single-factor explanations of diverse and complex change, by means of allowing multiple new technologies to be connected and discussed under a single heading: an innovation and its imitations. Many examples of such connections can be found, in a diverse range of sources; the examples below focus on cooking vessels:

- '[Steatite] pots were imitations of bronze cauldrons and consisted of lightly curved bottoms and nearly vertical sides. Some of the later examples have vertical fluting on their exterior surfaces, which was another attempt to imitate metal pots' (Harms 1996, 75).
- '[I]mitations of steatite vessels of the 9th century reinforce the probable date of importation of this Arabian artifact' (Whitcomb 1995, 494; referring to imitations in ceramic).
- '[B]lack steatite bowls from the Hijaz in Arabia, dating to the 8th century, have been found as far north as Jerusalem, with black ceramic imitations occurring sporadically across the whole of Palestine' (Wickham 2005, 775).
- 'The stone and imitation stone bowls ... should therefore also be assigned to the 8th and 9th centuries' (Magness 1994, 203; again, 'imitation stone' refers to ceramic).
- '[T]he flat based steatite serving bowls, appealingly decorated with intricate geometric and floral designs, gained sufficient popularity that an imitative form in pottery soon appeared to meet demand at the lower end of the market' (Walmsley 2000, 332; see also 2007, 68-9, which ascribes the growing popularity of decorated steatite vessels 'intended as inexpensive substitutes for metal ones' to 'an expanded educated and merchant group in early Islamic society', whose '[h]ouseholds sought to acquire goods that emulated in function and, to some extent, appearance the high-value consumer goods in precious metals popular among the wealthier levels of society').

The regular assigning of the term 'imitation' in these descriptions is notable, and many more such passages can be found in archaeological publications.[2] Indeed, it can be hard to deny the existence of those features of form and finish that are cited as evidence for an intention by ancient artisans to create an object resembling something characteristically made in a different material, or to provide a visual reference to particular morphological features associated with other industries, a concept sometimes labelled 'skeuomorphism'. Carl Knappett has investigated the connections between skeuomorph and prototype, with the former being an 'icon' or 'index' of the latter (2002, 108-10). These connected relationships are not, Knappett argues, restricted to the objects, but extend to those groups habitually using them, themselves symbolically represented by the vessels they consume. Thus, by these complex chains of mimesis and resemblance, '[i]n its consumption, the skeuomorph becomes an icon of the group that the [prototype] item refers to, but only in the context of its consumption by a group in *emulation* or mimicry of the relationships between another group and its icon' (Harrison 2003, 316). Knappett furthermore notes that the relationship between skeuomorph and prototype, and their associated consumers, is two-way, with imitation/emulation having power over the cultural meanings associated with the original and its social group (2002, 111).

Knappett discusses emulation as the primary explanation of imitation within the sphere of material culture, an idea which has been further investigated by David Hinton within a medieval context (2005). These ideas, especially in combination with terminology such as that in the quotes above, sets up or reinforces a hierarchy of perceived value and quality, with (in the case of our cooking pots) metal above stone, and ceramic, typically, firmly at the bottom. It is unclear to what extent this modern perception, often implied or assumed rather than explicitly stated, reflects any medieval reality.

Sociological approaches to emulation, in particular that taken by Colin Campbell (1987), have exposed the weaknesses of imitative behaviour reflecting aspirations for increased social status as a single-factor explanation for changes in consumptive activity. Campbell argues that the aspiration to a higher social level may be as much connected with a desire for a higher standard of living for its own sake, as with social competition by emulation (1987, 53); those artefacts associated with that higher standard of living are thus desirable not simply because of their connection to a particular social group, but because of their own material and cultural qualities. The acquisition of cooking pots of a particular type is thus something to which people might have aspired for diverse and complex reasons, certainly connected with other reference groups (not necessarily restricted to those further up the social scale) but also with concepts such as 'taste', 'style', and the disparate cultural meanings taken on by artefacts at different times. The extent to which cooking pots can be considered as objects for display – arguably more the case in households at the lower end of the socio-economic scale – surely has implications for the idea of social emulation as an explanation for their appearance. Campbell's argument that '[t]here seems to be no reason ... to assume that private or inconspicuous consumption should be any less culturally meaningful than its public counterpart nor any the less expressive of basic cultural values' (1987, 55) suggests that we should look beyond

---

[2] Vickers, Impey and Allen's volume, entitled *From Silver to Ceramic: the Potter's Debt to Metalwork in the Graeco-Roman, Oriental and Islamic Worlds*, presents ceramics as an almost entirely derivative industry, suggesting that 'their manufacturers followed the rule which seems to have applied in most other cultures and ages, and imitated forms and decorative effects originally created for another medium' (1986, first page of introduction – volume has no page numbers; a similar argument is presented by Vickers and Gill 1994).

emulation to try to understand more fully the motivations behind choices of vessel.

Cooking vessels of various materials are attested for the medieval Middle East both archaeologically and in historical sources, although with inverse frequency. Few metal vessels of the early Islamic period survive as archaeological artefacts, although some are mentioned in inventories such as those found in the Geniza archive (see below). Conversely, ceramic pots are ubiquitous on archaeological sites, but they almost never appear in written records of the period. It is therefore not entirely straightforward to bring comparable evidence to bear upon metal, stone and ceramic cooking pots, in order to elucidate their relationships.

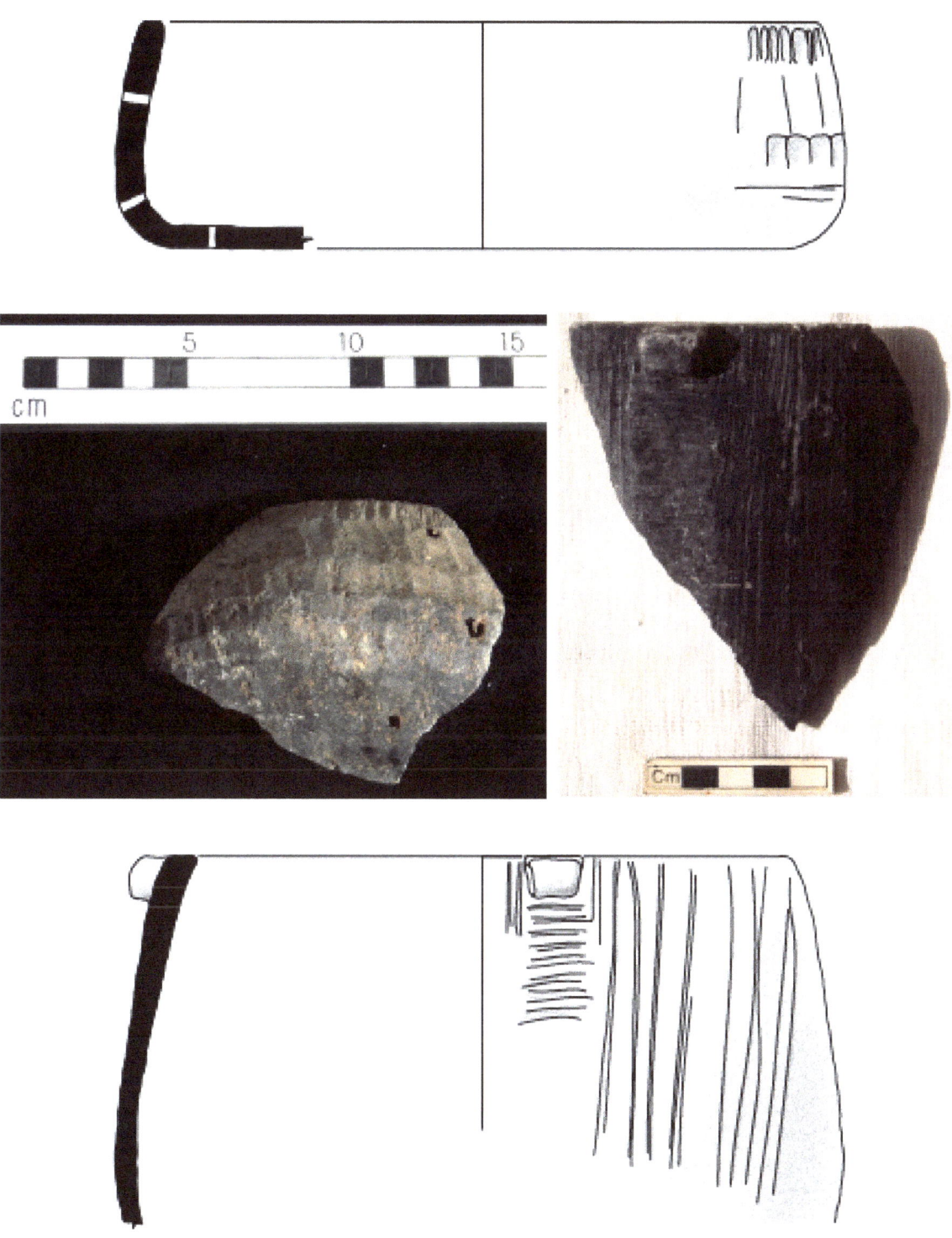

Figure 1 – Two very different forms of stone cooking vessels from the site of Jam in central Afghanistan, both broadly 12th century in date: find number 05/30 (upper drawing and left photograph Ø 19cm) and 05/68 (lower drawing and right photograph Ø 19cm). Photograph from the Minaret of Jam Archaeological Project; drawings, based on MJAP field records, by Elizabeth Postgate.

Metal cooking vessels comprise those made from bronze, copper alloy or copper, sometimes tinned; iron; or lead/lead alloy. Pots were made by various techniques including casting or smelting (primarily lead alloy) or hammering and beating (copper/copper alloy). This diversity of materials and manufacturing techniques, as well as differences in form, must have resulted in products that were distinct from each other, and that had a variety of different properties from the perspective of cooking methods. In light of this, the extent to which 'metal cooking pots' can be regarded as a coherent category in itself must be questioned.

As stated above, few medieval examples of plain, functional metalwork are known from the Middle East, despite numerous published catalogues of outstanding collections of metal 'art' (Allan 1986; 1999; 2002; Fehérvári 1976, *inter alia*). An Umayyad copper vessel from Umm al-Walid, Jordan, was apparently used for boiling and/or serving water (Bujard 2005, fig. 4). Several large copper and copper-alloy cooking pots or cauldrons were found on board the 11th-century Serçe Limanı wreck, and have been demonstrated to have an origin in the Islamic world (Allen, Brill and Bass 2004). A significant hoard of metalwork, dated to *c*. 1100 AD, was found buried in large jars beneath a workshop floor in Tiberias; a number of cooking pots and frying pans were found alongside a series of fancy objects such as candelabras, lamps and incense burners (Hirschfeld *et al*. 2000, fig. 3; Hirschfeld 2007; Khamis and Amir n.d.). The excavations of Nishapur recovered a single bronze frying pan, made of sheet metal (Allan 1982, 49, 89; Allan notes on p. 49 that '[s]uch objects must have been common enough, but, being of thin sheet metal and of no commercial or artistic value, they almost never survive'). The presence of multiple cooking vessels within single assemblages in Tiberias and on the Serçe Limanı wreck is of note, and such vessels were thus, as Allan suggests, presumably considerably more common than their low level of survival would indicate.

Fragments of stone cooking pots (Figure 1), such as those exported from the Hijaz and widespread throughout the Middle East in early Islamic times, are attested in moderate quantities on archaeological sites covering a wide range of time and space. The production of stone cooking vessels is known to have continued until recent times in various parts of the Islamic world, for example in Egypt's eastern desert, in the uplands of northwest Yemen, in northeast Iran and possibly in Afghanistan (Harrell and Brown 2008; Weir 2004/forthcoming; Simpson 2004/forthcoming; personal observation). The antiquity of these industries is rarely clearly understood. Vessels could be lathe-turned or chiselled from metamorphic rock such as steatite, soapstone, softstone, talc-stone, or chlorite/schist, and were sometimes decorated with geometric motifs. The geological properties of stones such as steatite are ideally suited to cooking-pot production: soft and easy to carve, it hardens on contact with heat. More significantly, steatite has good heat resistance and transmission, and resistance to thermal shock (a property also recognised by potters, who at various times would crush and add it as temper to ceramic cooking pots; see for example Ownby *et al*. 2004).[3] More artefactual and petrographic analysis is needed to distinguish the multiple production centres of these artefacts and to clarify their chronology. Steatite cooking vessels often show signs of repair by means of metal rivets or staples, indicating that they held some level of value in the eyes of their users (Figure 1, upper drawing and left photo).

Of course, the most common cooking pots of the medieval Middle East were those made of clay. These were produced in multiple variations: handmade or wheelmade; shallow, open forms in addition to deep, globular vessels with restricted mouths; cut or modelled rims; horizontal or vertical handles, and so on. Some vessels have glazed interiors; some have painted decoration – swags of colour around the exterior wall, or complex geometric designs. Again, they represent a diversity of traditions and culinary applications. Certain specific wares, in particular 'Kerbschnitt' ware, are often described as imitative of steatite vessels (Magness 1994, fig. 4). The primary technological characteristic of clay cooking pots, however, is the use of a fabric mixed with common coarse tempering particles to aid thermal shock resistance, and often reasonably thin walls to facilitate heat transmission (Tite, Kilikoglou and Vekinis 2001).

The price of cooking pots

As argued above, modern archaeologists constructing material hierarchies have tended to assume, perhaps reasonably enough, that metal cooking pots were the most costly to purchase, and ceramic vessels the cheapest, with stone somewhere in the middle. What evidence can we bring to a discussion of the prices of cooking wares during medieval times? Despite lacking a large or detailed body of data, the sources do allow us to gain at least an impression of the contemporary and comparative value of these wares.

The Geniza archive from the Synagogue of Ben Ezra in Old Cairo includes manuscripts which contain trousseau lists, marriage contracts or inventories of household objects or merchants' stock, and these often include lists of utensils, especially copper vessels. However, the interpretation of these data is complicated by our poor understanding of the diverse labels applied to these objects, and their characteristics and presumed variability. Some of the values listed can be quite high, implying fancy vessels – *objets d'art* – for display, or ewers and basins for the washing of guests' hands. Furthermore, the value of metals fluctuated in line with their availability, with much of the Middle East's copper being imported from central and

---

[3] These properties are still recognised: a website selling modern steatite cooking wares from Brazil (http://www.fantes.com/soapstone.html, accessed 20 Jan 2010) lists among other advantages, their suitability for low-fat cooking; that they are virtually non-stick and easy to clean; that they keep an even and constant heat, and preserve food temperature (hot or cold) much longer than metal cookware; that they do not react with acidic foods; have a beautiful appearance; and last for generations. Likewise, steatite cooking ware, or *pietra ollare*, is still used today in north and central Italy (M. Caroscio, personal communication).

western Europe during later medieval times (Ashtor 1971), and we must assume that the cost of raw materials was reflected in the price of finished products. The editor of the Geniza manuscripts, Shelomo Goitein, states that 'pieces of regular kitchenware, such as pots, kettles, and caldrons, were rarely brought in by brides' (1983, 143) – referring to metal pots, kettles and cauldrons as noted in trousseau lists – but some pieces associated with the kitchen are mentioned occasionally in the manuscripts (and there are clearly more of these than Goitein's inevitably abridged synthesis of the diverse Geniza material discusses). Cooking pots worth 2 dinars are inventoried in one 11th- and two 12th-century trousseau lists. Two more trousseau lists, dated *c.* 1170 AD and *c.* 1230 AD, include cooking pots worth 4 dinars, which, as Goitein remarks, is a high price – we might visualise even the cheaper of these as of superior quality to the average purely functional cooking pot (Goitein 1983, 143, 391 n. 32).

Stone cooking pots are mentioned specifically only in one trousseau list: a stone frying pan, paired with one of iron (Goitein 1983, 143, 391 n. 33). No value is given, but the fact that the artefact was considered worth listing is interesting in itself. (Stone jars for storing wheat or water are also occasionally mentioned, for example Goitein 1983, 141, 339.) Clearly stone cooking vessels were not inventoried in the trousseau lists with anything like the frequency of metal vessels, which could indicate either their lower cost and reduced importance, or their greater rarity. Some insight into the comparative monetary values of stone and iron frying pans, however, might be inferred from a letter sent from one Jewish merchant in Aden to another in India, after 1138; this document again ended up in the Geniza archive in Old Cairo. Regarding an order for household objects to be bought and sent to the letter's recipient in India, the Aden-based merchant wrote that: '[y]ou asked me to buy a frying pan of stone in a {lit., 'and its'} case. Later on its case broke {alt. tr.: … pan of stone, and I wrapped it and after I wrapped it, it broke}, whereupon I bought you an iron frying pan for a *niṣâfi*, which is, after all, better than a stone pan {lit., 'more recommended than the stone one'}' (Goitein and Friedman 2008, 600-1; Goitein 1973, 189). There is much of interest in this brief passage. Why was the stone pan no longer useful once the *case* was broken (but see Goitein and Friedman 2008, 601, n. 37 for Friedman's alternative reading in which no case was present)? Why was the iron pan 'better', or for what was it 'more recommended'? Given the lack of detail on the cost of the stone pan, was the higher regard for the iron pan stated in defence of its price, which was not trivial?[4] How would the purchase price of this iron vessel have compared with the bronze example excavated in Nishapur? Clearly we do not as yet have evidence to address these intriguing questions.

Ceramic vessels, according to Goitein, are not commonly listed in the Geniza documents, since 'inexpensive crockery was not brought in by the bride for obvious reasons' (1978, 129). Goitein's suggestion that pottery was not transported by women to new marital homes may overlook the human tendency to prefer familiar things over strange ones, and it seems equally probable that ceramic vessels were simply not included in the inventories, which served an explicitly financial purpose, securing the brides' portion of the household goods in the event of a divorce. The fragility of ceramics, and their generally shorter lifespan than more durable objects, may have been another factor behind their omission from such documents.[5] Indeed, those ceramics that are listed seem in general to be glazed wares, especially Chinese porcelains or other top-end-of-the-market table pieces. For these Goitein does not list values, but Eliyahu Ashtor cites prices from Geniza trousseau lists of ½ to 1 dinar for a porcelain cup, and sometimes as much as 2, 4 or even 5 dinars (1969, 180). However, cheaper and presumably coarser wares are noted occasionally in merchants' correspondence or accounts at much lower prices: 20 bags or bales of pottery cost a single dinar in the second half of the 11th century; in 1229 a pot sold for ¾ to five-eighths of a dirham (= 1/10 of a dinar), on average; while in an unknown year, 130 jugs were valued at five-eighths of a dinar, equal to less than 0.005 of a dinar apiece. Although I have not found any prices specifically associated with cooking pots, two ceramic jugs for the storage of fat (and so presumably fairly unspecial vessels) sold in 1229 for 1½ dirhams (Ashtor 1969, 180).

So although few prices for cooking vessels are easily available, there are far more metal items than ceramics listed in the Geniza documentation. Those prices that we do have support the often-made assumption that basic metal vessels cost considerably more to buy and were worth more in financial terms than basic ceramic ones. Stone is more enigmatic, but it was worth listing on one occasion, indicating either moderate financial value, or perhaps scarcity value.

The culinary value of cooking pots

So much for the monetary value of these different cooking wares. Their prices, we assume, reflected the cost of the materials from which they were made, in addition to the time and skill required to produce them. But the value of artefacts can be measured in multiple ways. To what extent, for example, does the cost of the pots reflect their culinary value? Clearly, cooking pots made of different materials, with a range of associated properties, would have been suited to a variety of culinary techniques. A recent scientific study of schist cooking-pot fragments from 5th- to 13th-century deposits at Merv demonstrated the successful application of absorbed-residue analysis to the vessels (Namdar, Stacey and Simpson 2009); such

---

[4] A *niṣafi* is half a Maliki dinar, equal to a little more than a single Egyptian dinar (Goitein 1973, 182, n. 5; 189, n. 12). The letter writer goes on to detail what he purchased for another *niṣafi*: 68 goblets, 10 bowls and 5 cups, all of glass, with a basket to contain them.

[5] Ethnographic studies have suggested that the average lifespan of regularly used ceramic cooking vessels is a year or two (Shott 1996, 466-7, table 2; Tani and Longacre 1999).

FIGURE 2 – 20TH-CENTURY 'RICE POT' FROM KABUL BUT ACCORDING TO THE SHOP-OWNER ORIGINALLY FROM KANDAHAR.

results may present interesting comparisons with those that might be gained from ceramic vessels, and allow more in-depth analysis of the uses to which each type of cooking-pot was put. In the meantime, we must fall back on ethnographic research, examining contemporary situations where cooking pots of metal, ceramic and even stone are regarded as especially suitable for the preparation of different foods or dishes. James Skibo's work among Kalinga villagers in the Philippines recorded many households where rice is cooked in aluminium pots and vegetables and meat in more traditional ceramic ones (1992). Conversely, in some parts of Afghanistan, thick-walled, heavy, stone pots are labelled 'rice pots', and used accordingly (personal observation: see Figure 2). However, in neither of these cases is it clear that vessel choice is made purely on the basis of efficient matching of culinary task to pot techno-function. In Kalinga households, the metal pots are kept shiny even though this is both hard work, and not advantageous in terms of their culinary performance, since, when hung in prominent positions in the houses, they act as status symbols reflecting the wealth and modernity of the inhabitants (Skibo 1992, 29). Equally, the Afghan 'rice pots' can be carved with elaborate designs and are clearly more than functional objects. This raises the question of the extent to which members of pre-modern societies might have selected cooking vessels on the basis of characteristics other than their technological fitness for the job in hand.

One source that does seem to provide a primarily culinary judgement is Muhammad ibn al-Karim al-Katib al-Baghdadi's *Kitab al-Tabikh* [Book of Cookery], written in Baghdad in 623 AH (1226 AD). Al-Baghdadi offers the following advice on cooking-pot selection: 'Of cooking pots let him [the cook] choose those made of stone, or as a second-best those of earthenware: only as a last resort should he use pots of tinned copper. There is nothing more abominable than food cooked in a copper pot which has lost its tinning' (Rodinson, Arberry and Perry 2001, 38). Al-Baghdadi thus sets up a four-tier hierarchy with stone at the top, followed by ceramic. Even well maintained metal pots are considered barely adequate, and poorly maintained ones quite unusable (not least because food prepared in untinned copper vessels can endanger health). One suspects that al-Baghdadi might have approved of Skibo and Schiffer's view that archaeologists fail to appreciate adequately the qualities and technological complexities of ceramic cooking pots (1995, 82-3); that

Pot type	Views of archaeologists	Medieval financial value	Culinary value
Copper alloy[1]	Highest status	Fairly expensive	Worst
Stone	Medium status	Unclear (no data)	Best
Ceramic	Lowest status	Cheap	Good

[1] It remains unclear where iron vessels should be placed in most or all of these categories.

FIGURE 3 – SUMMARY OF THE VALUES OF DIFFERENT COOKING WARES WITHIN DIFFERENT SPHERES.

the very characteristics that make such pots ugly and unappealing in some eyes also make them fit for purpose, and that ceramic cooking pots represent significant skill in their production.[6]

Al-Baghdadi's is not the only extant culinary work that sheds light on cooking-pot choices in the medieval Middle East. The elite cuisine of Baghdad was recorded in detail, probably in the 940s or 50s AD, by Ibn Sayyar al-Warraq in his *Kitab al-Tabikh*, a detailed treatise on cooking, containing many recipes and much information on utensils, oven types and culinary processes (Nasrallah 2007; see also Ozaki 2010 for discussion of this and other relevant sources). Al-Warraq emphasises that the best cooking pot is one that has been well cleaned, using clay smeared on the walls to draw out oils from previous uses, preventing 'greasy odors' from contaminating the next meal; a final rinse with parsley is also recommended. Cleaning with clay needed to be repeated multiple times before the pot was considered acceptable, and was particularly necessary for soapstone vessels (and perhaps ceramic ones). Al-Warraq furthermore notes the need to replace 'Meccan soapstone pots' quite often, since, once cracked, broken, patched or fixed, they were impossible to keep clean (Nasrallah 2007, 81-2). For the authors of two culinary treatises from 13th-century al-Andalus, cleanliness dictated that ceramic cooking pots in the kitchens of the rich should be replaced frequently, ideally even after a single use, although if interiors were glazed, then their use up to five times was acceptable. However even at this elite level, it is acknowledged that such disposability may not be practical, and instructions on the regular washing of pots with hot water and bran follow (Marín 2002 [1996], 293). At anything other than the highest economic level, it seems very unlikely that such profligacy was generally practised.[7] Tin-lined pots are also regarded as difficult to keep clean and tending to spoil food flavour as a result (Nasrallah 2007, 85).

Al-Warraq ascribes value to different types of cooking pot in a more nuanced way than al-Baghdadi, matching vessels to dishes and/or cooking processes rather than simply ranking pots of different materials in preferential order. According to al-Warraq, soapstone pots are best for cooking meat, soups, and for dishes baked or simmered in a *tannur* oven, while soapstone frying pans are most suitable for omelettes and rounded soapstone pans for stir-fried dishes. Ceramic vessels are good for baking in the *tannur*, since they have already been fired and retain their properties as a result; copper is contrasted as a bad material for such a means of cooking, and food left standing in metal vessels of any type will quickly spoil. Brass vessels are recommended for certain puddings involving large amounts of oil, and for deep frying (fritters) on a low heat (Nasrallah 2007, 85-6).[8] There is also an element of practicality in choice of vessel: porridges should be cooked in tin-lined copper pots, not because these are better than stone ones in culinary terms but because the dish needs to be vigorously beaten, which might cause the latter type of container to break. An additional factor in the coupling of vessel material and dish, according to al-Warraq, is their Galenic humoural relationships: fish are best when fried in an iron pan 'because both of them are cool and fire and oil are hot. Mixing the two will result in a happy medium of balanced properties.' Al-Warraq immediately goes on to discuss the heat-transmission characteristics of the iron pan, and the way in which it crisps the fish skin; clearly, humours were considered an integral part of vessel functionality (Nasrallah 2007, 85). The emphasis on stone vessels in al-Warraq's writings, and the limitations he ascribes to copper, brass and even iron vessels, would indicate that his views might broadly concur with al-Baghdadi's less detailed statement of his cooking-pot preferences.

So which pot is best?

The purpose of this paper has been to flag up the hierarchy of value attributed to cooking pots by archaeologists, which is based primarily on modern perceptions of the importance of monetary worth as reflecting social status (arguably rooted in a capitalist mindset), as dominating other possible valuable qualities (see Figure 3). Perhaps particularly in our post-colonial era, this needs to be revisited. Stone and ceramic cooking pots were clearly

---

[6] Al-Baghdadi also provides interesting guidance on how to protect stone pots in the event of culinary mishap such as boiling over: apparently the cook should stick dampened sheets of paper to the vessel's exterior surfaces (Rodinson, Arberry and Perry 2001, 304).

[7] The height of the social strata to which these Andalusi works relate is emphasised by their recommendation of gold and silver vessels for cooking (Marín 2002 [1996], 292).

[8] Al-Warraq's translator even describes a dish of sparrows, chickpeas and vegetables simmered very slowly and gently throughout a drinking session, in a *glass* cooking pot, to provide snacks for the drinkers but more importantly to amuse the onlookers with the bobbing up-and-down of the sparrows in the boiling water (Nasrallah 2007, 692). Glass cooking pots also appear in a recipe for brains (Marín 2002 [1996], 293). These vessels were clearly used for their novelty value rather than for their culinary practicality.

regarded much more highly than metal vessels by at least a few cooks in the medieval Middle East, and matching the appropriate utensil to the planned dish or cooking method was of considerable importance. We must therefore aim for a more nuanced interpretation of 'value', in light of the multiple factors behind the selection of one pot over another.

Functionality is one factor behind choices of cooking wares in the medieval Middle East, but it seems likely that there were others too: the affordability of the pots; the status, identity, tastes and attitudes of the purchasers and/or users. We can only speculate about associations that *might* have become attached to certain types of pot, since these are difficult or impossible to demonstrate. Steatite, for example, in the immediate post-conquest period, was exported from the Arab-Muslim heartlands in the Hijaz, an origin perhaps having different implications for expressions of identity within particular religious communities, or reflecting the various socio-economic networks within the region (see Northedge 2012 for a possible example of this in the Amman Citadel). Equally, Harrell and Brown's steatite industries in Egypt, flourishing in the 15th century (when the wares were exported outside Egypt) and still functioning into the 19th century, were apparently associated with Eastern Desert nomadic groups such as the Ababda, with whom the Nile Valley inhabitants have traditionally had a somewhat antagonistic relationship (2008). How far any such associations were held by, and travelled with, the pots, is unknown, and it is doubtful that we shall ever be able to shed light on this. We should consider, though, that medieval cooking wares might have shared the sort of resonances that we connect with their modern counterparts, for example brands such as Le Creuset, which arguably has particular class and/ or lifestyle associations in modern Britain. Equally, our modern choices in the culinary sphere reflect different attitudes as well as abilities in the kitchen: some regard stainless steel pans as superior, while others prefer to cook in pans with a non-stick coating; some will disregard superficial qualities such as colour or style, while for others this might be important in dictating an acquision. There is no reason why the choices of cooking pots in the medieval Middle East could not have been dictated by similarly complex factors.

As archaeologists, then, I would argue that we need to leave aside our hierarchy of assumed values, and instead to think about how we might unpick what lay behind the selection of such vessels during the medieval period. Valuable approaches to this complex issue might include a consideration of the processes of food preparation and consumption, and their social meaning within the diverse communities of the medieval Middle East. An interrogation to this end of a diverse dataset of well contexted material, with increased application of techniques such as residue analysis, might also provide insights. Clearly, significant further research will be required before we can start to distinguish between culinary choice (what produces the best food) and social choice (what best suits the lifestyle the owner has or wishes to project). Nonetheless, when asking the question 'which pot is best?' or 'which pot is worth more?' we need to make it explicit what exactly we are asking.

Bibliography

Allan, J. W. 1982. *Nishapur: Metalwork of the early Islamic period*. New York, Metropolitan Museum of Art.

Allan, J. W. 1986. *Metalwork of the Islamic World: the Aron Collection*. London, Sotheby's.

Allan, J. W. 1999. *Islamic Metalwork: the Nuhad Es-Said Collection*. London, Philip Wilson.

Allan, J. W. 2002. *Metalwork Treasures from the Islamic Courts*. Doha/London, Museum of Islamic Art/Islamic Art Society.

Allen, J. W., Brill, R. H. and Bass, G. F. 2004. Metal vessels. In G. F. Bass, J. W. Allan, J. R. Steffy and S. Matthews (eds), *Serçe Limanı: the ship and its anchorage, crew and passengers*, 344-360. College Station, TX, Texas A&M University Press.

Ashtor, E. 1969. *Histoire des Prix et des Salaires dans l'Orient Médiéval*. Paris, S. E. V. P. E. N.

Ashtor, E. 1971. *Les Métaux Précieux et la Balance des Payements du Proche-Orient à la Basse Époque*. Paris, S. E. V. P. E. N.

Bujard, J. 2005. Les objets métalliques d'Umm al-Walid (Jordanie). *Antiquité tardive: revue internationale d'histoire et d'archéologie (IVe - VIIIe s.)* 13, 135-140.

Bulliet, R. 1979. *Conversion to Islam in the Medieval Period: an essay in quantitative history*. Cambridge MA, Harvard University Press.

Campbell, C. 1987. *The Romantic Ethic and the Spirit of Modern Consumerism*. Oxford, Blackwell.

Decker, M. 2009. Plants and progress: Rethinking the Islamic agricultural revolution, *Journal of World History* 20.2, 187-206.

Fehérvári, G. 1976. *Islamic Metalwork of the eighth to the fifteenth century in the Keir Collection*. London, Faber and Faber.

Goitein, S. D. 1973. *Letters of Medieval Jewish Traders*. Princeton, NJ, Princeton University Press.

Goitein, S. D. 1978. *A Mediterranean Society: The Jewish Communities of the Arab World as Portrayed in the Documents of the Cairo Geniza, volume 3: The Family*. Berkeley/Los Angeles/London, University of California Press.

Goitein, S. D. 1983. *A Mediterranean Society: The Jewish Communities of the Arab World as Portrayed in the Documents of the Cairo Geniza, volume 4: Daily Life*. Berkeley/Los Angeles/London, University of California Press.

Goitein, S. D. and Friedman, M. A. 2008. *India Traders of the Middle Ages: Documents from the Cairo Geniza ('India Book')*. Leiden/Boston, Brill.

Harms, W. H., 1996. Aqaba. In T. Ring, K. A. Berney, R. M. Salkin, S. La Boda, N. Watson and P. Schellinger (eds), *The International Dictionary of Historic Places*, vol. 4, 72-75. London, Taylor and Francis.

Harrell, J. A. and Brown, V. M. 2008. Discovery of a medieval Islamic industry for steatite cooking vessels in Egypt's Eastern Desert. In Y. M. Rowan and J. R. Ebeling (eds), *New Approaches to Old Stones: Recent Studies of Ground Stone Artifacts*, 41-65. London/Oakville, Equinox Publishing Ltd.

Harrison, R. 2003. The magical virtue of these sharp things: colonialism, mimesis and knapped bottle glass artefacts in Australia, *Journal of Material Culture* 8.3, 311-336.

Hinton, D. A. 2005. *Gold and Gilt, Pots and Pins: People and Possessions in Medieval Britain*. Oxford, Oxford University Press.

Hirschfeld, Y. 2007. Post-Roman Tiberias: between East and West. In J. Henning (ed.), *Post-Roman Towns, Trade and Settlement in Europe and Byzantium vol. 2: Byzantium, Pliska, and the Balkans*, 193-206. Berlin/New York, Walter de Gruyter.

Hirschfeld, Y., Gutfeld, O., Khamis, E. and Amir, R. 2000. A hoard of Fatimid bronze vessels from Tiberias, *Al-Usur al-Wusta* 12.1, 1-7, 27.

Khamis, E. and Amir, R. (n.d.), *The bronze hoard from Tiberias*, available online from http://micro5.mscc.huji.ac.il/%7Emsjan/hoard.html (accessed 10 Feb 2010).

Knappett, C. 2002. Photographs, skeuomorphs and marionettes: some thoughts on mind, agency and object, *Journal of Material Culture* 7.1, 97-117.

Magness, J. 1994. The dating of the black ceramic bowl with a depiction of the torah shrine from Nabratein, *Levant* 26, 199-206.

Magness, J. 2010. Early Islamic pottery: a revolution in diet and dining habits?, S. R. Steadman and J. C. Ross (eds), *Agency and Identity in the Ancient Near East: New Paths Forward*, 117-126. London, Equinox Publishing Ltd.

Marín, M. 2002 [1996], Pots and fire: the cooking processes in the cookbooks of al-Andalus and the Maghreb. In D. Waines (ed.), *Patterns of Everyday Life*, 289-302. Aldershot, Ashgate Variorum.

Namdar, D., Stacey, R. J. and Simpson, St J. 2009. First results on thermally induced porosity in chlorite cooking vessels from Merv (Turkmenistan) and implications for the formation and preservation of archaeological lipid residues, *Journal of Archaeological Science* 36.11, 2507-2516.

Nasrallah, N. (tr.) 2007. *Annals of the Caliphs' Kitchens: Ibn Sayyār al-Warrāq's Tenth-Century Baghdadi Cookbook*. Leiden/Boston, Brill.

Northedge, A. 2012. The contents of the first Muslim houses: Thoughts about the assemblages from the Amman Citadel. In R. Matthews, J. Curtis, M. Seymour, A. Fletcher, A. Gascoigne, C. Glatz, St J. Simpson, H. Taylor, J. Tubb and R. Chapman (eds), *Proceedings of the 7th International Congress on the Archaeology of the Ancient Near East*, Wiesbaden, Harrassowitz Verlag, 633-659.

Ownby, M. F., Ownby C. L. and Miksa, E. J., 2004. Use of scanning electron microscopy to characterize schist as a temper in Hohokam pottery, *Journal of Archaeological Science* 31.1, 31-38.

Ozaki, K., 2010. Medieval Islamic pots and pans: their uses as described in contemporary sources on dietetics and cooking, In M. Kawatoko and Y. Shindo (eds), *Artifacts of the Medieval Islamic Period excavated in al-Fustat, Egypt*, 51-65. Tokyo, Research Center for Islamic Area Studies, Waseda University.

Parker, S. T. 1998. The Roman 'Aqaba project: the 1996 campaign, *Annual of the Department of Antiquities of Jordan* 42, 375-394.

Rodinson, M., Arberry, A. J. and Perry, C. 2001. *Medieval Arab Cookery*. Totnes, Prospect Books.

Rowley-Conwy, P. 1989. Nubia AD 0-550 and the 'Islamic' agricultural revolution: preliminary botanical evidence from Qasr Ibrim, Egyptian Nubia, *Archéologie du Nil Moyen* 3, 131-138.

Shott, M. J., 1996. Mortal pots: On use life and vessel size in the formation of ceramic assemblages, *American Antiquity* 61.3, 463-482.

Simpson, St J., 2004/forthcoming. Changing patterns of manufacture and circulation from Kush to Merv in the Sasanian and Islamic periods, abstract for 2004 conference, *Softstone in Arabian and Iran*, available online (http://www.britishmuseum.org/pdf/Softstone%20in%20Arabia.pdf, accessed 10 Feb 2010); publication forthcoming in Society for Arabian Studies monograph series, edited by Carl Phillips and St John Simpson.

Skibo, J. M., 1992. *Pottery Function: a Use-Alteration Perspective*. New York, Plenum Press.

Skibo, J. M. and Schiffer, M. B., 1995. The clay cooking pot: an exploration of women's technology. In J. M. Skibo, A. E. Nielsen and W. H. Walker (eds), *Expanding Archaeology*, 80-91. Salt lake City, University of Utah Press.

Tani, M. and Longacre, W. A., 1999. On methods of measuring ceramic uselife: a revision of the uselife estimates of cooking vessels among the Kalinga, Philippines, *American Antiquity* 64.2, 299-308.

Tite, M. S., Kilikoglou, V. and Vekinis, G. 2001. Strength, toughness and thermal shock resistance of ancient ceramics, and their influence on technological choice, *Archaeometry* 43.3, 301-324.

Tomber, R. 2008. *Indo-Roman Trade: from pots to pepper*. London, Duckworth Debates in Archaeology.

Vickers, M. and Gill, D. 1994. *Artful Crafts: Ancient Greek Silverware and Pottery*. Oxford, Clarendon Press.

Vickers, M., Impey, O. and Allan, J. 1986. *From Silver to Ceramic: the Potter's Debt to Metalwork in the Graeco-Roman, Oriental and Islamic Worlds*. Oxford, Ashmolean Museum.

Vroom, J. 2003. *After Antiquity: Ceramics and Society in the Aegean from the 7th to the 20th century AD*. Leiden, Faculty of Archaeology, Leiden University.

Walmsley, A. 2000. Production, trade and regional exchange in the Islamic east Mediterranean: old structures, new systems?. In I. L. Hansen and C. Wickham (eds), *The Long Eighth Century: Production, Distribution and Demand*, 265-343. Leiden, Brill.

Walmsley, A. 2007. *Early Islamic Syria: an archaeological assessment.* London, Duckworth Debates in Archaeology.

Watson, A. M. 1983. *Agricultural innovation in the early Islamic world: the diffusion of crops and farming techniques 700-1100.* Cambridge, Cambridge University Press.

Weir, S. 2004/forthcoming. Contemporary stone work in the Yemen Highlands, abstract for 2004 conference, *Softstone in Arabian and Iran*, available online (http://www.britishmuseum.org/pdf/Softstone%20in%20Arabia.pdf, accessed 10 Feb 2010); publication forthcoming in Society for Arabian Studies monograph series, edited by Carl Phillips and St John Simpson.

Wickham, C. 2005. *Framing the Early Middle Ages: Europe and the Mediterranean, 400-800.* Oxford, Oxford University Press.

Whitcomb, D. 1995. Islam and the Socio-Cultural Transition of Palestine – Early Islamic Period (638-1099 CE). In T. E. Levy (ed.), *The Archaeology of Society in the Holy Land*, 488-501. London, Continuum International Publishing Group.

Rural Society in Al-Andalus during the Late Middle Ages.
Ceramic Assemblages and Social Dynamics in Eastern Andalusia

Alberto García Porras
Universidad de Granada

Abstract

The fortified medieval village known as "El Castillejo" (Los Guájares, Granada, Spain) shows specific archaeological features that make possible our undertaking different kinds of analysis from a variety of viewpoints. For example, it is possible to compare qualitative and quantitative data on sherd assemblages with the features of the buildings they where recovered in.

Keywords: Fortified Settlement, Andalusí House, Ceramics (13th-14th century)

1. Introduction

The settlement known as *El Castillejo de Los Guájares* (Granada) (Figure 1), is located in the mid Toba river valley, opposite to Guájar Faragüit but very close to it and above Guájar Fondón, on a cliff about 400 metres on the sea level (M.T.N.E., E. 1/25.000, hoja 1.041–IV, Los Guájares; $4_{4.730}/ 4_{07.701}$).

Several excavations have taken place during the last few decades. A wide area in the inner part of the settlement was excavated.[1] As a result, quite a few papers and essays have been published so far. These works discuss different points, including the relationship between this site and the regional settlement system it was part of. Furthermore, the building techniques used, the settlement patterns and the features of private and public buildings have been analysed (Barceló *et al.* 1987; Bertrand *et al.* 1990; Cressier, Malpica and Rosselló 1987; Malpica *et al.* 1986).[2] The ceramic sherds recovered during the excavations have been also studied and published (Cressier, Riera and Rosselló 1986). My PhD dissertation, defended a few years ago, included a detailed study of the pottery recovered during the numerous archaeological excavations undertaken on the site during the last two decades. When the research was still at an early stage, it was clear that in order to get reliable results there should be a rigorous approach. To get a complete understanding of the context the assemblage should be studied as a whole, analysing the features of the ceramics recovered and their relationship with the type of house the sherds were found in (García 2001). Actually, thanks to this approach it was possible to achieve results leading to a broader understanding of the context. As we have pointed out in earlier works (García 2002), this kind of research provides information not strictly related to ceramics in themselves.

Because of its unique features, "El Castillejo" can be regarded as a *unicum* and analysed as a case study. Usually, this is not the case for settlements dating to the same period. This paper aims to provide a complete analysis of these features that can be summarised as follows:

- Patterns related to building techniques, layout and spatial organisation of the settlement.
- A closed context showing minimal post-depositional alteration and perturbation
- The layers corresponding to the phase when the village was deserted show clear signs as to how the settlement was inhabited. We are talking about ceramic sherds that were recovered *in situ* and in a closed context as the settlement was abandoned.
- The pottery recovered shows homogeneous features concerning shapes and the technical devices used in making it.

Thanks to an integrated analysis of the settlement and of the archaeological assemblage, it was possible to reconstruct social aspects and the daily life of the community living in the village.

2. El Castillejo, a fortified settlement

This settlement was defended by walls with three small squared towers, delimiting an oval area (120x 130 m) oriented W-E that fitted the irregular shape of a hilltop (Figure 2). The main gate was located on the western edge of the enclosure. There was, actually, only one access to the settlement: a bent entrance with a side bastion, erected for guarding and defending the village. The space inside the walls is not divided into different areas: there are houses as well as other buildings, like a cistern for communal use that is joined to the inner side of the southern wall. All the buildings are, in fact, made of extremely thick lime and with a stone foundation, following the technique used for building mud walls. The use of this building technique exclusively, conveys to the settlement an extremely uniform aspect. There was a pond and a hydraulic system just outside the walls, but it does not seem that these structures were related to the water supply system existing inside the village.

El Castillejo can be defined as a fortified settlement, more precisely as a 'fortified village'. Thanks to the archaeological excavations it was possible to ascertain the

---

[1] Four archaeological excavations were undertaken in 1985, 1986, 1987 and 1989 as part of a research project directed by Antonio Malpica Cuello. Further research was carried on at different times during the same period.
[2] The bibliography quoted does not pretend to be a full list of all publications on *El Castillejo*, but includes the most important ones.

FIGURE 1 – *EL CASTILLEJO* PICTURED FROM THE EASTERN EDGE OF THE SETTLEMENT.

number of houses present in the settlement and that all of them were built inside the same enclosure. Even though *El Castillejo* can be defined as a village, it was fortified in the same way as some castles in Andalusia. The walls, the towers and the bastion are a clear sign that the site needed to be defended.

As far as we know, *El Castillejo* was inhabited between the late 12th and the beginning of the 14th centuries, at a time when the Almohad kingdom was playing an important role in the Iberian Peninsula. The major development of the settlement took place at that time. Nevertheless, it was still inhabited when the Nasrid kingdom was established in Granada during the second half of the 13th century. The analysis of the ceramic sherds recovered suggests that *El Castillejo* was abandoned between the end of the 13th and the beginning of the 14th century. The settlement was abandoned at once, but there is no sign of a catastrophic event: neither ash layers as a consequence of a fire, nor evidence that the buildings fell down abruptly. Apparently, there is no sign of a fight but, truth be told, we do not know why the village was abandoned. The inhabitants left behind all their belongings.

Nevertheless, a few centuries later this site recovered its original function; in fact, it was used again as a fortified settlement during the 16th century, but it was not inhabited any longer on a permanent basis. The chronicle of Luís del Mármol Carvajal mentions this phase: '*Pasando el rio, caminó la gente toda en sus ordenanzas, y llegando á Guájar del Fondon, donde se veian las reliquias del incendio que los herejes habian hecho en la iglesia cuando mataron á don Juan Zapata, hallaron el lugar desamparado, aunque tenia un sitio fuerte donde se pudieran defender los moradores*' (Mármol 1946, 245).[3] This account has been confirmed by archaeological evidence (García 1995).

2.1 Houses in 'El Castillejo'

At first sight the farming settlement *El Castillejo* shows an extremely heterogeneous structure. The plan of the buildings could easily be recognised even before undertaking the excavation. Only one street crossed the settlement from east to west, reaching the edges of the hilltop. It divides the site into two areas: the south and the north. This street coincides with the crest of the hilltop.

Even though all the buildings show similar features, not all of them can be considered as houses or mansions. There are a few with two or three parallels naves that can be regarded as a distinguished feature. Possibly, these buildings were not part of the residential area; in fact, only a few ceramic sherds were recovered inside them. They have been interpreted as structures for communal use, probably storage places or stables, but their function is not yet clear. The analysis of the ceramic assemblages

---

[3] "They crossed the river and everyone walked orderly; when they reached Guájar Fondon they could see the signs of the fire put by the heretics when Juan Zapada was killed. The site was clearly abandoned but there were still some fortified structures that made it possible to defend it".

FIGURE 2 – OVERVIEW MAP OF THE FORTIFIED SETTLEMENT *EL CASTILLEJO* (CASA = HOUSE; MURO DE TAPIAL = MUD WALLS; BARRO COCIDO = FIRED MUD; MURALLA = TOWN WALLS; ALJIBE = CISTERN; ESTRUCTURA DEFENSIVA = DEFENSIVE STRUCTURE).

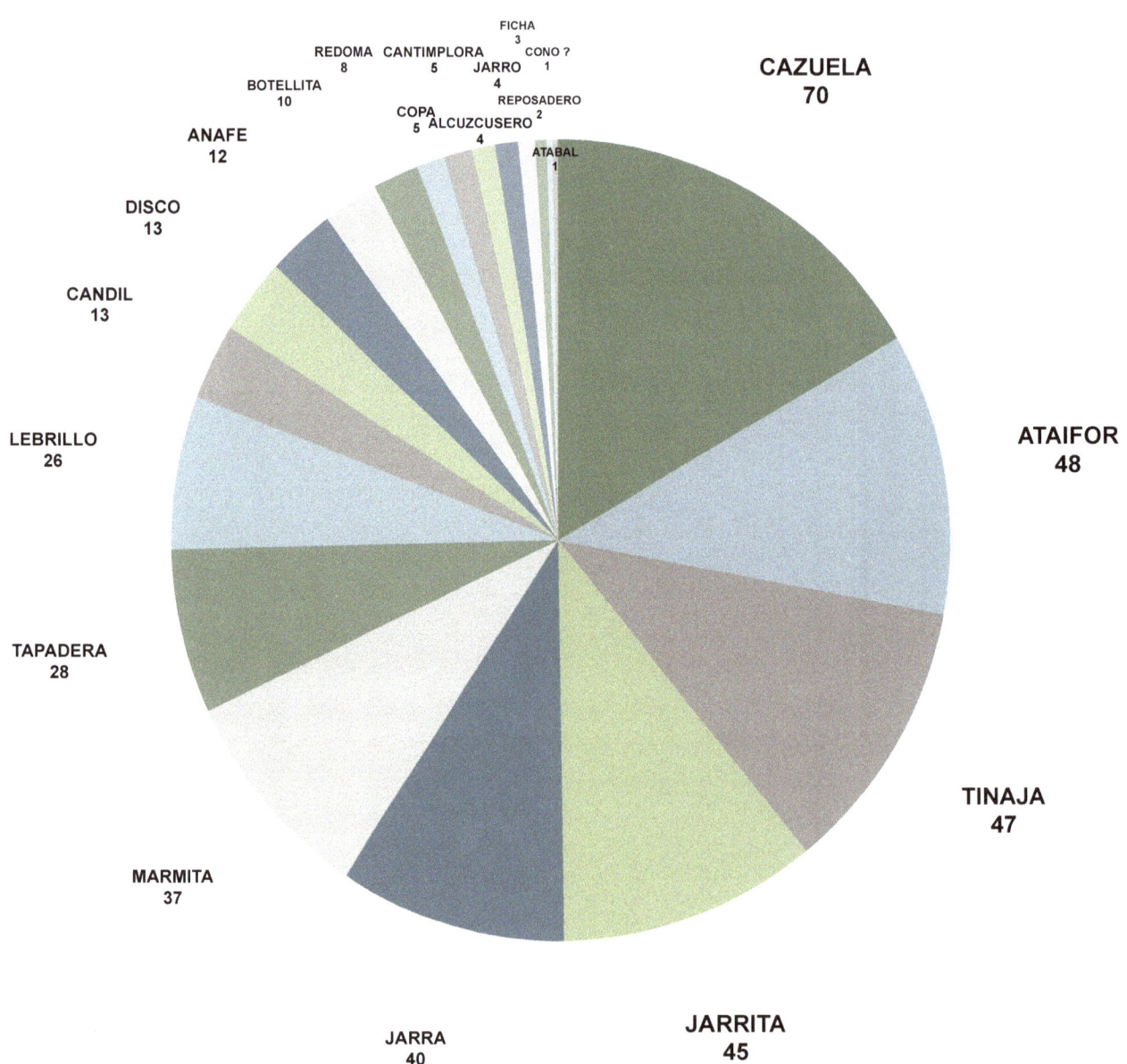

Figure 3 – Ceramics types recovered in *El Castillejo* (cazuela = casserole; marmita = saucepan; cuscusera = pan for cooking couscous; jarra = jug; tinaja = earthenware storage jar; cono de azucar = sugar cone; lebrillo = washbasin; candil = oil lamp; anafe = portable stove; ataifor = tray; jarrita = small jug; jarro = pitcher; copa = cup; botellita = small bottle; redoma = cruet; atabal = small drum; cantimplora = water bottle; tapadera = lid; reposadero = support).

recovered in the areas interpreted as public buildings shows that all the sherds are part of pots with the same function. It appears that some buildings had a defensive function, while others were possibly used as stables or storage places.

Turning to analyse the houses, they show differences in terms of layout, plan and dimensions (Bertrand *et al.* 1990; Malpica *et al.* 1986). Even though the building technique employed was always the same, it was possible to make a typological analysis of houses and buildings in *El Castillejo*, as summarised below:

A. Simple houses
   AI. Single-room houses
   AII. Houses with an inner court
      AIIa. A small house of approximately 40 sm with an L layout and a central court
      AIIb. A big house of approximately 70-80 sm with four or five rooms with a U layout and a central court
   AIII. Buildings with parallel naves
      AIIIa. Buildings with two naves
      AIIIb. Small buildings (sup. $\leq$ 22 sm) with two squared areas
B. Complex houses
   BI. With a central structure like AIIa
   BII. With a central structure like AIIb
C. Houses with an unidentified structure

Most of the houses are type AII or B (with an inner court or complex structure) and all of them had a central court that was the major source of light and air. Thanks to stairs, possibly made of perishable materials as they have not been preserved, it was possible to access the upper floor. A large amount of tiles has been recovered, suggesting that these buildings had a double-sloped roof.

2.2 Pottery assemblages at 'El Castillejo'

During the archaeological excavations undertaken at the site, large assemblages of ceramic sherds were recovered. The analysis and preliminary restoration of these materials make it possible to state that the pottery recovered on the site shows homogeneous features concerning forms, functions and technical devices used; moreover, it dates to the same period. We are talking about ceramics for daily use with marked functional features, but made with little attention to aesthetic patterns.

Twenty-one different types of vessels have been classified (Figure 3) and divided into eight functional groups (Figure 4). On the one hand, the pottery used for cooking and storing food, like pans and big storage jars, does show small variations in forms; on the other hand, jars, plates and other objects used for food consumption and display on the table show wider variations. Nevertheless, these variations are not as marked as in town centres. Generally speaking, the pottery recovered at *El Castillejo* shows homogeneous patterns and was made in an extremely

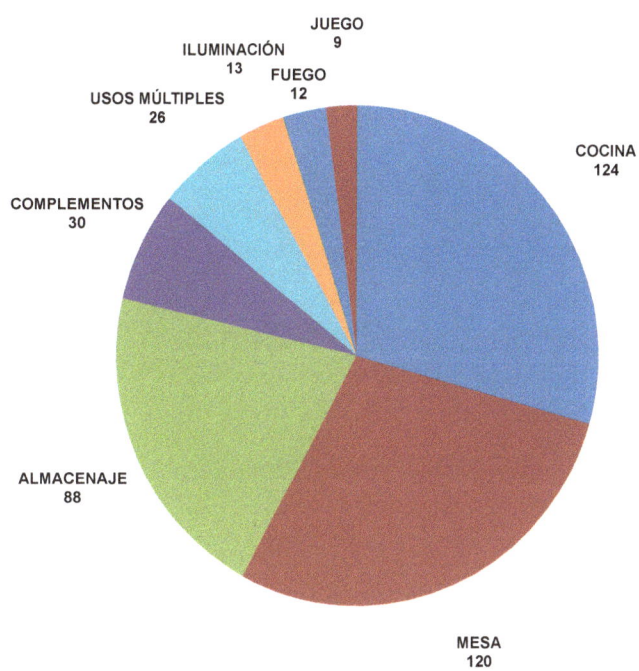

VAJILLAS

Cocina	124
Almacenaje	88
Usos múltiples	26
Iluminación	13
Fuego	12
Mesa	120
Juego	9
Complementos	30
TOTAL	**422**

FIGURE 4 – CERAMICS RECOVERED IN *EL CASTILLEJO* DIVIDED BY FUNCTION (COCINA = VESSELS USED IN THE KITCHEN; ALMACENAJE = STORAGE VESSELS; USOS MÚLTIPLES = MULTIPLE FUNCTIONS; ILUMINACIÓN = LIGHTING; FUEGO = COOKING VESSELS; MESA = TABLEWARE; JUEGO = GAMES; COMPLEMENTOS = SUBSIDIARY OBJECTS).

accurate way. These objects were nicely shaped: as several scholars have pointed out, with the ratio between different dimensions being well balanced (Fernández 2003, 444). This accuracy might be the result of a perfect control of technical devices during the different phases of pottery making: clay selection and processing, modelling with the wheel, firing, use of glazes, finishing etc. All these techniques were mastered by the potters who made the objects recovered at *El Castillejo*, but more generally the same can be stated about all potters working during the Almohad period (Fernández 2000).

As stated above, there are small variations in objects' form and all the pottery dates between the late 13th and

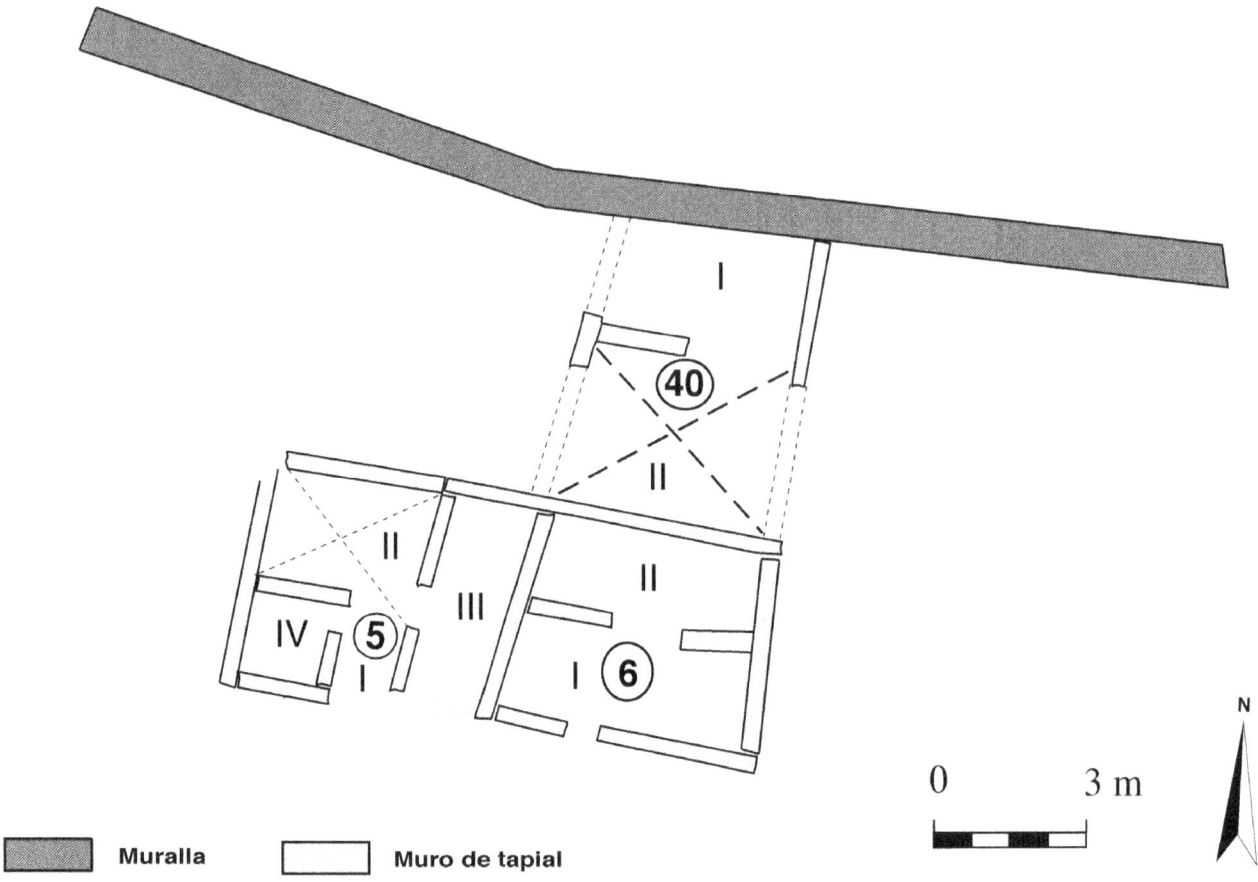

FIGURE 5 – A GROUP OF HOUSES IN *EL CASTILLEJO*: HOUSE 5, 6 AND 40
(MURALLA = TOWN WALLS; MURO DE TAPIAL = MUD WALL).

the beginning of the 14th century, corresponding to the phase when *El Castillejo* was deserted and the inhabitants left behind their belongings. It is worth noting that most of the pottery recovered was *in situ*; actually, in the very same place where it was normally kept or used. This made it possible to reconstruct the majority of the objects and to get a deeper understandig of daily life on the site just before it was abandoned.

To get a clear picture of this phase a comprehensive quantitative analysis of the ceramics was carried out, taking into account known typlogies as well as the functional groups.

3. Ceramic sherds and buildings: a comparative analysis

As discussed above, the buildings, as well as the ceramics assemblages recovered inside them, show similar features across the whole settlement. All the sherds were found in primary deposition. The relationship between pottery use and the possible function of the building it was found in has been analysed. The discussion that follows does not concern ceramic features and building techniques only, but aims to be a complete study of the context. The case studies below have been chosen as examples.

3.1 Buildings with 'special function': House 5

House 5 is located in the central area of the settlement (Figure 5), between House 4-4bis and House 6. It is a small square house of 42sqm (a detailed description is in Malpica *et al.* 1987, 488).

The rooms are arranged with an L plan and give on to an inner courtyard, which is connected to the main entrance thanks to a small and narrow passageway (room I, measuring 3,6sqm). Actually, the inner courtyard (room II) is the largest room of the house (11,7sm) and there is a room on each side of the entrance: the one on the western side is smaller (room IV, about 3,5sqm), while the on the opposite side (room III) is bigger (9,4sqm). The floor was made of the natural rock, smoothed so as to make the surface more regular. A stone bench was used for craft activities.

The archaeological assemblage recovered inside this building is extremely well preserved. Worth mentioning is a gilded and embossed necklace made of copper, possibly used as an amulet (Malpica *et al.* 1987, 488). Concerning ceramic sherds, 29 different objects were found (Figure 6). As in every house at *El Castillejo*, the majority of sherds (31%) are cooking pottery, while storage jars are 7%, and

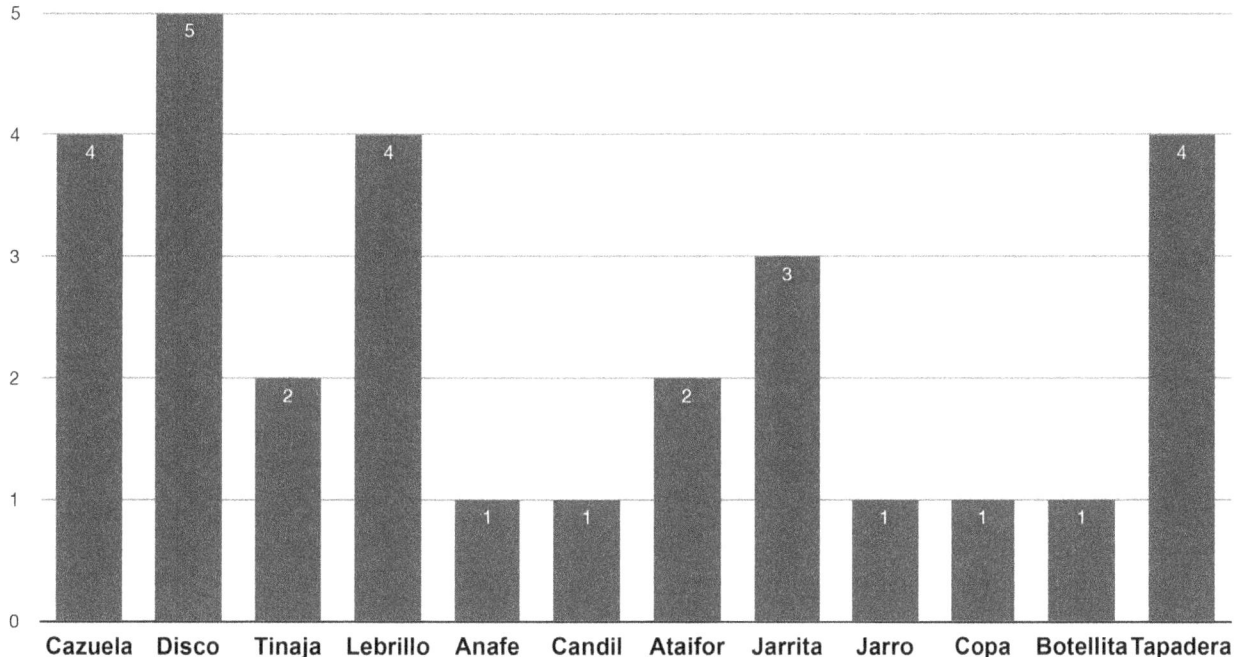

Figure 6 – Ceramic types recovered in house 5 (cazuela = casserole; disco = disk; tinaja = earthenware storage jar; lebrillo = washbasin; anafe = portable stove; candil = oil lamp; atafoir = tray; jarrita = small jug; jarro = pitcher; copa = cup; botellita = small bottle; tapadera = lid).

pottery used for eating and displaying food is 27,6% of all sherds recovered. A portable stove, a big basin and four lids were found also, and some of these objects show distinctive features.

Even though this house is similar to other buildings excavated on the site, a few elements can be regarded as unusual. Vessels that are usually quite common in al-Andalus, like pans and jars, were not recovered inside this building; round ceramic discs were used instead. These objects were found in large amounts and could be used for different purposes: as lids for big storage vessels (two lids in House n° 5) or for preparing food (all the other discs in House n° 5), including for baking bread (as suggested by Rosselló 1992, 255). Several objects recovered in this house can be related to bread preparation, like the big basin and a type of unglazed pan (type VIII in García 2001, 202-204). Several pans of this kind were actually found in House n° 5 (Figure 7).

Turning to analyse the spatial distribution of the sherds, it can be said that most of the pottery was found in the courtyard (about ¾ of the total amount of sherds). Furthermore, pottery used for different purposes was found there, implying that this space was used for a variety of activities. As the majority of pans, discs and the basin were found in the courtyard, it is clear that most daily activities related to food preparation (cooking and preparing bread) were carried out there. Food was consumed in the court; water and wheat were stored. The variety of ceramics sherds recovered shows that the court was a multi-functional space that could be used for resting, as a storage place and even as a kitchen. As all the other

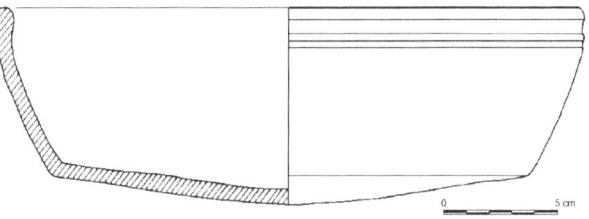

Figure 7 – Casserole possibly used in the oven.

houses, it possessed an upper floor that could be reached thanks to stairs, and a double-sloped roof.

3.2 The development of the houses in 'El Castillejo': House 4-4bis and House 00-00bis

3.2.1 House 4-4bis

This house is located in the western area of the settlement (Malpica et al. 1987, 443-44; Figure 8). On the southern side it gives onto the main street of the settlement, on the eastern side it adjoins the wall of House 3, and on the western side it borders on House 5. This building consists of two parts: one is the inner courtyard and is located in the northern area; the southern wall of the other part adjoins the courtyard. There is no connection between the two parts.

The northern part has the same structure as the other buildings of the village: the rooms are arranged in an L layout around an inner courtyard. The main entrance is located on the south-west corner and gives direct access to an inner rectangular courtyard (room I). The floor is

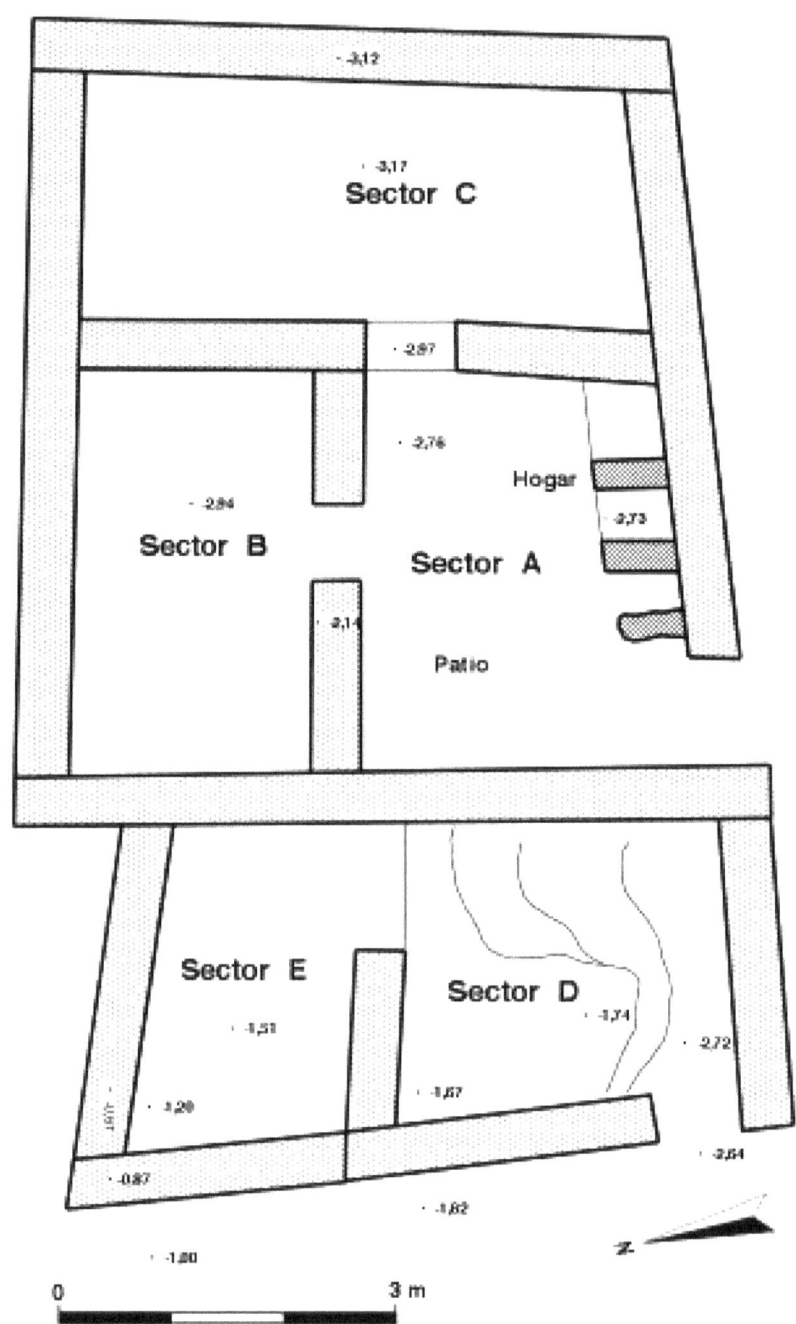

FIGURE 8 – HOUSE 4-4BIS: HOUSE WITH A COMPLEX STRUCTURE (SECTOR = AREA ;
PATIO = COURTYARD; HOGAR = FIREPLACE).

extremely poorly preserved, but on the eastern side of the perimeter wall there are traces of a structure, possibly a larder, divided in two parts by two masonry walls. The larder was very close to the fireplace: a layer of ashes and a considerable amount of ceramic sherds are the only evidence left.

The house consists of two rooms: one on the eastern and one on the northern side of the courtyard. The one located on northern side is larger (room II) and has a rectangular plan (10,9sqm). This room could be accessed through a small room and two steps fill the height difference existing between the two areas. Only a minimal part of the floor was preserved. The room on the eastern side of the building (room III) has a slightly trapezoidal plan (7,8sqm) and access to it is through a very small room. The floor was made of lime and it is badly preserved. Next to the northern wall there are traces of ashes that have interpreted as a small fireplace with edges made of stone and bricks, and with a coating. The postholes left in the walls by some beams clearly show that there was an upper floor that could be reached thanks to a stair made of wood or of any other perishable material. The large amount of tiles recovered indicates a single-sloped roof.

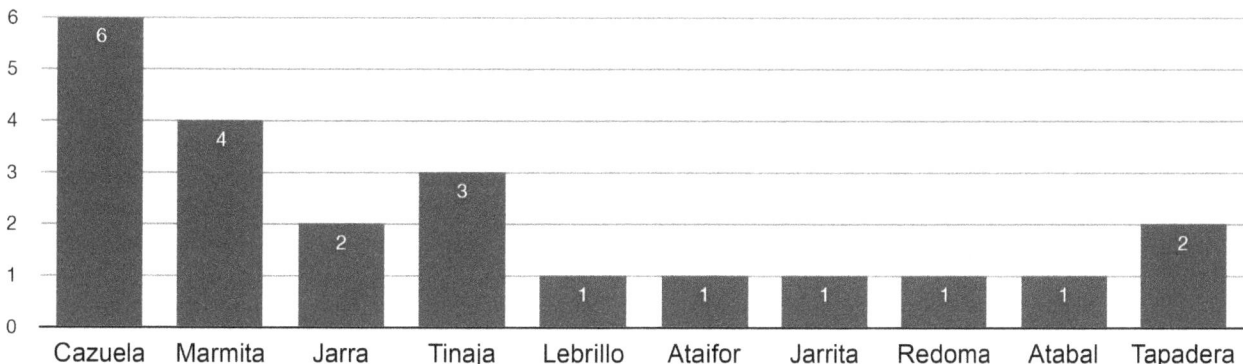

FIGURE 9 – CERAMIC TYPES RECOVERED IN HOUSE 4-4BIS (CAZUELA = CASSEROLE; MARMITA = SAUCEPAN ; JARRA = JUG; TINAJA = EARTHENWARE STORAGE JAR; LEBRILLO = WASHBASIN; ATAIFOR = TRAY; JARRITA = JAR; REDOMA = CRUET; ATABAL = SMALL DRUM; TAPADERA = LID).

Two more rooms adjoin the southern side of the house described above and were named as '4bis'. Access to this area was from the south-east. Firstly, we are going to describe the room located on the south-east (D area). It is a very small room (5,4sqm) located next to the court and possibly without a roof. A grey layer, probably the fireplace, was found there together with ceramic sherds, unfired clay and metal waste. The room on the south-west edge (E area) was even smaller (5,4sqm); a dark layer was found there. Most of the pottery was actually recovered in this room.

The relationship between the two buildings is not yet clear. It might be possible to shed new light on this point by analysing the spatial distribution of ceramics in connection with the stratigraphy (Figure 9). A total amount of 22 ceramic objects were found: 7 inside House 4 (31,8%) and 15 in House 4-bis (68,2%). The pottery recovered in House 4 can be divided into three groups according to its function: cooking pottery is the largest group (71,4%) followed by pottery with multiple functions (14,3%, i.e. the big basin) and objects used as part of a seat (the lid, 14,3%). It is apparent that objects commonly used for storing or consuming food were not present in this house.

Turning to analyse pottery recovered in House 4-bis, we find that a larger amount of sherds was recovered; furthermore, these objects could be used for a broader range of functions. About 33% of the vessels recovered in House 4-bis were used for cooking and 20% for consuming and displaying food, implying a lower rate of the latter in comparison to the assemblages recovered in all the other houses of the settlement. It is worth noting that a vessel used as a small drum was found (6,7%). The pottery recovered in House 4-bis was used for a variety of purposes and shows similar figures: there are pans (20%), pots (13,3%) and jars (13,3%). Surprisingly, big storage jars (*tinajas*) are the objects present in the highest amount (20%).

These vessels responded to a wide range of daily needs. As objects used for displaying and storing food were not found in House 4, this house should be regarded as part of a larger building that included House 4bis. Actually, in House 4 it would not have been possible to carry on certain domestic activities because some objects are lacking. For this reason, to get a better understanding of this area, the ceramics recovered in House 4 and 4bis should be analysed as if they were two different parts of the same building. As a result, the quantitative analysis of the sherds gives different figures. Cooking pottery is 45,5% of the total amount, about twice the average figure of a standard house in this settlement. Pans are the large majority of cooking pots (27,3%), followed by other pots (18,2%), while objects used for food consumption are 13,6% of the total amount of sherds (with an average of 28,4% in the rest of the village). Furthermore, in all the other houses jars and trays are the majority of objects used on the table, while in House 4-4bis they represent 4,5% each of the total amount of sherds.

We believe that the large number of cooking vessels might be related to the presence of two fireplaces. As they were located in two different spots and a complete seat of kitchen pottery was associated to each of them, we can assume that the two fireplaces might have been used at the same time. Nevertheless, it is not clear why there is so little tableware.

Anyway, if we analyse the distribution of the sherds recovered inside House 4-4bis it clearly shows that there are two different groups of kitchenware, each one related to one of the two fireplaces. One fireplace was located next to the northern wall of the inner courtyard in the building numbered as House 4 and close to the larder. The other fireplace was recovered in the first room (Room E in D area) of House 4bis: two saucepans, two cooking pots, one jar and a lid were found there. About 27,3% of the total sherds recovered was found in each fireplace, but a larger amount of pottery was recovered in room O in building 4bis (40,9%). Most of this assemblage consisted of storage jars (2 big jars and 3 storage vessels: *tinajas*). Furthermore, there were a few objects that were not used on a regular base (a saucepan, a jar and a small globular pot) or that were employed on special occasions (a small drum). Room O has been interpreted as the storage room.

Only a few sherds were recovered in the rest of House 4-4bis. Evidence of daily activities was recorded in the room located in the northern area of building 4, where a glazed lid was found. These rooms were probably resting areas.

Summing up, a house with IIa plan was built and it was enlarged later on. The old fireplace was kept in use, but a new one was added. It might be possible that the presence of two fireplaces implies that two related conjugal units were living in the building. As the analysis of the ceramic assemblage has shown, we cannot talk about two separate houses. Furthermore, the presence of a shared storage room implies that the two conjugal units were closely related.

3.2.2 House 00-00bis

House 00-00bis is possibly the most peculiar building in *El Castillejo* (see Malpica and Cressier 1991, 287-288) (Figure 10). Together with house 4-4bis, it belongs to the group defined above as 'complex houses'. New rooms (annex IV and 00bis) were added to the older part (00); the result was a more complex building.

This building is located close to the main gate, adjoining the inner side of the village walls. Entrance to the building is from the main road, just after the gate and crossing a porch. The courtyard (9,5sqm) was the central part of the house; access to it was through the passage I. Three rooms were arranged in an L layout around the courtyard. The rooms located on the south or on the western wings could be accessed through the southern side of the patio: room VI (south-west), room V (south) and room VII (west). Room VI and V were probably rest-rooms while the ceramics recovered in the Room VII show that it was a kitchen or a place for food consumption. Two rooms with a trapezoidal plan were added on the western side (group IV, adjacent to building 00). Their shape adjusted to the empty area left around the original building. Access to the new rooms was from the same street. As there were scant sherds in these two rooms, they have been interpreted as storage rooms.

The 'group 00bis' is located south of House 00. The two buildings are strictly related: there was a stair between room V in House 00bis and room III in House 00bis. The connection between the two buildings and the complex structure of 00bis led to further research to understand the relationship between the two parts of the building. The relationships between these two buildings, their role and their possible use at the same time have been analysed. House 00bis was built on a rectangular plot: four

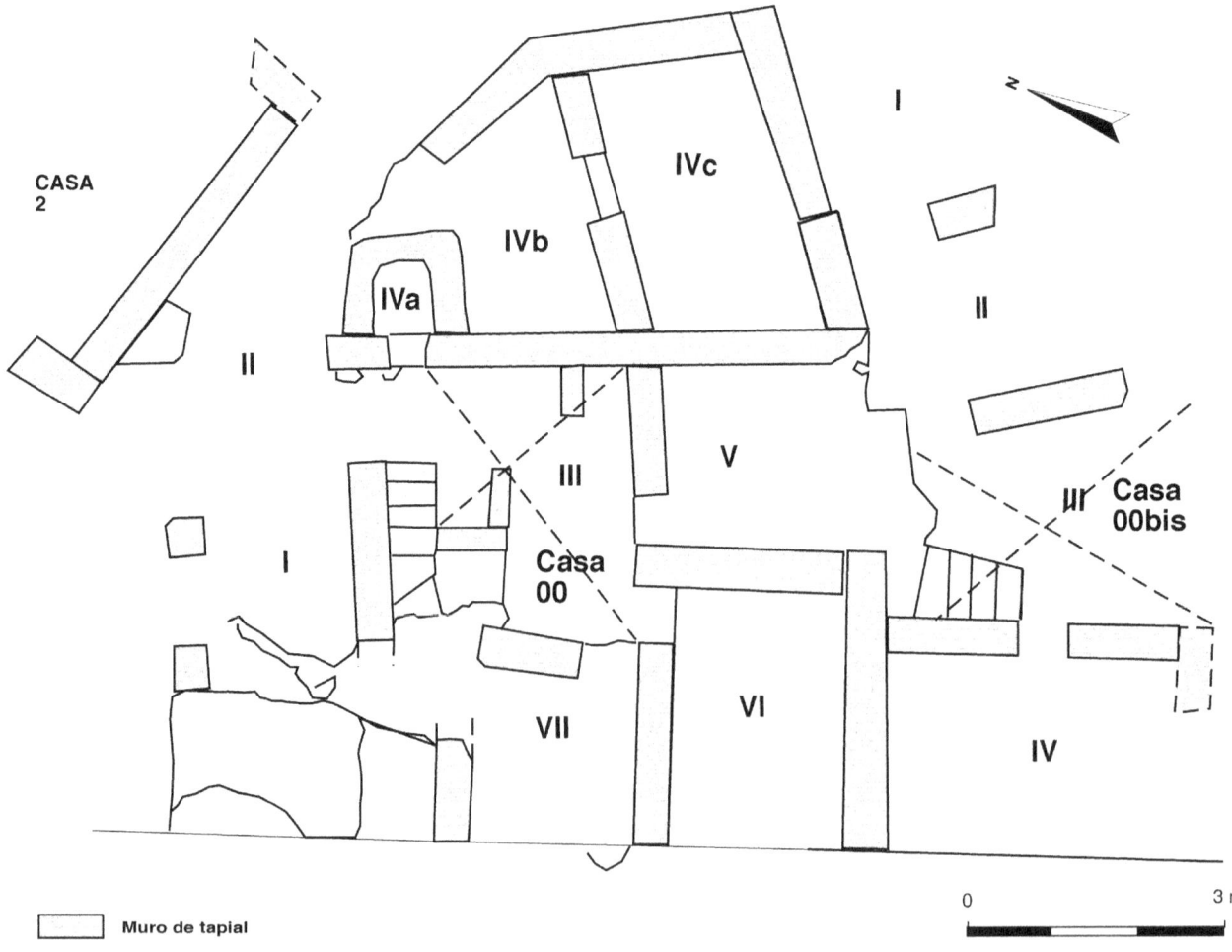

FIGURE 10 – HOUSE 00-00BIS: HOUSE WITH A COMPLEX STRUCTURE (CASA = HOUSE; MURO DE TAPIAL = MUD WALL).

rectangular rooms were built in a row. Access to this new area was from an alley on the eastern side of the building. Building 00 was not well preserved because of the sloping ground it was built on. The ground was preserved only in room III and IV. In room III, actually the patio, there was a stair connecting it with building 00. The latter adjoins the village walls: a stone bench covered with plaster was built there, showing that it was a resting room.

This building was made with the same technique used in all the settlement: earthen walls were erected on a masonry base. Despite the differences in the material used in the two phases and comparisons made with the other houses in the settlement, it was not possible to establish when the building 00-bis was added. The walls of bulding 00bis adjoin the southern side of House 00. Thus, it is clear that the latter was built at an earlier stage. Furthermore, it seems that not much time passed between the erection of the two buildings.

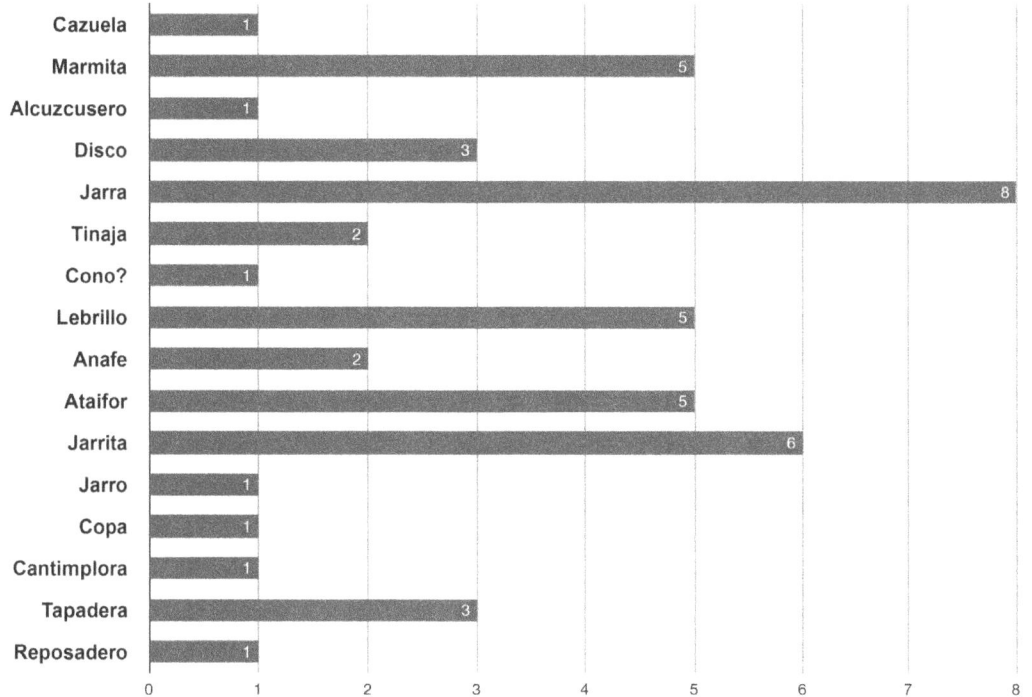

FIGURE 11 – CERAMIC TYPES RECOVERED IN HOUSE 00 (CAZUELA = CASSEROLE ; MARMITA = SAUCEPAN; CUSCUSERA = PAN FOR COOKING COUSCOUS; DISCO = DISK; JARRA = JUG; TINAJA = EARTHENWARE STORAGE JAR; CONO DE AZUCAR = SUGAR CONE; LEBRILLO = WASHBASIN; ANAFE = PORTABLE STOVE; ATAIFOR = TRAY; JARRITA = SMALL JUG; JARRO = PITCHER; COPA = CUP; CANTIMPLORA = WATER BOTTLE; TAPADERA = LID; REPOSADERO = SUPPORT).

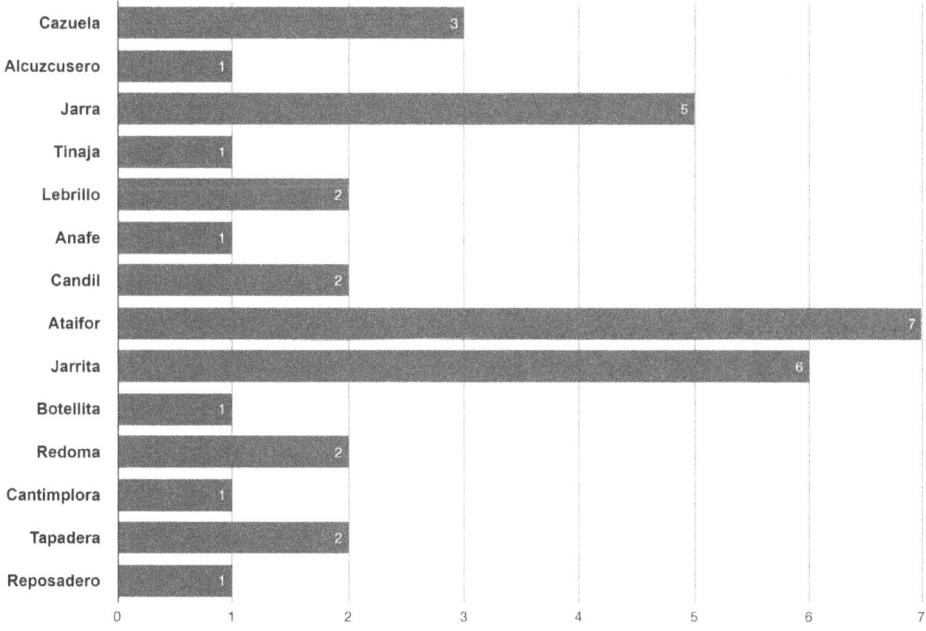

FIGURE 12 – CERAMIC TYPES RECOVERED IN HOUSE 00BIS (CAZUELA = CASSEROLE; CUSCUSERA = PAN FOR COOKING COUSCOUS; JARRA = JUG; TINAJA = EARTHENWARE STORAGE JAR; LEBRILLO = WASHBASIN; ANAFE = PORTABLE STOVE; CANDIL = OIL LAMP;

Turning to analyse the relationship between the two buildings, it is important to take into account the distribution of ceramics (Figures 11 and 12). The assemblage recovered in House 00 shows features similar to most of the buildings in the settlement. Nevertheless, there are a few differences concerning cooking pottery (21,7%) and possibly storage pottery (23,9%). The ceramics recovered in House 00bis show a different distribution. Neither cooking pottery (11,4%), nor storage pottery (17,1%) show figures similar to the rest of the settlement. Most of the ceramics recovered in this building are tableware (nearly half of the total number of sherds). Basins (20%) and small jars (17,1%) were next, while other objects were present in the same quantities as in the rest of the settlement.

If we analyse the ceramics present in House 00 and 00bis as one assemblage instead of considering them as two separate assemblages, the differences mentioned above do not appear so marked anymore. The sum of the ceramics recovered in both buildings could satisfy completely daily needs. Spatial anlysis shows that food preparation and cooking were carried on in the courtyard of House 00, just next to House 00bis and room IV. Food was mostly stored in House 00bis (annex IV) and consumed in the two courtyards. All the other rooms were resting areas.

Coming to a conclusion, it can be said that this house with a complex structure was inhabited by the same family group, possibly an extensive familiar group made up of two conjugal nuclei. Thus, the existence of a duplicated ceramic assembly can easily be explained.

4. Ceramic production centres

4.1 Ceramics from nearby urban centres

A variety of pottery made in different places reached *El Castillejo*. So far it has not been possible to reconstruct the trading network between production centres and the sites where the pottery was used. It is difficult to draw a picture of the market without written sources available. This being the case, the only way to reconstruct ceramic trade is to analyse the features of the vessels recovered both in production centres and in the places where they were used. The best way to approach this kind of research is to udertake a quantitative analysis of all the materials recovered in key-sites, such as *El Castillejo* proved to be.

El Castillejo shows unique features: it is a closed context and the ceramic assemblage dates entirely to one phase, corresponding to the time when the settlement was deserted. Thus, typologies and quantitave data can be used as reference (García 2001, 416-420). The number of sites with similar features is extremely low; in fact, there are only a few settlements with such a degree of precision. Moreover, there are even fewer sites we can take into account if we wish to analyse this specific period.

Luckily, there is an extremely interesting site dating approximately to the same period and located in a town centre, thus it can be discussed as a case study for a comparative analysis of the assemblages recovered at *El Castillejo*. We are talking about the excavation undertaken a few years ago on the site known as *casa de San Nicolás* in Murcia (Navarro 1991, 69).

The sherds recovered in the two contexts are clearly different. Differences involve both features and functions of the objects. The vessels recovered in rural settlements are in fact very different from those present in urban contexts. Generally speaking, the number of big storage vessels is higher in the countryside, as larger amounts of water and wheat needed to be stored. As countryside settlements were remote place from the main trade routes, storage vessels like *tinajas*, as well as siloes, were largely employed to store food. *Tinajas*, as well as jars could be used for storing water, as there was no systematic water supply. In town centres wheat, other kinds of grain and food in general, as well as water, were kept in jars and *tinajas*, but different storage systems could be used. As town centres were closer to marketplaces, it was easier to get access to food supplies; moreover, the inhabitants could count on public water supplies.

There are further differences between settlements in the town centre and in the countryside. For example, lids are more widespread in urban sites than in villages. This represents a kind of object that can be considered of minor importance, but the difference shows up. The number of lamps is higher in urban contexts; this was possibly related to the the larger dimensions of the houses located in town centres. In *El Castillejo* there was only one lamp in each house.

Turning to analyse functions, if we compare urban and rural sites, differences involved not only the number of sherds but also the variation in features relating to each functional group. Even though the same objects were present both in town and in rural settlements, in urban sites like the *casa de San Nicolás* the difference between ceramic forms is more marked and the objects are distributed in a more uniform way. It is important to underline that the ceramics produced in town centres reached also rural settlements. The same objects present in urban contexts in al-Andalus were widespread in the countryside, but their percentages differed responding to different needs.

4.2. Long-distance trade objects

Thanks to the comparative analysis undertaken so far, it has been possible to ascertain that immediately after the establishment of the kingdom of Granada, objects produced in town workshops were traded to far distant settlements, including *El Castillejo*. In doing so, general features, quantitative and qualitative data have been taken into account. Among the sherds recovered in the settlement, some can be regarded as rather 'uncommon'. These vessels are useful in reconstructing the trade network *El Castillejo* was part of.

Especially one object caught our attention while studying this assemblage: the rim of a big storage vessel. It has a tronco-conical shape, with a broad and flat rim, thicker in the outer side and with a thin edge. There is a thin incision all around the neck.

We are presenting an umpublished piece that could not be included among the ceramic types identified at *El Castillejo*. Even though only a few fragments were recovered and it was not possible to reconstruct this object, it was probably a big storage vessel made in the Valencian area between the 13th and 14th centuries (Mesquida 2002, 208-209). This kind of storage vessel or tinaja has been recovered on several sites far away from Valencia; in fact, they were used as containers for trading food. We are not going to list all the places where these vessels were found, but it is worth mentioning that some were recovered in Tuscany (Francovich and Gelichi 1984, 28-39) and Majorca (Coll 1993, 1071-1074) while others in closer sites, like on Gibraltar (Torremocha 2004).

It is worth pointing out that in this case the tinaja described above was found in a rural settlement far away from the main trade routes of the late middle Ages. It is only a few sherds but important nonetheless.

5. Conclusions

There is no doubt that *El Castillejo* was a rural settlement. The features of the buildings and the building technique used show that the village can be regarded as a uniform site. Despite that, the difference existing between the buildings in the southern and in the northern area of the settlement might imply certain social difference: a point that is worth further analysis.

The features of the ceramic assemblages confirm the picture drawn starting by the analysis of the buildings. Generally speaking, the objects recovered in different houses within the settlement show similar features and functional needs were far more important than any aesthetic aspect. This can help reconstructing the social context these objects were used in.

Despite that, it should be said that the forms show a certain degree of variation but without reaching the diversification achieved in urban contexts next to the production centres.

The difference existing between assemblages recovered in a rural site like *El Castillejo* and in an urban context like *Casa de San Nicolás* in Murcia make clear the functional purposes that these objects served in different contexts. Thus, differences should not be related to the distance from production centres and trading networks. Technical devices, forms and, whenever present, decorative patterns are actually the same in both contexts.

As mentioned above, the ceramics produced in urban workshops rather close to settlements like *El Castillejo* were commonly traded to rural areas. Obejcts produced in different regional areas could also reach the countryside: this is the case of the storage jar from the Valencian area used for shipping goods (Amigues *et al.* 1995) that could circulate over a wide area thanks to trading networks.

It can be said that, if on the one hand, objects and more generally goods circulating on a long distance basis reached *El Castillejo*, on the other hand, products and especially food stuffs produced in the area controlled by *El Castillejo* were not necesseraly consumed on a local base and could also reach urban centres. During the 13th and 14th centuries *El Castillejo* might have been part of a broader network, and even though the inhabitants lived from agriculture their production might have not been uniquely for self-consumption.

Bibliography

Barceló, M., Cressier, P., Malpica, A. and Rosselló-Bordoy, G. 1987. Investigaciones en El Castillejo. (Los Guájares–Granada). In G. Rosselló Bordoy (ed), *Actas de V Jornades d'Estudis Històrics Locals. Les illes orientals d'al–Andalus i les seves relacions amb Sharq al–Andalus, Magrib i Europa cristiana (ss. VIII–XIII)*, 359–74. Palma de Mallorca.

Bertrand, M., Cressier, P., Malpica. A., Rosselló-Bordoy, G., 1990. La vivienda rural medieval de "El Castillejo" (Los Guájares, Granada). In J. Bermúndez López, A. Bazzana (eds) *La casa hispano–musulmana. Aportaciones de la Arqueología*, 207–27. Granada.

Cressier, P., Malpica, A., Rosselló-Bordoy, G., 1987. Análisis del poblamiento medieval de la costa de Granada: el yacimiento de "El Castillejo" y el valle del río de la Toba (Los Guájares). In *Actas del II Congreso de Arqueología Medieval Española*. Vol. III, 149–60. Madrid.

Cressier, P., Riera Frau, Mª M., Rosselló-Bordoy, G., 1991. La cerámica tardo almohade y los orígenes de la cerámica nasrí. In *A cerâmica medieval no Mediterrâneo Occidental*, 215-46. Lisboa.

Fernández Navarro, E. 2000. Estudio tecnológico de la cerámica nazarí de Granada. In *Cerámica nazarí y mariní* (Transfretana – Monografías, Revista del Instituto de Estudios Ceutíes, 4). 41-70. Granada.

Fernández Navarro, E. 2003. Relación entre las formas y el uso en la cerámica de agua. In *Cerámicas islámicas y cristianas a finales de la Edad Media. Influencias e intercambios*. 433-58. Granada.

García Porras, A., 1995. Cerámica nazarí tardía y cristiana de "El Castillejo" (Los Guájares, Granada), *Arqueología y Territorio Medieval* 2, 243–57.

García Porras, A., 2001, *La cerámica del poblado fortificado medieval de "El Castillejo" (Los Guájares, Granada)*. Granada.

García Porras, A., 2002. La organización del espacio doméstico en el poblado fortificado medieval de "El Castillejo" (Los Guájares, Granada). Una lectura desde el análisis de la cerámica. In C. Trillo (ed.),

Asentamientos rurales y territorio en el Mediterráneo medieval, 422-55. Granada.

García Porras, A., 2008, Caracterización de una producción cerámica "comercializable". La cerámica almohade. In N. Ferreira Bicho (ed.) *Actas del IV Congresso de Arqueología Peninsular*, 139-55. Faro.

Malpica Cuello, A., Barceló, M., Cressier, P., Roselló-Bordoy, G. 1986. La vivienda rural musulmana en Andalucía oriental: el hábitat fortificado de "El Castillejo" (Los Guájares, provincia de Granada). In *Arqueología espacial. Coloquio sobre el Microespacio*, Vol. IV, 285–309. Teruel.

Malpica Cuello, A., Barceló, M., Cressier, P., Roselló-Bordoy, G. 1987. Informe de la campaña de excavación sistemática del yacimiento medieval de El Castillejo (Los Guájares, Granada), *Anuario Arqueológico de Andalucía/1986*, 487-92.

Malpica Cuello, A., Cressier, P. 1991. Informe sobre la campaña de excavación sistemática de "El Castillejo" (Los Guájares, provincia de Granada). Año 1989, *Anuario Arqueológico de Andalucía/1989*, 287-89.

Mármol Carvajal, L. del, 1946. Historia del rebelión y castigo de los moriscos de Granada. In *Historiadores de sucesos particulares*, Vol. I, Madrid.

Roselló Bordoy, G., 1992. Precisiones sobre terminología cerámica andalusí. In J. Bermúndez López (ed.) *I Coloquio Hispano–Italiano de Arqueología Medieval*, 253–62. Granada

Considering a Rural and Household Archaeology of the Byzantine Aegean: The Ceramic Spectrum

Athanasios K. Vionis
Department of History and Archaeology
University of Cyprus

Abstract

The purpose of this short study is to quantify, evaluate and interpret recently collected and processed ceramic evidence about settlement location, rural- and domestic-life throughout the Greek Early Middle Ages in the Aegean region, i.e. during the so-called 'Dark Ages' or Early Byzantine times (mid 7th – mid 9th centuries) and the Middle Byzantine era (mid 9th – early 13th centuries). More specifically, it explores the spatial expression of peasant communities in the Byzantine countryside, and examines the socio-economic identity and functional character of rural sites (e.g. hamlets and villages) under the spectrum of domestic ceramic assemblage-composition. This paper demonstrates a methodological exercise for the processing, detailed study and interpretation of complete collections of medieval ceramic finds that comprise the largest part of material culture evidence from Byzantine deserted villages in central Greece, the Aegean islands and southwest Anatolia.

Keywords: Byzantium, landscape history, rural archaeology, ethnicity, diet, ceramics

Introduction

Large amounts of surface ceramic finds collected during the intensive archaeological survey carried out by the 'Ancient Cities of Boeotia Project' in the region of Tanagra, central Greece (Figure 1), by the Rijksuniversiteit Leiden in the Netherlands, a project in which the author has been involved since 2000 (Vionis 2004-2005; 2006a), form the basis of this case study. Comparative references are made to evidence from two other projects in the Eastern Mediterranean, namely the 'Naxos Survey Project' of the 2nd Ephorate of Byzantine Antiquities of the Hellenic Ministry of Culture on the island of Naxos in the Cyclades (Vionis forthcoming), and the 'Sagalassos Archaeological Research Project' in southwest Turkey carried out by the Katholieke Universiteit Leuven in Belgium (Vionis et al. 2009a; Vionis et al. 2010).

The ongoing 'Ancient Cities of Boeotia Project', which began its systematic Survey Programme at the site of the ancient city of Tanagra and its surrounding territory in 2000 (led by Prof. J.L. Bintliff, Leiden University and Prof. B. Slapšak, Ljubljana University), aims at the detailed examination of past human activity at the site of the ancient city and in the countryside in its proximity (Bintliff et al. 2004-2005). Surface survey in the surroundings of

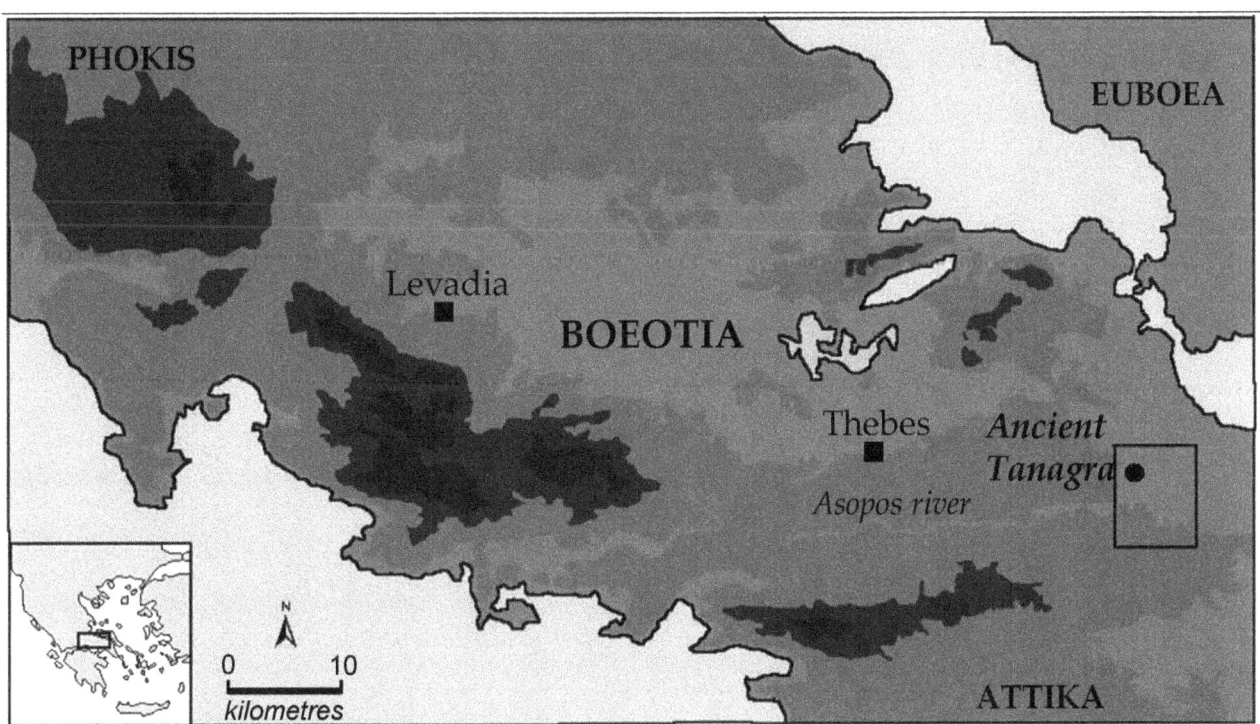

FIGURE 1 – THE PROVINCE OF BOEOTIA IN CENTRAL GREECE, WITH THE REGION OF TANAGRA TOWARDS THE EAST.

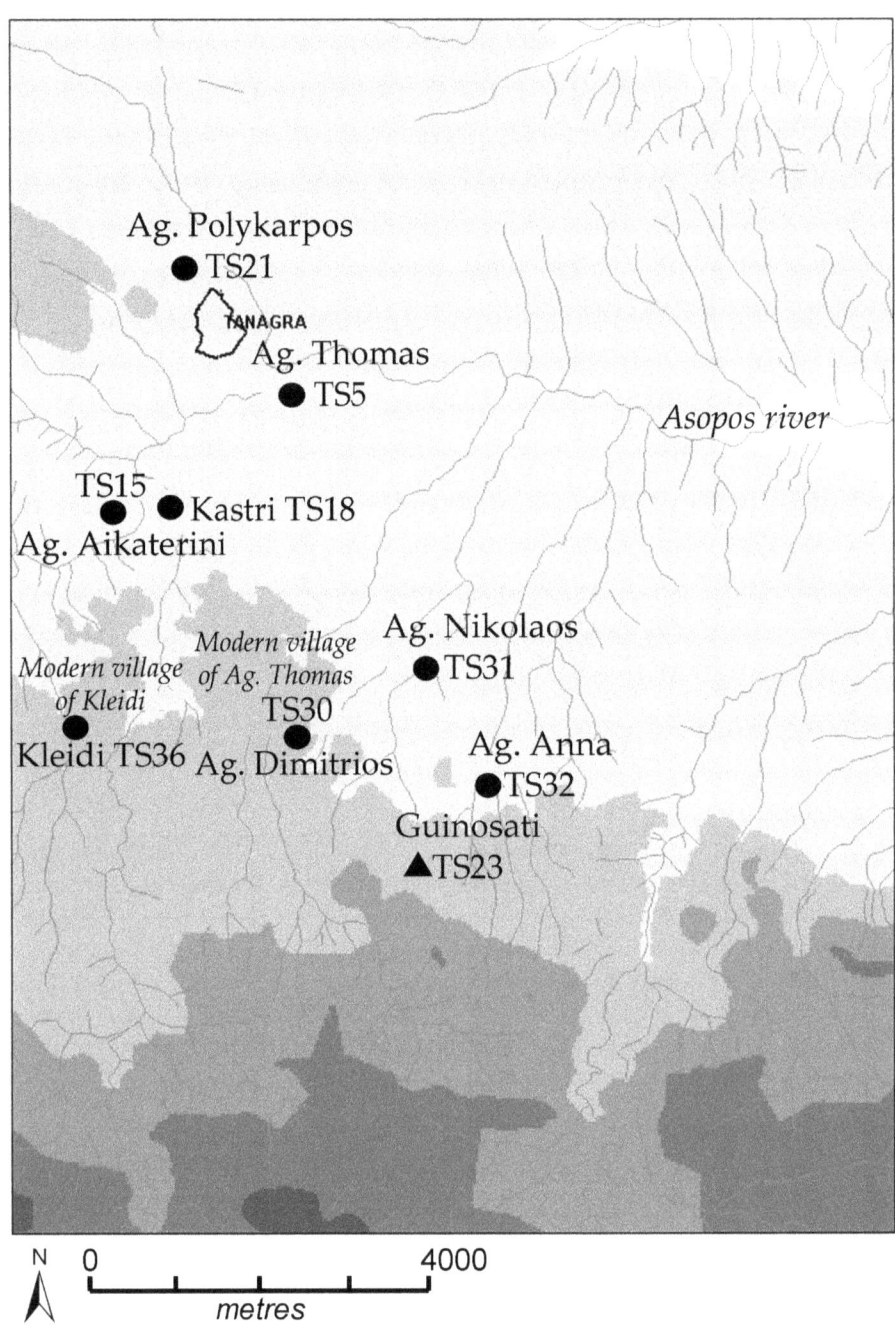

FIGURE 2 – THE REGION OF TANAGRA WITH IDENTIFIED BYZANTINE SETTLEMENT SITES (BLACK CIRCLES).

Tanagra (henceforth cited as the Tanagrike) has revealed the remains of a number of deserted villages dated to the Byzantine, Frankish and Ottoman periods (Figure 2), granting the author the potential to further investigate and interpret the material culture of this neglected period in the area, in an attempt to provide a more complete picture of regional settlement history and domestic life (Vionis 2006a, 84).

The presence of a number of isolated humble rural chapels on the island of Naxos (Figure 3), some of them dated (on the basis of their aniconic wall-fresco decoration) to the period of the *Iconoclast controversy* (8th – 9th centuries), provided the initial impetus for the exploration of the territory around those monuments (200m radius) in order to determine their use. Thus, to understand if they were once associated with a settlement and to what period they are to be dated. Although the characteristics and chronology of such aniconic decoration in several churches in Crete, the Peloponnese and western Mainland Greece are still debated (Chatzidakis 1989, 9-16; Brubaker and Haldon 2001, 24-28), their association with Islamic art of the same period and their approximate dating to the so-called 'Dark Ages' provided the initiative for an extensive surface survey around those monuments by the 2nd Ephorate of Byzantine Antiquities (coordinated by the author). Indeed, pottery fragments dated to the 'Dark Ages' (Early Byzantine period) and to later periods

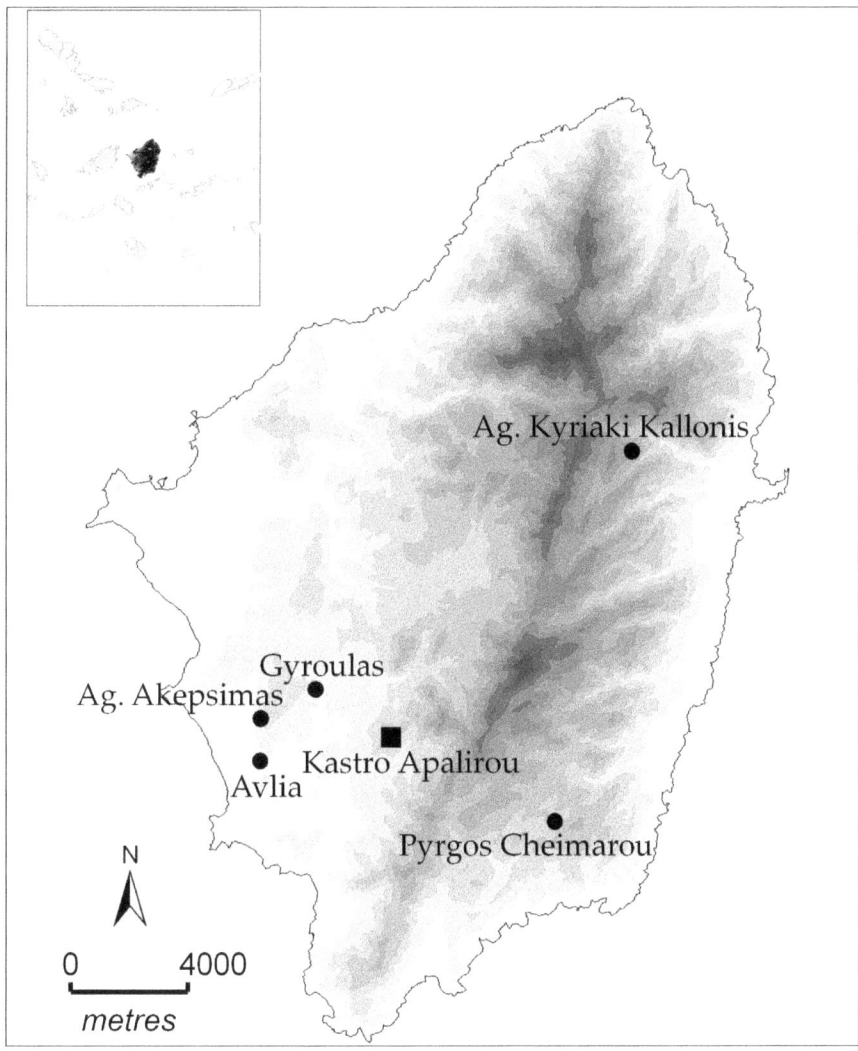

FIGURE 3 – THE ISLAND OF NAXOS IN THE CYCLADES WITH SITES MENTIONED IN THE TEXT, BYZANTINE CHURCHES MAKED BY BLACK CIRCLES.

(Middle and Late Byzantine times) that were identified in the territory around those chapels, provide evidence for the existence of small or larger settlements associated with these ecclesiastical monuments.

Systematic excavations and surveys undertaken at the ancient city site of Sagalassos and in its territory in the modern province of Burdur, in south-western Turkey (110km north of the city of Antalya), carried out since 1990 by the 'Sagalassos Archaeological Research Project' (directed by Prof. M. Waelkens, Leuven University) have discovered rich ceramic assemblages dated between the 7th and 13th centuries. At the city itself this research has revealed continuous occupation from Late Antiquity to the Late Middle Ages at three sites in Sagalassos: on Alexander's Hill, at the Temple of Hadrian and Antoninus Pius, and at the former Temple of Apollo Klarios (Figure 4).

The study of medieval ceramic assemblages

Ceramic vessels used for food preparation, cooking, serving, consuming, storage and transport have been the main evidence for dating and studying social changes during all periods and at all social levels. Although long-considered as essentially a dating agent on archaeological sites, ceramics also offer an indirect indicator of economic, social and cultural behaviour. The foundation of the 'Medieval Pottery Research Group' in Britain in the 1950s promoted the study of medieval and post-medieval ceramics and porcelain, including theoretical, methodological and analytical aspects of pottery research. Thus, for example, the British medieval ceramic specialists Gaimster and Nenk (1997, 171) have argued that changes in domestic ceramics in northwest Europe during the late medieval to early modern period are linked to broad economic and cultural trends. The refinement of dining manners and changes in dietary habits are the result of cultural-economic trends in northwest Europe at that time, with an increasing emphasis on the individual, resulting in the use of personal serving settings. A similar shift from multi-functional to separate rooms dedicated to different household activities, and with a greater degree of comfort and privacy, has also been noted in the study of vernacular architecture for the period following the High Middle Ages (Gaimster and Nenk 1997; Johnson 1996).

SAGALASSOS

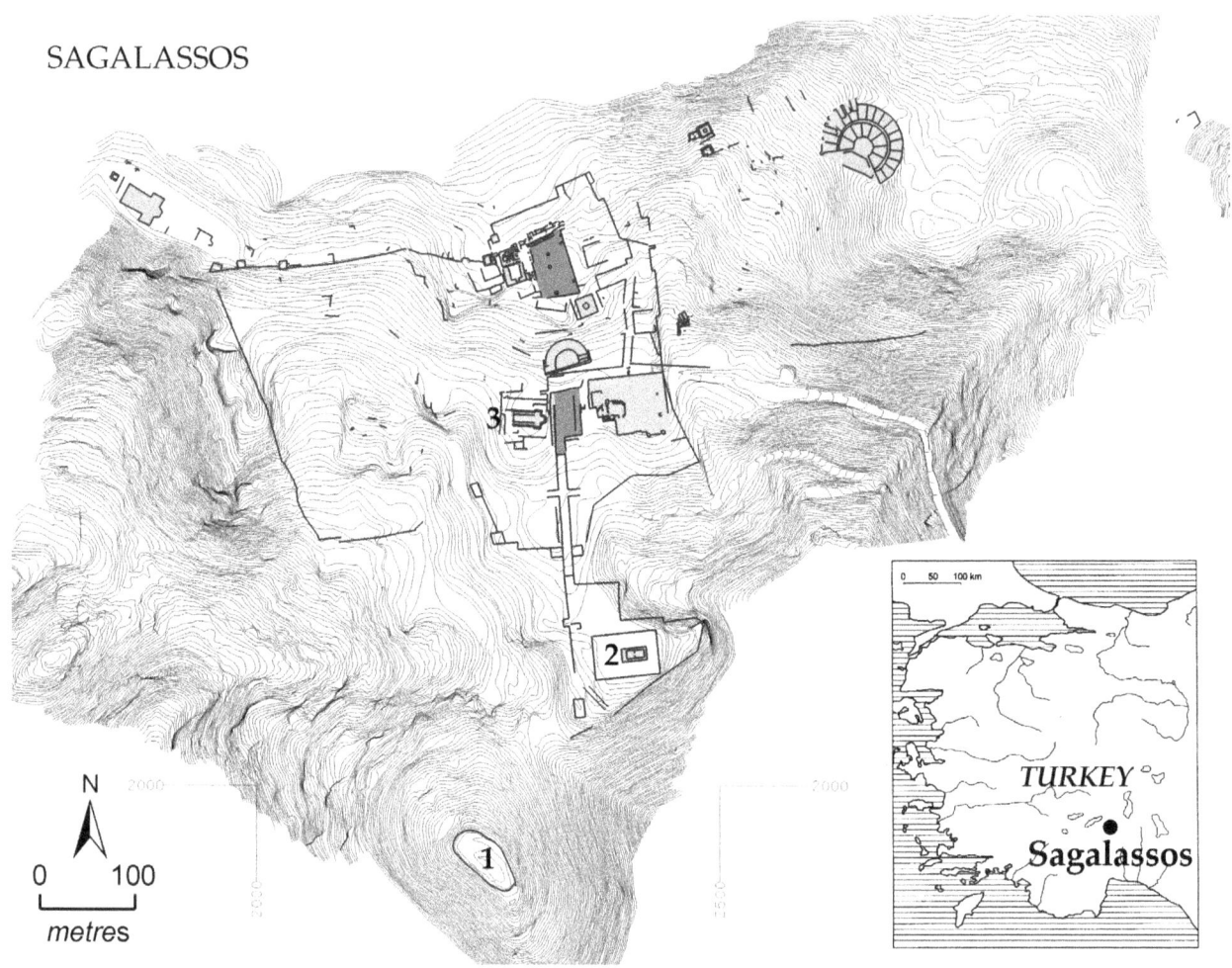

FIGURE 4 – PLAN OF THE ANCIENT CITY OF SAGALASSOS. 1: ALEXANDER'S HILL, 2: THE TEMPLE OF HADRIAN AND ANTONINUS PIUS, 3: THE FORMER TEMPLE OF APOLLO KLARIOS.

In Greece and in the largest part of southern Europe, the study of medieval and post-medieval ceramics was the aspect of those period's domestic material culture that mainly attracted the scientific interest of archaeologists since the 1930s. Although, as far as the Byzantine/medieval period is concerned, primary interest and attention was always given to glazed decorated table wares, as opposed to the bulk of plainer body sherds of unglazed common wares, the study of all medieval ceramics has seen a growing development up to the present time. Apart from the monumental publication by Hayes (1992) on the Late Roman and post-Roman pottery excavated at Saraçhane in Constantinople/Istanbul, recent excavations at Corinth seem to have provided answers to most problems involving glazed tableware chronology and classification, thanks to the association of ceramics and coins in the same stratigraphic sequences (Sanders 1987; 2000; 2003). In parallel attempts have also been made by ceramic specialists and other scholars to analyze pottery typo-chronology, technology, function, exchange and social change in the Aegean region (Armstrong 1989; 1996; 2002; Bakirtzis 1980; 1989; François and Spieser 2002; Hahn 1989; 1996; Papanikola-Bakirtzi 1996; 1999; Spieser 1989; 1991; Vionis 2001; 2006a; 2006b; Vroom 1998a; 1998b; 2003).

Special focus on the medieval and later periods in Greece, with an emphasis on the systematic study and publication of surface pottery, was given by survey projects in eastern Phocis in central Greece (Armstrong 1989), northern Keos in the Cyclades (Cherry *et al.* 1991), Methana (Mee and Forbes 1997) and Laconia in the Peloponnese (Armstrong 1996; 2002). The 'Cambridge-Durham Boeotia Project' in central Greece remained a notable exception within this group of existing intensive survey projects in developing specific survey methodologies for the post-Roman era, paying close attention to written sources and standing monuments, and in taking into account post-Roman period-subdivisions, such as Early and Middle Byzantine, Frankish etc. (Bintliff 2000, 38-41). A number of experts on Byzantine, Frankish and Ottoman history, archaeology and architecture, such as Fred Aalen, Archibald Dunn, John Hayes, Machiel Kiel and Peter Lock became actively involved in the Boeotia Programme for a number of years. They all contributed to the synthesis of information on the development of post-Roman rural life in central Greece, mainly published in article-form (Kiel 1992; 1997; Lock 1986; 1997).

In northwest Europe and in the United States, the long-established fields of medieval and post-medieval archaeology have been pioneers in linking contemporary pictures of everyday life, textual descriptions and material culture. Taking their inspiration from historians of daily life and of lifestyles, eating habits and other aspects of social behaviour have been sought in ceramic assemblages and their changes over time. One of the first archaeologists in Greece to follow these studies was Vroom (2003), who together with Sigalos (2004) and the author of this paper worked within the framework of the Cambridge-Durham Boeotia Project. In this context, the large amounts of finds from deserted villages were approached from the viewpoint of the north-western European tradition. Vroom (2003) borrowed the concept of image and ceramics to link Byzantine and post-Byzantine icons to tableware assemblages from the Boeotia Project collections. Vroom's published study remains a pioneer work with reference to post-Roman eating habits in Boeotia and in the Aegean area. It is, however, difficult to read further aspects of medieval archaeology in her work, such as the character and function of single sites and the relation between the ceramics collected during the survey and the development of medieval rural settlement. The sharp decline in local ceramic production that Vroom (2003) suggests for the Early Byzantine period (with the exception of the crude handmade 'Slavic ware'), the selected presentation of diagnostic wares, and the omission of site context make her work of limited value for studying individual sites and the total of their associated assemblages.

Byzantine settlement in the Aegean

The Early Byzantine 'Dark Ages'

The inability to recognise the material culture of the period after the end of Late Antiquity has resulted in the general assumption by both archaeologists and historians that the beginning of the Middle Ages in the 7th century is marked by the transformation and ruralisation of the Late Antique city and the impoverishment of the countryside in the Aegean and in the Eastern Mediterranean, caused by waves of Slav tribes invading from the north, and Arab naval forces raiding coasts and islands (Foss 1977; Laiou and Morrisson 2007). The picture emerging from the limited material traces recovered or securely dated by

FIGURE 5 – POTTERY FRAGMENTS DATED TO THE 7TH-9TH CENTURIES; A1: PATTERN-BURNISHED WARE FROM THESPIAE, A2: HANDMADE WARE FROM THE TANAGRIKE, B1: PATTERN-BURNISHED WARE FROM SAGALASSOS, B2: HANDMADE WARE FROM SAGALASSOS.

archaeologists points to a declining urban and rural life, with the acropolises of shrinking ancient cities functioning as refuge spots for Byzantine Greek populations (that seem to have remained on or near the former *foci* of settlement) during the late 7th and 8th centuries. This seems to have been the general pattern for urban centres (such as Athens, Corinth and Ephesus) and the countryside (Bintliff 2001, 38; 2012). Although it remains plausible that cities of the Late Antique era ceased to be the dominant unit of social and commercial organisation and that villages and fortresses became the dominant settlement cells of the Early Medieval world (Bintliff 2008, 1283-84; Mitchell 2000, 145), it should not be taken for granted that at that time the countryside was necessarily overtaken by barbarian tribes whose only contribution was crude handmade pottery and the disruption of technology and trade (Vionis 2008, 34).

Past research by the Cambridge-Durham Boeotia Project and recently by the Leiden Ancient Cities of Boeotia Project in central Greece has shown that during the Early Middle Ages the territories around known Late Antique towns were inhabited into the transitional 7th-9th centuries. In the Tanagrike, the small fortified hilltop of Kastri (TS18) has been identified as a 'refuge settlement' of the period, after the abandonment of the ancient city of Tanagra 2 km to the northeast (Figure 2), where a crudely-built surrounding defensive wall and fragments of the so-called 'Slav' handmade pottery (Figure 5, a2) dated between the late 6th and the 8th centuries have been recovered (Vionis 2008, 34). A number of Slav toponyms surviving in the province of Boeotia should provide hints for settlement continuity with possible replacement of the Greco-Roman place-names with Slav ones (Bintliff 2000, 42). The ancient city of Hyettos in northern Boeotia was the only site in the region (surveyed by the Cambridge-Durham Boeotia Project) where handmade pottery of the 'Slavic' tradition was identified (by John Hayes) in the past (cf. Vroom 2003, 107-08, 141-43). The fact that similar handmade vessels with a flat base and flaring rim made of coarse fabric have been found in association with wheel-thrown vessels (such as amphorae and imported wares) at a number of sites, mainly in the Peloponnese in southern Greece, could indicate the peaceful merging of local populations with the 'invaders' creating Slavo-Hellenic communities through intermarriage (Avraméa 1997, 86; Bintliff 2001, 37-38; 2012; Gregory 1993, 155; Vroom 2003, 143).

An ongoing re-examination of the Cambridge-Durham surface survey ceramic assemblage by the author has so far revealed a number of fragments from wheel-made vessels (i.e. pattern-burnished jugs, plain jugs, amphorae) dated to the period of the 'Dark Ages' (Figure 5, a1) from two further sites in Boeotia (Thespiae and Klimataria) with ceramics (as well as sculptural evidence) dating to the 7th and 8th centuries (Vionis in peer review). This evidence confirms the initial hypothesis of the project directors (Bintliff *et al.* 2007, 179) that occupation, at least in the case of the ancient city of Thespiae and its *chora* (site THS 14), continued into the Early Byzantine period. This new information reinforces even more the theory that the long-lasting tradition of wheel-made pottery was not lost in a region that produced locally almost all the pottery in use during every other period (Bintliff 2000, 43); it also suggests that urban centres of Late Antiquity were replaced by small rural communities, not necessarily formed by a Greco-Roman population fleeing from a Slav-dominated countryside (Bintliff 2001, 38; 2012). These centres had access to local and regional markets for pottery supply that included the well established wheel-thrown pottery and products of the 'new' handmade pottery technology.

Recent excavations at the ancient site of Sagalassos in southwest Turkey have also provided evidence for continuous habitation after the catastrophic earthquakes of the late 6th century that ravaged its civic centre. Ceramic evidence from the walled site of the sanctuary of Hadrian and Antoninus Pius on the large commanding terrace to the southeast of the lower city (Figure 4) suggests that the site must have remained in use as a defended hamlet or *kastron* (considering its strategic location), providing shelter to surviving populations during the troubled late 7th and 8th centuries (Vionis *et al.* 2009a). As is the case for Boeotia, handmade cooking vessels have also been identified at Sagalassos in association with wheel-made pottery (both kitchen and table wares) made of a coarse clay (Figure 5, b1-b2). A limited number of imported amphorae for long-distance transport (Late Roman 1 amphora variants), dated from the 7th to the 8th and 9th centuries, are also present in the assemblage, possibly suggesting economic links with places where the distribution of such amphorae has been identified, such as the inner Aegean area, Crete, Cyprus, the Levant, Sicily and southern Italy (Poulou-Papadimitriou and Nodarou 2007), rather than suiting an isolated community in the Anatolian interior confined to the household production of handmade pottery.

During the 'Naxos Extensive Survey Project', pottery fragments dated to the transitional 'Dark Ages' were identified at a number of sites on the island of Naxos (Figure 3) around chapels with aniconic decoration, as well as at a few excavated sites throughout the island (excavations directed by O. Hadjianastasiou-Filaniotou, KA' Ephorate of Prehistoric and Classical Antiquities). Surface ceramic evidence from the site of Agia Kyriaki Kallonis (surveyed by the author), and excavated pottery from Gyroulas (displayed at the museum of the site), Avlia and Pyrgos Cheimarou (studied by the author at the Archaeological Museum of Naxos) are of special significance, since they provide direct evidence for the economic links between the island and other parts of the eastern Mediterranean, as well as with Constantinople, thanks to securely dated amphorae of the LR1 variant-types and of Hayes's (1992, 71) 'Sarachane type 36' (Vionis in peer review; forthcoming). The picture about settlement during the period of Arab raids in the Aegean, emerging through the case study analysed, contradicts previous historical views about desolation of coastal regions and retreat of populations to the mountains and into island interiors (Malamut 1988, 67-68). Ceramic evidence from Naxos shows that settlements during the late

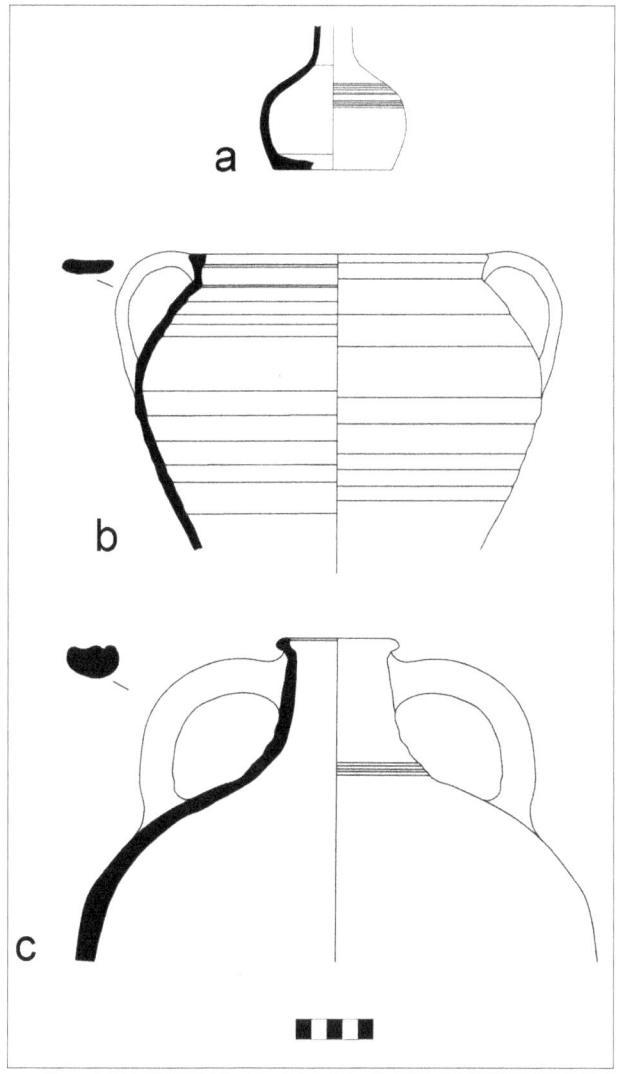

FIGURE 6 – POTTERY OF THE 7TH-9TH CENTURIES FROM THE SITE OF PYRGOS CHEIMAROU IN NAXOS; A: JUG, B: COOKING POT, C: AMPHORA.

7th and 8th centuries were not confined to the mountainous regions of the island but were also located very close to the coast, with island populations participating in a maritime trade that connected the Aegean and parts of the eastern Mediterranean to Constantinople and southern Italy. These must have been permanent settlements, as indicated by the variety of ceramic forms (for transport, storage, food processing), implying that we are not dealing with random finds but with an almost complete domestic assemblage of the troubled 'Dark Ages' (Figure 6).

The Middle Byzantine revival

The period between the 10th and the 12th centuries has been characterised as a time of great Byzantine accomplishments, with an increased growth in demography, economy and socio-cultural achievements (Harvey 1989; Bintliff 2012). Farming was the prime occupation during the Byzantine era (Laiou 2002, 49); agricultural settlements and villages were scattered across the Byzantine countryside and it seems that the provinces were focusing upon, and were connected to, urban centres administratively, ecclesiastically and commercially. A number of archaeological surface surveys throughout Greece (Armstrong 1989; 1996; Bintliff and Snodgrass 1985; Cherry *et al.* 1991; Davis *et al.* 1997; Mee and Forbes 1997) have provided material evidence for relevant recovery and re-settlement of the rural landscape during the Middle Byzantine period. Similarly, excavations at provincial urban centres such as Corinth (Sanders 2000, 171; Scranton 1957, 82-83), Thebes (Symeonoglou 1985) and Athens (Camp 2001, 240; Thompson and Wycherley 1972, 216) have revealed Middle Byzantine layers of thriving life and re-organised settlement plan/layout.

The model of a Byzantine village or *chorion* (defined as a cluster of houses surrounded by farming land/fields) published by Ducellier and based on textual evidence

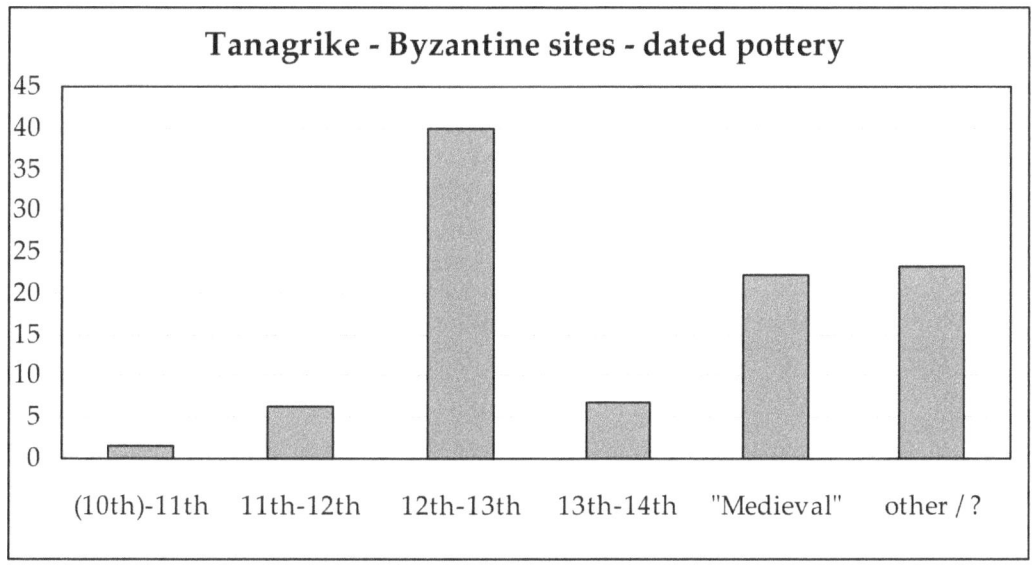

FIGURE 7 – DATED SURFACE POTTERY FROM BYZANTINE SITES IN THE TANAGRIKE.

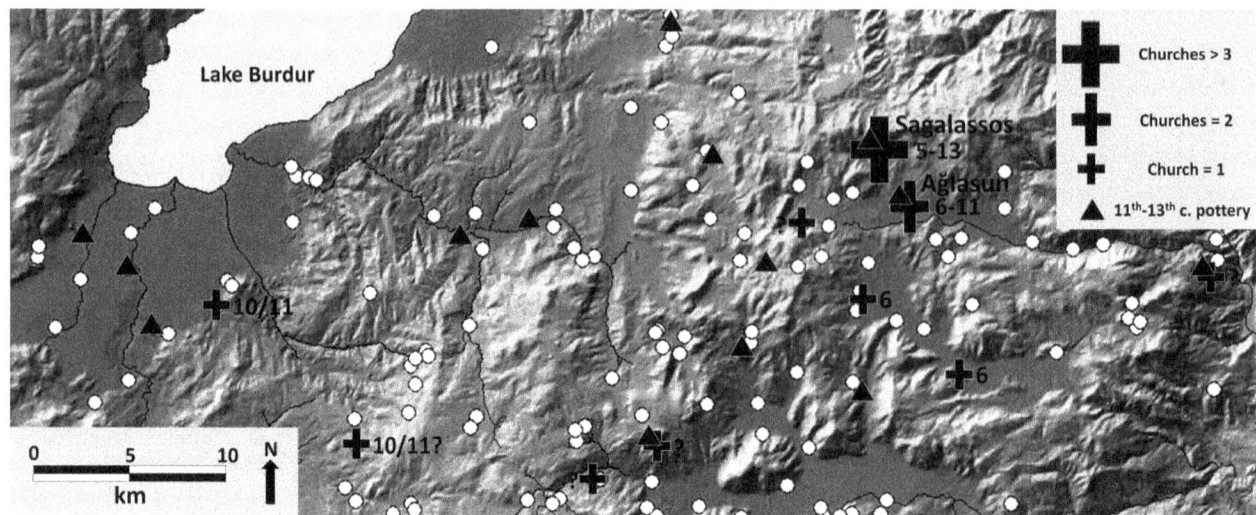

FIGURE 8 – BYZANTINE SITES AND CHURCHES IN THE TERRITORY OF SAGALASSOS
(COURTESY OF THE SAGALASSOS ARCHAEOLOGICAL RESEARCH PROJECT).

(1986, 187-88) is probably the closest example to Byzantine reality: a 'village' was made of surrounding vegetable gardens, a wider area of cultivable fields, pasturelands, and isolated farmsteads and hamlets (occupied by peasants/ serfs). However some scholars have argued that population in Byzantine Greece temporarily declined during the 11th century, recovering during the 12th century and later.

Ceramic sherds recovered during the intensive surface survey in the Tanagrike (Figure 2) have shown widespread signs of recovery in the Byzantine countryside between the 11th and the early 13th centuries (Vionis 2008, 35). Middle Byzantine settlements are well attested in the territory with diagnostic surface pottery reaching its peak between the mid 12th and the mid 13th centuries (Figure 7). These new settlements of different size established across the countryside are interpreted as small nucleated hamlets and villages located at regular intervals (Figure 2), reminiscent of the modern nucleated village pattern. The locations of these settlements are both lowland (non-defensive), and hilltop (defensive), usually concentrated around churches, which possibly functioned as parish-churches for each settlement (J.L. Bintliff, pers. comm.; Vionis 2008, 35).

According to historical sources, such as the 11th-century *Cadaster* or Land Register of Thebes (Svoronos 1959), there was a process of expanding estate formation, though at a primitive stage, but increasingly there arose a predominance of major landowners against independent peasant producers. What this settlement density across the Middle Byzantine countryside might suggest is that the fertile lands after the 'Dark Ages' have begun to act as a sought-for resource, and a rising population became available to exploit this land and to be exploited by others as a workforce (Vionis 2008, 35). Agricultural intensification in Tanagrike and Boeotia as a whole was intended to meet the growing demand of major urban centres (e.g. Constantinople) for agricultural goods, namely wheat, especially from the 11th century onwards (Dunn 1995).

In Asia Minor a similar pattern of settlement (or re-settlement) is to be identified. As mentioned above, the city-site of Sagalassos continued to be inhabited from the Early Byzantine to the Middle Byzantine period, with the wall-fortified site of the former temple of Antoninus Pius functioning as a small *kastron* (Vionis *et al.* 2009a). In addition, excavations on Alexander's Hill, outside the south entrance of the ancient city (Figure 4), have unearthed a small fort with evidence of occupation between the 12th and mid 13th centuries (Vionis *et al.* 2010). Parallel surface survey in the surrounding territory has also identified a number of small Middle Byzantine settlement sites (Figure 8) (Vanhaverbeke *et al.* 2009; Vanhaverbeke and Waelkens 2003, 304-5).

This evidence of human occupation during the Middle Byzantine era needs to be compared to the Pisidian Middle Byzantine pattern of occupation based on villages, sketched by Mitchell (2000, 145). According to this model (as also mentioned above), the Classical city-state ceased to be the dominant unit of social and commercial organisation, with villages superseding cities, the cities themselves becoming large or minor villages. However, the settlement hierarchy may be more complicated in the period after Antiquity, including so-called *kastra*, consisting of hamlets, of which at least one was fortified, emerging within the walls of imperial cities or as small hilltop *kastra* in its environs, close to urban foci of Late Antiquity (such as the aforementioned Kastri in Tanagrike) and keeping their ancient names (Vionis *et al.* 2009b, 201).

One of the suburban sites at Sagalassos with surface evidence for human activity dated to the Middle Byzantine period is on the outskirts of the present-day İlçe of Ağlasun, 6 kilometres south of Sagalassos (Vanhaverbeke *et al.* 2009; Vanhaverbeke and Waelkens, 2003). It has been widely accepted that another type of ancient evidence that points to continuous occupation is the survival of local place names (Mitchell 2000, 147). The place-name

FIGURE 9 – DISTRIBUTION OF MIDDLE BYZANTINE DATED POTSHERDS AT THE SITE OF AGIOS AKEPSIMAS IN NAXOS.

of the village of Ağlasun is very likely to have derived from the classical Sagalassos; the last listed bishop of Sagalassos is known to have been present at *Agalassou* (the 'Byzantine' version of present-day *Ağlasun*?) as early as the 11th century (Belke and Mersich 1990; Waelkens 1993). Therefore, it goes without saying that there must have been continuity of settlement and population in the territory, so to make possible that the ancient place name survived (even in a Turkish-like version) from the Late Roman era to the time of the Seljuk establishment in the area during the 13th century. A hamam dated to the Seljuk period, that is to the 13th century, was identified during the surface survey in the present-day village of Ağlasun (Vanhaverbeke *et al.* 2005). It is very likely that a number of villages were established in the region during the Middle Byzantine period, being administered by a settlement of higher status (such as the defended site on the promontory of the Sanctuary of Hadrian and Antoninus Pius), possibly protected by a fort (such as the one on Alexander's Hill).

The case of Naxos is no different to that of Tanagrike and Sagalassos. It is worth noting that all the surveyed sites on the island of Naxos (Figure 3) that have revealed extensive or limited evidence of occupation in the 7th-9th centuries (including that of Agia Kyriaki Kallonis), bear evidence for extensive occupation during the previous Late Roman period in the 5th-7th centuries and the succeeding Middle and Late Byzantine eras in the 10th-14th centuries. Intensive survey projects on the Greek Mainland (such as the aforementioned Durham-Cambridge Boeotia Project and the Leiden Ancient Cities of Boeotia Project) seem to have identified a very similar picture of ceramic and settlement continuity from Late Antiquity to the High Middle Ages, in the form of an exact overlay of Middle Byzantine sites on Late Roman nucleated settlements (Bintliff 2000; Bintliff *et al.* 2007). On Naxos, Agios Akepsimas is one of the sites with ceramic evidence dating between the 11th and the 14th centuries, which overlies the Late Roman predecessor of the same site, and occupies an area of 1.0 hectare (Figure 9). It could be characterised as one of the many large hamlet sites located around Byzantine churches in the countryside of Naxos. Agios Akepsimas is a three-aisled barrel-vaulted basilica church dated to the 6th century with many later constructions.

Discussion: the Byzantine ceramic spectrum

Byzantine Boeotia

An interesting issue arose concerning assemblage composition, after the complete study of surface ceramic finds from five Middle Byzantine hamlet-sites in the Tanagrike (Boeotia) had shown that the countryside reached its post-Roman settlement density peak between the mid 12th and the mid 13th century, with pottery of this period representing 40% of the total assemblage (Figure 7).

A great proportion of the pottery from these assemblages is indicative of food and beverage consumption, with a relatively high percentage of glazed table-wares (42%) in comparison to the unglazed common wares (58%). It is surprising that tableware used for food and beverage consumption reaches more than 40% of the total assemblage from the Tanagrike (Figure 10). One would have expected an assemblage supposedly typical of a rural community living entirely off the land, with a greater emphasis on vessels used for storage and for food preparation rather than for meal times. Ceramics may thus indicate that glazed tableware would be rated as objects of daily use rather than objects reserved only for special

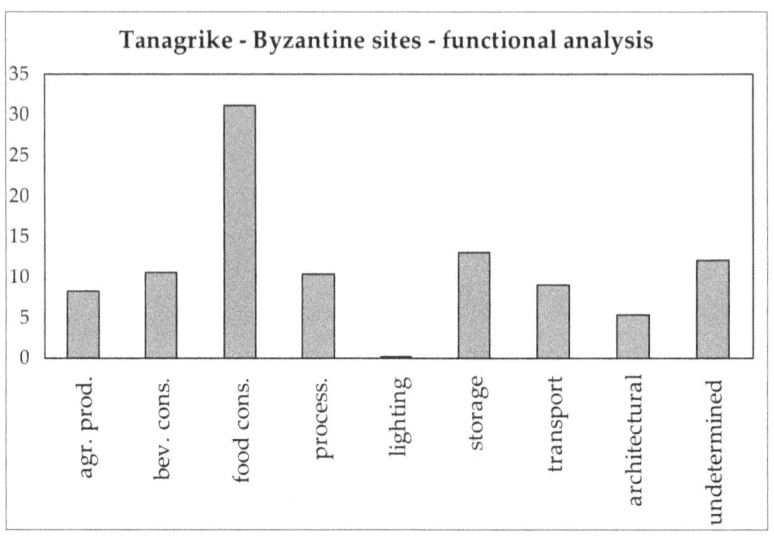

FIGURE 10 – FUNCTIONAL ANALYSIS OF POTTERY FROM MIDDLE BYZANTINE SITES IN THE TANAGRIKE.

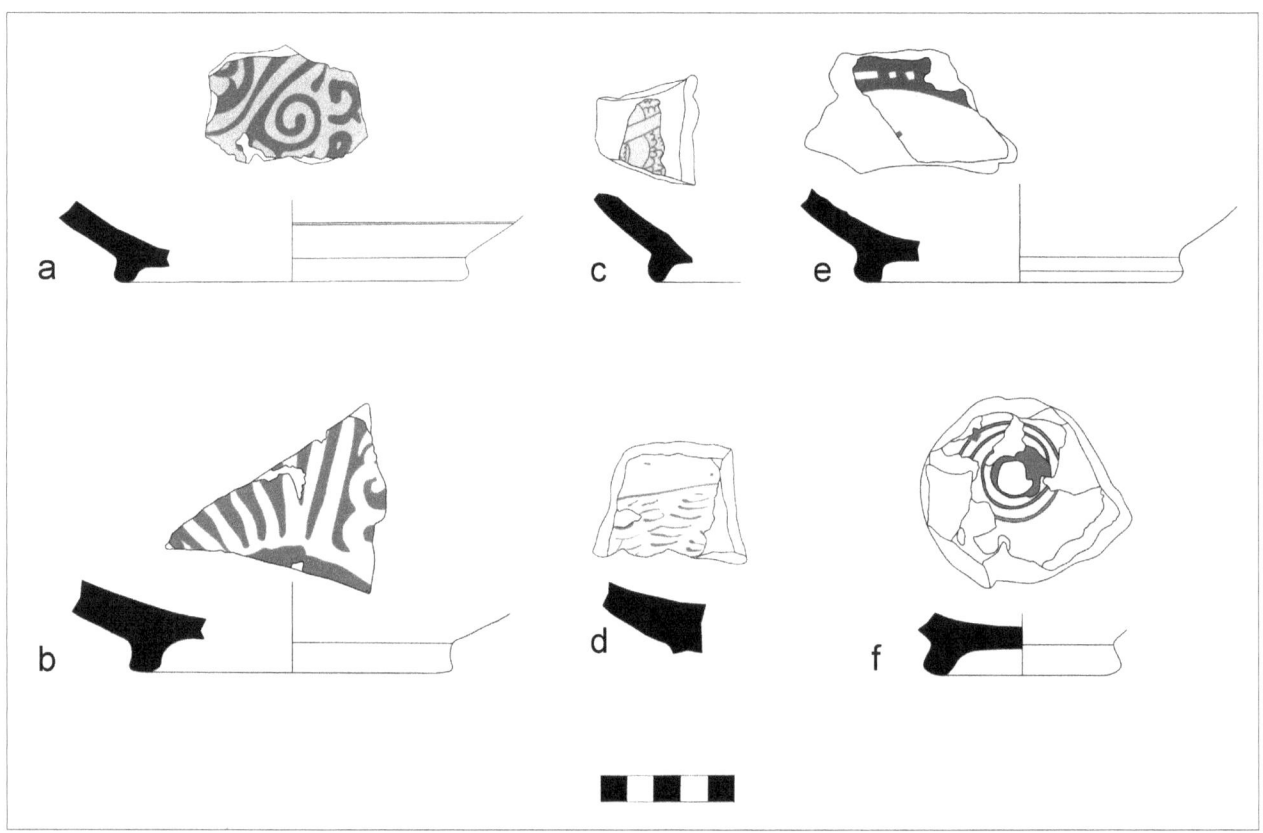

FIGURE 11 – BASE FRAGMENTS OF MIDDLE AND LATE BYZANTINE POTTERY FROM SITES IN THE TANAGRIKE.

occasions, further suggesting that peasants in the Middle Byzantine countryside were possibly better-off. It is worth noting that ceramic assemblages of excavated Middle (and Late) Byzantine contexts from the neighbouring town of Thebes are identical to our rural surface survey pottery; no differences can be identified between the urban and rural samples of ceramic wares (Figure 11).

Studies of the history of food and cooking in medieval Britain have linked archaeological finds and contemporary depictions of domestic life and have concluded that large, deep bowls for fish and meat were used communally by all diners sitting around the table (Black 1985). Similar conclusions have been drawn for the typical strong survival of glazed ring-foot base fragments discovered at medieval sites in the Tanagrike; communal open form bowls on the table, possibly stressed the need for interior and highly visible ornament. This is clearly shown by the proportion of open forms present, such as bowls (12%) and dishes (17%), which are amongst the commonest pottery-

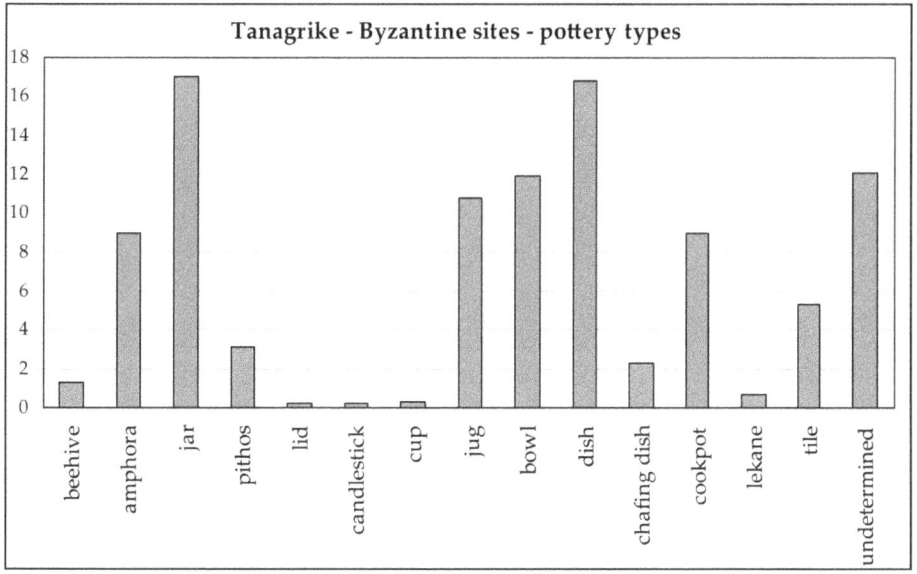

FIGURE 12 – POTTERY TYPES FROM MIDDLE BYZANTINE SITES IN THE TANAGRIKE.

types in the assemblage (Figure 12). Thebes has been suggested as a possible production centre of decorated glazed pottery; the Boeotian rural glazed tableware was most probably therefore locally-produced in the region and is indeed distinctly 'provincial' in appearance. Evidence for the production of glazed wares in a rural context has been identified by the Boeotia Project in the past from VM4, a Frankish-Late Byzantine era large village site (first recognized by Paul Spoerry) (cf. Vroom 1998a, 522). Imported glazed decorated wares identified in the Tanagrike assemblage come mainly from Corinth, Thessaloniki and possibly Lemnos, suggesting contact between rural Boeotia and other parts of the southern and northern Aegean.

It seems that contact between rural Boeotia and large urban centres is not merely highlighted by imported fine-wares but also by vessels used for transport, such as amphorae of the so-called 'Saraçhane 61' type, quite common in our assemblages. Transport amphorae represent 9% of the total assemblage (Figure 12). Amphorae are themselves evidence for transport and trade/export of agricultural products. Therefore, a first thought would be that rural Boeotia was probably exporting agricultural goods to large urban centres, such as Constantinople. These amphorae could have been used for the transport of oil or other substances, while it has also been suggested (Hayes 1992, 61) that 'Saraçhane 61' may have functioned as a beehive (Cherry et al. 1991, 357). Although amphorae are counted as mainly transport vessels, they could as well serve as storage containers in a secondary usage/reuse, while they must have gone out of use by the 14th century, having been replaced most probably by wooden barrels.

Matters concerning food storage are equally interesting. Storage represents 13% in our functional analysis, while storage containers such as jars and pithoi (very large clay containers used to store subsistence commodities) represent 10% and 3% respectively of pottery types in the Tanagrike assemblages (Figure 12). Clay storage containers are rarely moved from their original position after the abandonment of their context, mainly because of their weight and size. Thus, we could argue that the number of pithos and storage jars recovered closely represent the volume of storage goods in Middle (and Late) Byzantine rural Boeotia. However, the low percentage of pithos fragments (3%) is explained (Sanders 2000, 170) on the basis that these large ceramic containers were probably expensive to acquire and most people were expected to buy no more than two or three of them in a lifetime. It would seem logical to argue that a figure of 13% of storage vessels present in this functional analysis was sufficient to cover consumption needs, to avoid food shortage in case of an agricultural famine, and to meet tax obligations.

Byzantine Sagalassos

Functional analysis of the Middle Byzantine ceramics retrieved from Alexander's Hill reveals a pattern of a growing number of glazed table-wares towards the 12th and 13th centuries. This is a complete domestic assemblage on a possibly defensive site, with vessels for transport, storage, for the kitchen and the table (Figure 13). The occurrence of glazed table wares at the site, identical to glazed pottery produced and circulating at that time within the Aegean region and in Cyprus, is of special significance. Some of these glazed table vessels (such as fragments of *Champlevé* Ware decorated with hares) bear repair holes (Figure 14), possibly indicating their re-use after they were broken once, and showing their aesthetic and/or monetary value as imported items. This rising percentage of glazed wares, increasing steadily towards the 12th and 13th centuries, is a feature not only of Sagalassos and inland Anatolia, but also of urban centres and other rural regions in the Byzantine provinces, as revealed by on-going systematic excavations and intensive surface surveys (Hayes 1992; Sanders 2000; Vionis et al. 2009b).

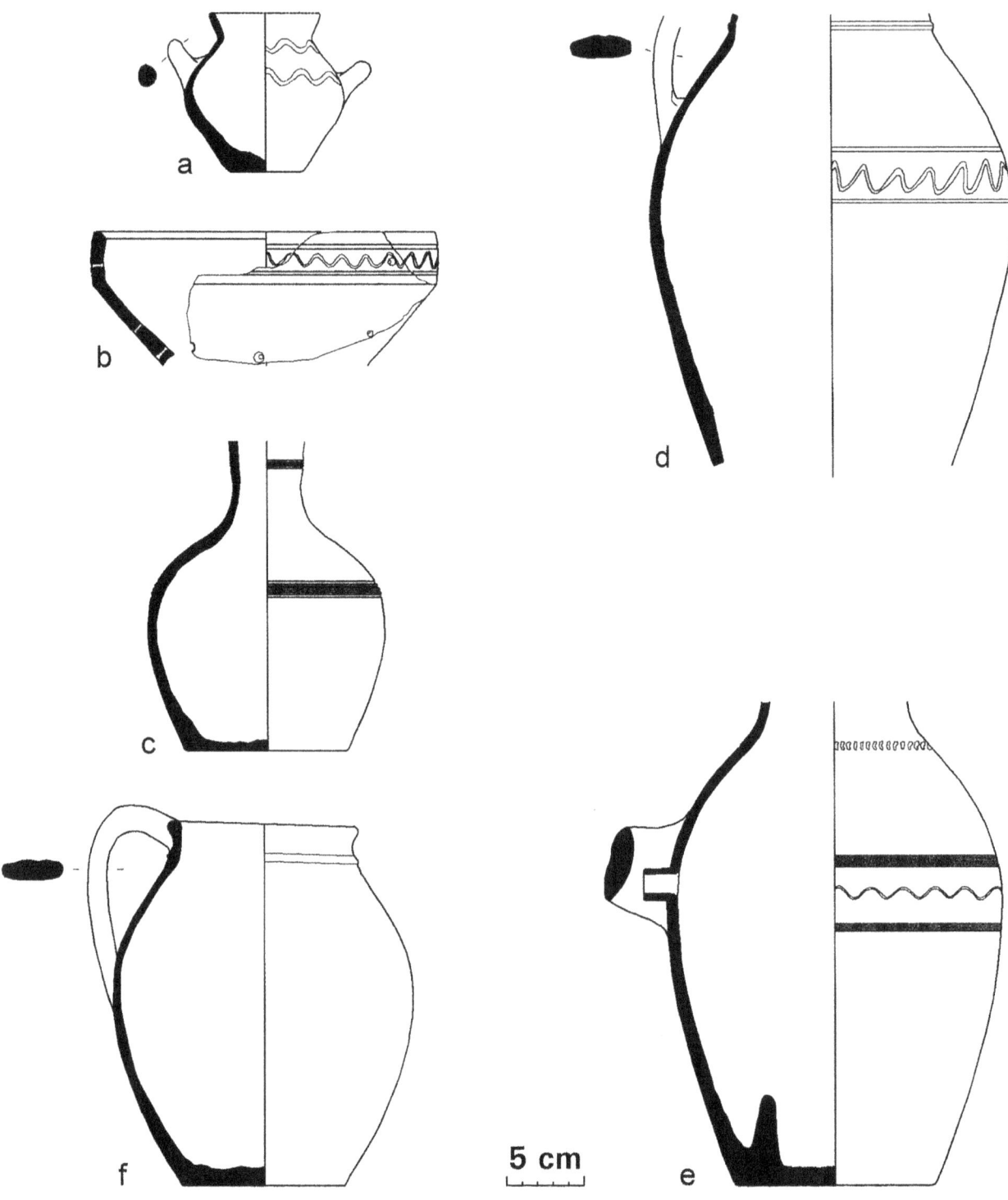

FIGURE 13 – REPRESENTATIVE COMMON-WARE TYPES FROM THE SITE OF ALEXANDER'S HILL IN SAGALASSOS.

Diet and Byzantine Ceramics

Apart from their meaning in terms of changing ceramic technology, economic and settlement patterns, new pottery forms should also reflect a changing pattern in cooking practices and eating habits. Indeed, the Early Medieval assemblage at Sagalassos is different from the Late Roman one in more ways than merely manufacture techniques and fabric: the number of retrieved Early Medieval (7th-9th century) vessel forms is noticeably more confined and the proportion of wares associated with food processing is larger than that associated with food consumption. Arthur's (2007) recent case-study on the distribution of open cooking pots or *casseroles* versus closed cooking vessels or *ollae* in combination with the distribution of sheep/goat- versus cattle- and pig-dominated faunal assemblages in Late Antique and Early Medieval Italy, is revealing in terms of environmental and cultural influences in cooking and diet. According to Arthur's model, throughout the ancient world the distribution of open cooking pots seems

FIGURE 14 – BASE FRAGMENT OF A *CHAMPLEVÉ* WARE DISH, WITH HARE IN A CENTRAL MEDALLION AND A SURVIVING REPAIR HOLE, EARLY 13TH CENTURY.

to closely match the distribution of areas of sheep/goat-dominated faunal assemblages, whereas closed globular cooking vessels are generally a feature of the North, from Britain across the Rhineland to central Europe where cattle- and pig-breeding were dominant (Arthur 2007, 18).

It is evident that the handmade and wheel-thrown closed cooking pots from post-7th-century contexts at Sagalassos dominate the ceramic assemblages; the equally-balanced presence of casseroles and closed cook-pot forms of the Late Roman period is no longer attested. Firmly dated evidence from the Aegean region and Constantinople in the period after the 7th century shows a preference towards closed round-bodied cooking pots (Hayes 1992). The same pattern is noted at Sagalassos not only in the Early Medieval assemblages from the former temple-sites but also from the Middle Byzantine occupation layers on Alexander's Hill, where flat-bottomed globular cooking pots with strap handles and small rim-diameter are the norm (Figure 13f). Whether this shift is a cultural phenomenon related to cooking practices changing from dry dishes to semi-liquid foods and stews, or an environmental change in the Middle Ages at Sagalassos, should be cross-checked with residue and faunal-remains analysis.

Indeed, lipid analysis of closed cooking pot fragments from the Middle Byzantine site on Alexander's Hill revealed a diet different from the one dating to the Late Roman civic occupation within the city of Sagalassos. According to this lipid analysis, food provisioning of a small military group, possibly stationed on the fort of Alexander's Hill during the Middle Byzantine period, was especially rich in beef, followed by pork and deer (Romanus *et al.* 2007; Vionis *et al.* 2010). Archaeozoological analysis of faunal remains from Alexander's Hill has demonstrated the same phenomenon (Vionis *et al.* 2010). This is a picture in contrast with recent conclusions about Middle Byzantine diet as comprising mainly fish and vegetables, based on the study of table-ware shapes and religious depictions of meals (Vionis 2006b, 488-91; Vroom 2003, 313-21, 367).

Bibliography

Armstrong, P. 1989. Some Byzantine and later settlements in Eastern Phokis. *Annual of the British School at Athens* 84, 1-48.

Armstrong, P., 1996. The Byzantine and Ottoman pottery. In W. Cavanagh, J. Crouwel, R. W. V. Catling and G. Shipley (eds), *Continuity and Change in a Greek Rural Landscape. The Laconia Survey, Volume* 2: *Archaeological Data*, 125-40. London, Annual of the British School at Athens Supplementary Volume 27.

Armstrong, P. 2002. The survey area in the Byzantine and Ottoman periods. In W. Cavanagh, J. Crouwel, R. W. V. Catling and G. Shipley (eds), *Continuity and Change in a Greek Rural Landscape. The Laconia Survey, Volume* 1: *Methodology and Interpretation*, 339-402. London, Annual of the British School at Athens Supplementary Volume 26.

Arthur, P. 2007. Pots and boundaries: on cultural and economic areas between Late Antiquity and the Early

Middle Ages. In M. Bonifay and J.-C. Tréglia (eds), *LRCW2. Late Roman Coarse Wares, Cooking Wares and Amphorae in the Mediterranean: Archaeology and Archaeometry*, 15-27. BAR (British Archaeological Reports) International Series 1662, I. Oxford, BAR Publishing.

Avraméa, A. 1997. *Le Péloponnèse du IVe au VIIIe Siècle: Changements et Persistances*. Paris, Publications de la Sorbonne.

Bakirtzis, Ch. 1980. Didymoteichon: un centre de céramique post-byzantine. *Balkan Studies* 21, 147-53.

Bakirtzis, Ch. 1989. *Byzantina Tsoukalolagina*. Athens, Archaeological Receipts Fund 39.

Belke, K. and Mersich, M. 1990. *Phrygien und Pisidien*. Tabula Imperii Byzantini 7. Wien, Österreichische Akademie der Wissenschaften.

Bintliff, J. L. 2000. Reconstructing the Byzantine countryside: new approaches from landscape archaeology. In K. Belke, F. Hild, J. Koder and P. Soustal (eds), *Byzanz als Raum. Zu Methoden und Inhalten der Historischen Geographie des Östlichen Mittelmeerraumes, 37-63*. Wien, Österreichische Akademie der Wissenschaften.

Bintliff, J. L. 2001. Recent developments and new approaches to the archaeology of medieval Greece. In M. Valor and M. Carmona (eds), *Fourth European Symposium for Teachers of Medieval Archaeology, 33-44*. Sevilla, University of Sevilla.

Bintliff, J. L. 2008. *Medieval and post-medieval*. In D. M. Pearsall (ed.), *Encyclopedia of Archaeology, 1280-98*. New York, Academic Press.

Bintliff, J. L. 2012. *The Complete Archaeology of Greece, from Hunter-Gatherers to the Twentieth Century AD*. Oxford-New York, Blackwell-Wiley.

Bintliff, J. L. and Snodgrass, A. M. 1985. The Boeotia survey, a preliminary report: the first four years. *Journal of Field Archaeology* 12, 23-161.

Bintliff, J. L., Ceulemans, A., De Craen, K., Farinetti, E., Kramberger, D., Music, B., Poblome, J., Sarri, K., Sbonias, K., Slapsak, B., Stissi, V. and Vionis, A. K. 2004-2005. The Tanagra Project: investigations at an Ancient Boeotian City and in its Countryside (2000-2002). *Bulletin de Correspondence Hellènique*, 128-129 (2.1), 541-606.

Bintliff, J. L., Howard, P., and Snodgrass, A. M., (eds) 2007. *Testing the Hinterland: The Work of the Boeotia Survey (1989-1991) in the Southern Approaches to the City of Thespiae*. Cambridge, MacDonald Institute Monographs.

Black, M. 1985. *Food and Cooking in Medieval Britain: History and Recipes*. Birmingham, English Heritage.

Brubaker, L. and Haldon, J. (eds) 2001. *Byzantium in the Iconoclast era (ca. 680-850): the sources*. Aldershot, Ashgate.

Camp, J. M. 2001. *The Archaeology of Athens*. New Haven and London, Yale University Press.

Chatzidakis M. (ed.) 1989. *Byzantini Techni stin Ellada: Naxos*. Athens, Melissa.

Cherry, J. F., Davis, J. L. and Mantzourani, E. 1991. *Landscape Archaeology as Long Term History: Northern Keos in the Cycladic Islands from Earliest Settlement until Modern Times*. Monumenta Archaeologica 16. Los Angeles: Cotsen Institute of Archaeology.

Davis, J. L., Alcock, S. E., Bennet, J., Lolos, Y. G. and Shelmerdine, C. W. 1997. The Pylos Regional Archaeological Project, Part I: overview and the archaeological survey. *Hesperia* 66, 391-494.

Ducellier, A. 1986. *Byzance et le Monde Orthodoxe*. Paris, Armand Colin.

Dunn, A. 1995. Historical and archaeological indicators of economic change in Middle Byzantine Boeotia and their problems. *Epetiris tis Etaireias Boiotikon Meleton* 2(II), 755-74.

Foss, C. 1977. Archaeology and the 'twenty cities' of Byzantine Asia. *American Journal of Archaeology* 81, 469-86.

François, V. and Spieser, J.-M. 2002. Pottery and glass in Byzantium. In A. E. Laiou (ed.), *The Economic History of Byzantium from the Seventh through the Fifteenth Century*. Dumbarton Oaks Studies 39, 593-609. Washington DC, Dumbarton Oaks Research Library and Collection.

Gaimster, D. and Nenk, B. 1997. English ouseholds in transition, c. 1450-1550: the ceramic evidence. In D. Gaimster and P. Stamper (eds), *The Age of Transition: The Archaeology of English Culture 1400-1600*, 171-95. Oxford, Oxbow.

Gregory, T. E. 1993. An early Byzantine (Dark Age) settlement at Isthmia: a preliminary report. In T. E. Gregory (ed.), *The Corinthia in the Roman Period*. Journal of Roman Archaeology Supplement Series 8, 149-60. Ann Arbor, Journal of Roman Archaeology.

Hahn, M. 1989. Byzantine and post-Byzantine pottery from the Greek-Swedish excavations at Khania, Crete. In V. Déroche and J.-M. Spieser (eds), *Recherches sur la Céramique Byzantine*, 227-32. Athens, Bulletin de Correspondence Hellénique Supplément 18.

Hahn, M. 1996. The Berbati-Limnes Project: the early Byzantine to modern periods. In B. Wells (ed), *The Berbati-Limnes Archaeological Survey 1988-1990*, 345-451. Stockholm, Åström.

Harvey, A. 1989. *Economic Expansion in the Byzantine Empire, 900-1200*. Cambridge, Cambridge University Press.

Hayes, J. W. 1992. *Excavations at Saraçhane in Istanbul: The Pottery*, II. Princeton, Princeton University Press.

Johnson, M. 1996. *An Archaeology of Capitalism*. Oxford, Blackwell.

Kiel, M. 1992. Central Greece in the Suleymanic Age: preliminary notes on population growth, economic expansion and its influence on the spread of Greek Christian culture. In G. Veinstein (ed), *Soliman Le Magnifique et Son Temps: Actes du Colloque de Paris Galeries Nationales du Grand Palais, 7-10 mars 1990*, 399-424. Paris, La Documentation Française.

Kiel, M. 1997. The rise and decline of Turkish Boeotia, 15th-19th century. In J. L. Bintliff (ed), *Recent Developments in the History and Archaeology of Central Greece*. BAR (British Archaeological Reports) International Series 666, 315-58. Oxford, BAR Publishing.

Laiou, A. E. 2002. Agrotiki zoi kai oikonomia. In D. Papanikola-Bakirtzi (ed.) *Kathimerini Zoi sto Vyzantio*, 49-57. Athens, Kapon.

Laiou, A. E. and Morrisson, C. 2007. *The Byzantine Economy*. Cambridge, Cambridge University Press.

Lock, P. 1986. The Frankish towers of central Greece. *Annual of the British School at Athens* 81, 101-23.

Lock, P. 1997. The Frankish period in Boeotia: problems and perspectives. In J. L. Bintliff (ed.) *Recent Developments in the History and Archaeology of Central Greece*. BAR (British Archaeological Reports) International Series 666, 305-13. Oxford, BAR Publishing.

Malamut, E. 1988. *Les Iles de l'Empire Byzantine, VIIIe-XIIe Siècles*, vol. I. Paris, Publications de la Sorbonne.

Mee, C. and Forbes, H. (eds) 1997. *A Rough and Rocky Place: The Landscape and Settlement History of the Methana Peninsula, Greece*. Liverpool, Liverpool University Press.

Mitchell, S. 2000. The settlement of Pisidia in Late Antiquity and the Byzantine period: methodological problems. In K. Belke, F. Hild, J. Koder and P. Soustal (eds), *Byzanz als Raum. Zu Methoden und Inhalten der Historischen Geographie des Östlichen Mittelmeerraumes, 139-52*. Wien, Österreichische Akademie der Wissenschaften.

Papanikola-Bakirtzi, D. 1996. *Medieval Glazed Ceramics from Cyprus: The Workshops of Paphos and Lapithos*. Thessaloniki, A.G. Leventis Foundation.

Papanikola-Bakirtzi, D. (ed.) 1999. *Byzantine Glazed Ceramics: The Art of Sgraffito*. Athens, Archaeological Receipts Fund.

Poulou-Papadimitriou, N. and Nodarou, E. 2007. La céramique protobyzantine de Pseira: la production locale et les importations, étude typologique et pétrographique. In M. Bonifay and J.-C. Tréglia (eds), *LRCW2. Late Roman Coarse Wares, Cooking Wares and Amphorae in the Mediterranean: Archaeology and Archaeometry*. BAR (British Archaeological Reports) International Series 1662 II, 755-66, Oxford, BAR Publishing.

Romanus, K., Poblome, J., Verbeke, K., Luypaerts, A., Jacobs, P., De Vos, D. and Waelkens, M. 2007. An evaluation of analytical and interpretative methodologies for the extraction and identification of lipids associated with pottery sherds from the site of Sagalassos, Turkey. *Archaeometry* 49(4), 729-47.

Sanders, G. D. R. 1987. An assemblage of Frankish pottery at Corinth. *Hesperia* 56, 159-95.

Sanders, G. D. R. 2000. New relative and absolute chronologies for 9th to 13th century glazed wares at Corinth: methodology and social conclusions. In K. Belke, F. Hild, J. Koder and P. Soustal (eds), *Byzanz als Raum. Zu Methoden und Inhalten der Historischen Geographie des Östlichen Mittelmeerraumes, 153-73*. Wien, Österreichische Akademie der Wissenschaften.

Sanders, G. D. R. 2003. Recent developments in the chronology of Byzantine Corinth. In Ch. Williams II and N. Bookidis (eds), *Corinth: Results of Excavations*, XX, 385-99. Athens, American School of Classical Studies at Athens.

Scranton, R. L. 1957. *Corinth: Medieval Architecture in the Central Area of Corinth*, XVI. Princeton, The American School of Classical Studies at Athens.

Sigalos, E. 2004. *Housing in Medieval and Post-Medieval Greece*. BAR (British Archaeological Reports) International Series 1291. Oxford, BAR Publishing.

Spieser, J.-M. 1989. Informatique et céramique: l'exemple de Pergame. In V. Déroche and J.-M. Spieser (eds), *Recherches sur la Céramique Byzantine*, 291-302. Athens, Bulletin de Correspondence Hellénique Supplément 18.

Spieser, J.-M. 1991. La céramique byzantine médiévale. In V. Kravari, J. Lefort and C. Morrisson (eds), *Hommes et Richesses dans l'Empire Byzantine VIIIe-XVe siècle*, 249-60. Paris, P. Lethielleux.

Svoronos, N. 1959. Recherches sur le cadastre byzantin et la fiscalité aux XIe–XIIe siècles: la cadastre de Thèbes. *Bulletin de Correspondance Héllenique* 83, 1-166.

Symeonoglou, S. 1985. *The Topography of Thebes from the Bronze Age to Modern Times*. Princeton, Princeton University Press.

Thompson, H. A. and Wycherley, R. E. 1972. *The Athenian Agora: The Agora of Athens*, XIV. Princeton, The American School of Classical Studies at Athens.

Vanhaverbeke, H. and Waelkens, M. 2003. *The Chora of Sagalassos: The Evolution of the Settlement Pattern in the Territory of Sagalassos from Prehistoric until Recent Times*. Turnhout: Studies in Eastern Mediterranean Archaeology 5.

Vanhaverbeke, H., Başagaç, Ö., Paul, K. and Waelkens, M. 2005. A Selçuk hamam at Ağlasun, Burdur Province, Turkey. *Turcica* 37, 309-36.

Vanhaverbeke, H., Vionis, A. K., Poblome, J. and Waelkens, M. 2009. What happened after the 7th century AD? A different perspective on Post-Roman rural Anatolia. In T. Vorderstrasse and J. Roodenberg (eds), *Archaeology of the Countryside in Medieval Anatolia*. PIHANS 113, 177-90. Leiden, Nederlands Instituut voor het Nabije Oosten.

Vionis, A. K. 2001. Post-Roman pottery unearthed: medieval ceramics and pottery research in Greece. *Medieval Ceramics* 25, 84-98.

Vionis, A. K. 2004-2005. The medieval and post-medieval pottery and Tanagra village-history. *Bulletin de Correspondence Hellènique* 128-129 (2.1), 570-78.

Vionis, A. K. 2006a. The archaeology of Ottoman villages in central Greece: ceramics, housing and everyday life in post-medieval rural Boeotia. In A. Erkanal-Öktü *et al.* (eds), *Studies in Honor of Hayat Erkanal: Cultural Reflections*. Istanbul, Homer Kitabevi, 784-800.

Vionis, A. K. 2006b. The thirteenth-to-sixteenth-century *Kastro* of Kephalos: a contribution to the archaeological study of medieval Paros and the Cyclades. *Annual of the British School at Athens* 101, 459-92.

Vionis, A. K. 2008. Current archaeological research on settlement and provincial life in the Byzantine and Ottoman Aegean: a case-study from Boeotia, Greece. *Medieval Settlement Research* 23, 28-41.

Vionis, A. K. (in peer review). A ceramic 'koine' as evidence for continuity and economy. In A. Vionis (ed.), *Byzantium in Transition: The Byzantine Early Middle Ages, 7th-8th centuries*. Cambridge: Cambridge University Press.

Vionis, A. K. (forthcoming). Katoikisi sti Byzantini Naxo: archaiologikes martyries apo tin erevna pediou. In Ch. Pennas (ed.), *Archaiologika Tekmiria gia tin Proimi Byzantini Naxo*. Athens: Archaeological Receipt Funds.

Vionis, A. K., Poblome, J. and Waelkens, M. 2009a. The *hidden* material culture of the *Dark Ages*: early medieval ceramics at Sagalassos (Turkey); new evidence (ca. AD 650-800). *Anatolian Studies* 59, 147-65.

Vionis, A. K., Poblome, J. and Waelkens, M. 2009b. Ceramic continuity and daily life in medieval Sagalassos, SW Anatolia (ca. 650-1250 AD). In T. Vorderstrasse and J. Roodenberg (eds), *Archaeology of the Countryside in Medieval Anatolia*. PIHANS 113, 191-213. Leiden, Nederlands Instituut voor het Nabije Oosten.

Vionis, A. K., Poblome, J., De Cupere, B. and Waelkens, M. 2010. A Middle–Late Byzantine pottery assemblage from Sagalassos: typo-chronology and sociocultural interpretation. *Hesperia* 79(3) 423-464.

Vroom, J. 1998a. Medieval and post-medieval pottery from a site in Boeotia: a case study example of post-classical archaeology in Greece. *Annual of the British School at Athens* 93, 513-46.

Vroom, J. 1998b. Early modern archaeology in central Greece: the contrast of artefact-rich and sherdless sites. *Journal of Mediterranean Archaeology* 11, 3-36.

Vroom, J. 2003. *After Antiquity: Ceramics and Society in the Aegean from the 7th to the 20th Century A.C.: A Case Study from Boeotia, Central Greece*. Leiden, Archaeological Studies, Leiden University, 10.

Waelkens, M. (ed.) 1993. *Sagalassos I: First General Report on the Survey (1986-1989) and Excavations (1990-1991)*. Leuven, Acta Archaeologica Lovaniensia Monographiae 5.

Poverty and resistance in the material culture of Early Modern rural households in the Aegean

John Bintliff
Department of Classical and Mediterranean Archaeology, Leiden University

Abstract

Contemporary descriptions in texts and images created by bourgeois urban visitors to the countryside, portray the peasantry of Early Modern Southern Europe as 'primitive' peoples. Their houses are frequently very unsophisticated single-storey dwellings, their material culture limited. They are often associated in the same sources with indolence, crime and an absence of any desire to 'improvement' or 'progress'. Exceptions to these generalisations are met with in three areas: dress and body ornaments, and the display of highly-decorated tablewares. This paper will investigate these conflicting attitudes through the material culture of the Greek Mainland and the Agean Islands in the Medieval and Early Modern period.

Keywords: Postmedieval Archaeologyy, rural society, dress, identity, tableware, vernacular architecture, Greek Archaeology

Regional dress within Europe still appears a surprise to most of us when we encounter it. What does it say today – pride in local identity for sure, and was it the same in the past? The international newspapers in 2009 showed Hungarian voters for the European elections wearing diverse traditional costumes. Ladies in my adopted home the Netherlands can easily match their Hungarian counterparts in making a big regional identity-impression, if we consider the complex costumes worn on special occasions in the island region of Zeeland (Dekker 2005). But we poor English do not have much left to offer in national dress, and even the London financiers no longer go to work in pinstripe suits and bowler hats with rolled-up umbrellas.

In this paper I want to draw some links between Early Modern ethnic dress and the expressive use of ceramics in the home, focussing on Greece from where the remarkable image of Figure 1 is derived (from Korre-Zographou 1995).

But we need to go back in time to the Aegean in the High Middle Ages. A common Greek Mainland settlement under Frankish-Crusader rule, consisted of a castle or tower for the lord with simple peasant houses loosely scattered below it (Bintliff 2012, Ch. 19). On the contemporary Aegean Islands Venetian rulers created more elaborate townships, centred also on towers but with more advanced townhouses below: two storeyed, single roomed, with animals and stores below, living quarters above, they mark the localised introduction of Italian urban culture (Vionis 2005, 2012). On the Mainland, in contrast, single-storey longhouses shared by animals and people dominated for all but the elite, also till recent memory. These two housing cultures still make up the dominant surviving historic domestic houses on the Southern Mainland and the islands, called by Sigalos in his splendid overview of historic Greek domestic homes the Agricultural style (longhouses) and the Aegean style (the island townhouses) (Sigalos 2004). In the Middle Ages, both societies however shared similar ceramic styles, also with areas of the Middle East: slipwares and sgraffito, and dining from shared pedestal bowls (Vionis 2001).

FIGURE 1 - INTERIOR OF A TRADITIONAL HOUSE ON THE ISLAND OF CARPATHOS, AEGEAN DODECANESE ISLANDS (FROM KORRE-ZOGRAFOU 1995).

The conquest of Continental Greece by the Ottoman Empire in the 15th century led to gradual economic and population growth and a growing emulation of Eastern culture for the more-deeply Orientalised Mainland. Low initial populations expanded by the late 16th century at a remarkable rate, paralleling a general European trend (Bintliff 1995). An example from our Boeotia Project in Central Greece is the deserted village site of Panagia in Early Ottoman times. There is evidence for great settlement growth on surface ceramic finds by the late 16th century, whilst the tax record lists more than 1000 inhabitants. Signs of prosperity at this and other contemporary village-sites include fine tableware imports, such as 16th century Italian majolicas and Anatolian fineware imports (Iznik Ware).

On the Aegean islands, Venetian rule lasted longer, whilst subsequent Ottoman rule was remote and allowed most islands to flourish under local government. Here population and economy largely flourished from the 15th through to the early 19th centuries (Vionis 2009, 2012). However similar access to Eastern and Western tablewares is found to that on the Greek Mainland for the Early Ottoman period. Both Mainland and Aegean Islands largely fit Hugo Blake's (1980) model for measuring rural wealth in Italy through access to ceramic fineware imports, with a highlight in the 14th-16th century Renaissance period, largely contemporary to their florescence in Early Ottoman Greece.

Mainland Greece was to suffer decline with the deterioration of the Ottoman Empire during the 17th-18th Centuries. Population collapsed and the formerly independent flourishing villages were converted into tied estates (the çiftliks) of poor tenants producing commercial crops for a dominant landowning class. Mainland rural communities became typified by these semi-feudal estates, whilst the estate-owner's home revived the Medieval Mainland tradition of towerhouses (Bintliff 2012, Ch. 21). Our survey of deserted 17th-18th century çiftliks found traditional longhouses and associated surface ceramics which mostly continued Medieval traditions (Vionis 2006). Such 17th-18th century Mainland peasants could still obtain cheap substitutes for metal and glass tablewares from 'peasant porcelain': Aegean imitations of Italian majolica jugs and the cheerful whitewares of Kütahya in Turkey, again fitting Blake's (1980) model of deteriorating ceramic standards in this era for Southern Europe

For most Mainland peasants then, possessions were few and life had reverted almost to Medieval conditions even in the 19th century, after freedom was achieved from Ottoman rule (Bintliff 2012, Ch. 22). In the 19th-early 20th century, however, peasant porcelain was being widely-obtained from a new source, the Çanakkale potteries in North-West Anatolia. Contemporary photographs nonetheless suggest pride in possessing it and interestingly also in wearing regional dress identifiers (Fig. 2 from Northern Greece, from Korre-Zographou 1995).

In the 19th to early 20th century a Western 'peasant porcelain' product also spreads throughout our now-deserted village sites, Grottaglie Ware from Southern Italy

FIGURE 2 – LADIES CA. 1900 AD WEARING TRADITIONAL DRESS AND DISPLAYING ÇANNAKALE CERAMIC JUGS (FROM KORRE-ZOGRAFOU 1995). LEFT: SOURPI IN THESSALY. RIGHT: NEA ANCHIALOS IN THRACE.

FIGURE 3 – GROTTAGLIE WARE, A 19TH TO EARLY 20TH CENTURY 'PEASANT PORCELAIN' MANUFACTURED IN APULIA PROVINCE, ITALY AND ALSO SUBSEQUENTLY IN THE IONIAN ISLANDS (COURTESY OF IKEA PICTURES).

and the Ionian Islands (Fig. 3, an image courtesy of IKEA). Nonetheless, our survey of deserted Mainland villages finds little change in the longhouse and village plan even into the late 19th century. And indeed a generation ago older village inhabitants still lived in such traditional accommodation.

During the 17th- early 19th centuries the Mainland elite, however, copied Ottoman urban lifestyles and Oriental mansion designs: many such 'archontika' survive in the once wealthy 18th century textile villages of Mount Pelion, Thessaly (Kizis 1994).

Despite impoverished physical circumstances, peasant pride on the Mainland was chiefly manifested in the preparation and inheritance of distinctive folk dress with ethnic and also local identifiers, as seen in a photo around 1890 of a proud young couple in their longhouse village of Erimokastro, Central Greece (Fig. 4, courtesy of the French School at Athens Photothèque). Today this folk dress, distinctive for each village of Greece, has been revived as a mark of local pride, as in the costume displayed in Figure 5 from the villages in central Attica (the Mesogaia, from Broufas n.d.). However in origin these clothes are local combinations of wider dress traditions, both Balkan and also Western and Oriental, whilst the fabrics and ornaments also derive from wide contacts. It is in the distinct details of such combinations that each village can be seen as unique from its neighbours. In essence local peasant communities became globalised, but reacted by adapting these components into a quite distinctive highly-local dress style, so as to create something of local pride despite their otherwise limited economic and social opportunities.

Some sectors amongst the Mainland peasantry began to achieve prosperity two generations after Greek Independence, in the late 19th century. Full rights over land and rising international commerce stimulated the rise of a new middle class of farmers, and this was linked to the provision of teachers and local government officers to service rural communities. This emergent middle class marked its social status, above the majority of the peasantry who still occupied the traditional longhouses, through elaborating their homes into a two-storey house with

Figure 4 – Photograph ca. 1890 of a young couple in traditional dress in the village of Erimokastro, Central Mainland Greece, amidst the standard single-storey longhouses of the community (courtesy of the French Institute of Archaeology at Athens, Photothèque).

internal room divisions emulating Western townhouses (Sigalos 2004; Bintliff 2012 Ch. 22). The culmination of the spread of Western urban styles into Mainland villages comes with their adoption of Neo-Classical house façades in the late 19th-early 20th centuries.

On the Aegean islands, commercial contacts and greater prosperity had led much earlier to more clearly-cosmopolitan dress codes (Vionis 2003): contemporary illustrations show Cycladic islanders in mixed Western and traditional Oriental dress during the 16th-18th century. Aegean Island elites however maintained their Western lifestyle, retaining table-chairs and introducing the custom of personal table sets from Italy together with ceramic and glass services in the 17th-18th centuries.

Although the Aegean islanders also consumed peasant porcelain like their Mainland cousins, their more prosperous economy, greater social independence (few çiftliks are known) and vigorous commerce with the West allowed them greater quantities and quality of imports in the 17th-19th centuries (such as majolica jugs from Pesaro, Italy). On the Aegean islands as we have seen, the period 1500-1900 was always more wealthy and cosmopolitan, and access to interregional ceramic imports remained higher (Korre-Zografou 1995). Although we do find occasional 19th century Western industrial ceramics on Mainland deserted village sites, their major market was the wealthier, more open communities of the Aegean Islands.

Figure 5 – Traditional dress of women from the villages of Central Attica, Mainland Greece (Mesogaia district) (from Broufas, n.d.)

FIGURE 6 – INTERIOR OF A HOUSE ON THE AEGEAN ISLAND OF SKYROS, IN THE SPORADES, SHOWING WESTERN TRANSFER-PRINTED WARES AND JUGS FROM PESARO, ITALY (FROM KORRE-ZOGRAPHOU 1995).

Transfer-printed wares were made by many Western factories for the Greek market with appropriate scenes and captions in Modern Greek, but called 'Syriana' as largely imported through the great Cycladic island trading centre of Syros.

If the less wealthy Mainlanders displayed their local pride and identity through distinctive folk dress, but largely remained in simple houses with few material possessions until the turn of the 20th century, the Aegean islanders had long enjoyed more sophisticated homes, which in the 19th to early 20th century became galleries of Western ceramics (Fig. 6, from Korre-Zografou 1995). Greater wealth combined with cheaper and more easily-available Western factory wares encouraged island communities to new forms of middle-class display. Just like Greek traditional folk costume on the Mainland and also on the Islands, the overabundant displays of imported pottery combine the effects of growing globalisation with a distinctive local cultural statement of family status and island pride.

Conclusion

In this paper I have tried to show how rural communities have striven to adapt to good and bad times by developing symbolically-important representations of pride in their local identity, in particular through costume and the obtaining and deployment of exotic ceramics.

Bibliography

Bintliff, J. L. 1995. The Two Transitions: Current Research on the Origins of the Traditional Village in Central

Greece, J. L. Bintliff and H. Hamerow (eds), *Europe Between Late Antiquity and the Middle Ages. Recent Archaeological and Historical Research in Western and Southern Europe*, 111-130. Oxford, BAR Publishing. BAR International Series 617.

Bintliff, J. L. 2012. *The Complete Archaeology of Greece, from Hunter-Gatherers to the Twentieth Century AD.* Oxford-New York, Blackwell-Wiley.

Blake, H. 1980. Technology, supply or demand?, *Medieval Ceramics* 4, 3-12.

Broufas, C. n.d.. *40 Greek Costumes from the Dora Stratou Theatre Collection*. Athens, Dora Stratou Theatre. Dekker, J. (ed.). 2005. *De Zeeuwse streekdrachten 1800-2000*. Zwolle, Wanders.

Kizis, G. 1994. *Pilioreitiki Oikodomia*. Athens, Politistiko Technologiko Idrima ETBA.

Korre-Zographou, K. 1995. *Ta Kerameika tou Ellinikou Chorou*. Athens, Melissa.

Sigalos, E. 2004. *Housing in Medieval and Post-Medieval Greece*. Oxford, BAR Publishing. BAR International Series 1291.

Vionis, A. K. 2001. Post-Roman pottery unearthed: Medieval ceramics and pottery research in Greece, *Medieval Ceramics* 25, 84-98.

Vionis, A. K. 2003. Much Ado About...a red cap and a cap of velvet. In search of social and cultural identity in medieval and post-medieval insular Greece, H. Hokwerda (ed.) *Constructions of Greek Past. Identity and Historical Consciousness from Antiquity to the Present*, 193-216. Groningen, Egbert Forsten.

Vionis, A. K. 2005. Domestic material culture and Post-Medieval archaeology in Greece: A case-study of the Cyclades Islands, *Journal of the Society for Post-Medieval Archaeology* 39, 172-185.

Vionis, A. 2006. The archaeology of Ottoman villages in central Greece: ceramics, housing and everyday life in post-medieval Boeotia, A. Erkanal-Öktu et al. (eds), *Studies in Honour of Hayat Erkanal: Cultural Reflections*, 784-800. Istanbul, Homer Kitabevi.

Vionis, A. 2009. Material Culture Studies: The case of the Medieval and Post-Medieval Cyclades, Greece (c. AD 1200-1800), J. Bintliff and H. Stöger (eds), *Medieval and Post-Medieval Greece. The Corfu Papers*, 177-197. Oxford, BAR Publishing. BAR International Series 2023.

Vionis, A. 2012. *A Crusader, Ottoman, and Early Modern Aegean Archaeology. Built Environment and Domestic Material Culture in the Medieval and Post-Medieval Cyclades, Greece (13th-20th Century AD)*. Leiden, Archaeological Studies Leiden University 22.

Town centre and minor settlements
Cultural and social implications of tableware use during the late Middle Ages in Florence and its environs

Marta Caroscio
The Medici Archive Project, Florence
caroscio@medici.org

Abstract

Is there any difference between tableware used in major town centres such as late Medieval Florence and vessels used and displayed in minor settlements? To what extent is the demand and circulation of certain models influenced by "fashion"? How does the political control over a certain area influence trade and the circulation of models? What can pottery use tell us about cultural and social differences within the sub-regional areas under study? This paper aims to discuss the social implications of tableware use in central Florence and in settlements that can be regarded as minor ones, either under its political control or not. Circulation of local products will be discussed in comparison with the impact and social meaning of long-distance traded vessels, which are normally regarded as "luxury" items. Concerning Florence, the use of materials other than pottery will be discussed. As ceramics represent the majority of archaeological finds, written sources dating between the late 14th and the beginning of the 17th centuries will also be taken into account to reconstruct daily use of tableware in different contexts, discussing in detail selected examples of monastic and hospital inventories.

Keywords: tin-glazed pottery, local production, imports, circulation, fashion, quality, cultural context, social meaning

Introduction

This paper wishes to raise debate on the actual use of diverse tablewares according to the social and cultural context they were used in.[1] Assemblages recovered in central Florence will be compared with those excavated in settlements that can be regarded as minor ones, either under Florence's political control or not. Concerning Florence as a town, the use of diverse materials on the table, and their functional role in relations with pottery use, will be discussed. At this stage of the research, about 20 monastic inventories have been analysed. What shows up is that at a time when tin-glazed and lead-glazed pottery was already quite widespread (as known from archaeological evidence), wooden and tin tableware were extremely common, possibly more than what is usually assumed.

Florence

The starting point of this research is the analysis of the tin-glazed pottery recovered during the excavations undertaken in central Florence from 2003 to 2006 (Figure 1).[2] It reveals that the finished products circulating in Florence were either made within the town-walls or in the area that has been identified as the "production district" of Florence (Caroscio 2009a), referring to the term as defined by Peacock (1982). We are talking about a space that can include different production models (single workshops, groups of workshops etc.) and diverse retailing systems (dealers, retail sales, market places). Nevertheless, workshops operating within the same district used the same raw materials and technical devices, and operated within the same trading network (Figure 2). The quality and quantity of objects produced within the district will be compared with that of goods imported on a long-distance basis and circulating within the same area. The research undertaken on written sources, especially on tax-accounts dating from the late 14th to the late 16th centuries, has clearly shown that pottery, as well as bricks and tiles, was being made within the town walls. As the aim of this paper is to analyse the actual use of the finished products (i.e. tableware), we are not going to discuss this point in detail. Further research made clear that from the late 14th century onwards there was a re-location of several production activities, such as pottery making; in the first instance, into assigned areas in the town, and then, outside the town-walls. Several craft activities, in fact, were regarded as polluting and dangerous because of the risk of fires (Figures 3-4).

The role of the town of Montelupo was central during the 16th century (Berti 2001), and by then the whole production of tin-glazed pottery previously in central Florence, was definitely relocated there. From the 15th century onwards, a large amount of its ceramics circulated on a local-market scale. Interestingly, the comparative analysis of written sources (with special reference to contracts) and of archaeological evidence points out that, from the 16th century onwards, vessels produced for this local market were usually of higher quality than those which were at

---

[1] This paper is a spin-off from my Ph.D. dissertation. While researching on tin-glazed pottery use in Renaissance Florence, I started investigating the actual use of diverse materials. What I presented at the EAA 15th Annual Meeting represents some preliminary results of this ongoing research and a summary of the research undertaken on the circulation of models in the area under Florence's political control during the transition from the Middle Ages to the Renaissance. I am indebted to Allen Grieco and to Lucia Sandri for the research undertaken at the Archivio degli Innocenti in Florence. I am extremely grateful to Graziella Berti for encouragement and comments on my work. Least but not last, I would like to thank John Bintliff for organising together the session 'Pottery and social dynamics in the Mediterranean and beyond in Medieval and post-Medieval times'. Thanks to him this session has been an extraordinary occasion of meeting and debate with scholars researching on a variety of regional contexts.
[2] Research on the assemblage was coordinated by Riccardo Francovich (University of Siena) and resulted in a publication of the whole context (Francovich *et al.* 2007).

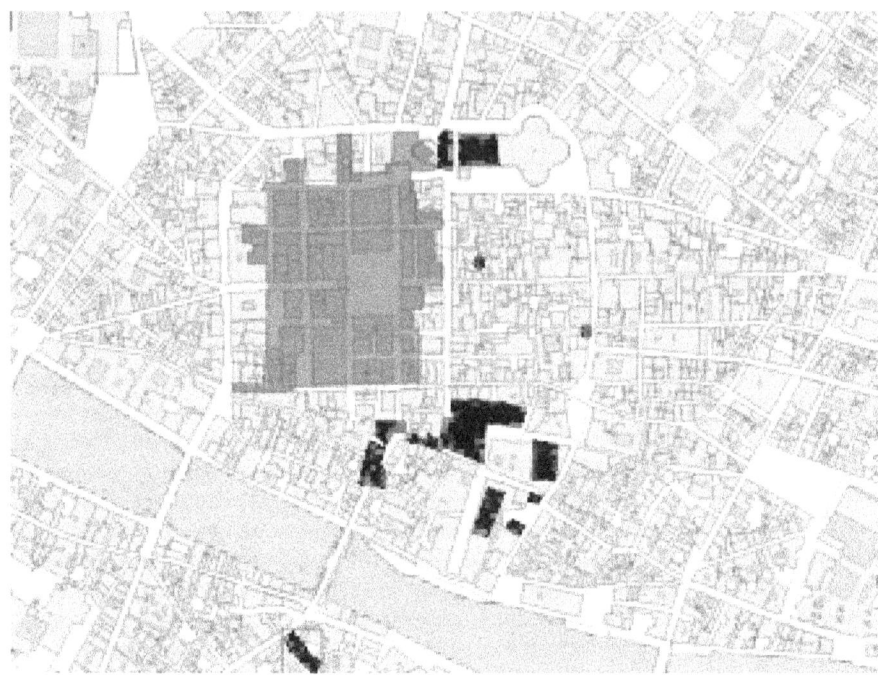

Figure 1 – Excavations in central Florence. 19th century excavations (shaded in grey); excavations employing stratigraphic technique (shaded in black).

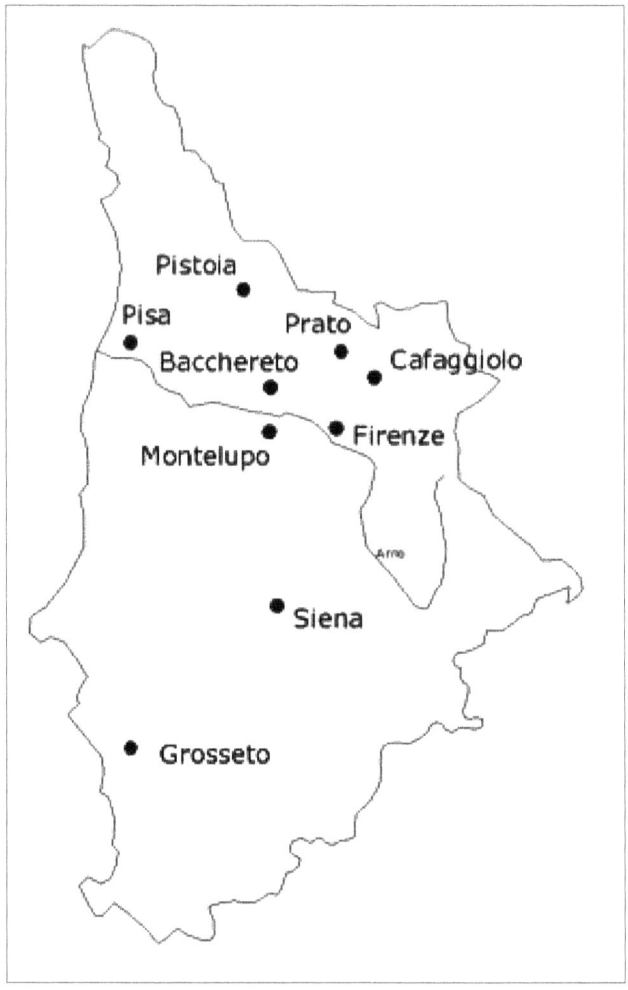

Figure 2 – The Florence (Firenze) production district.

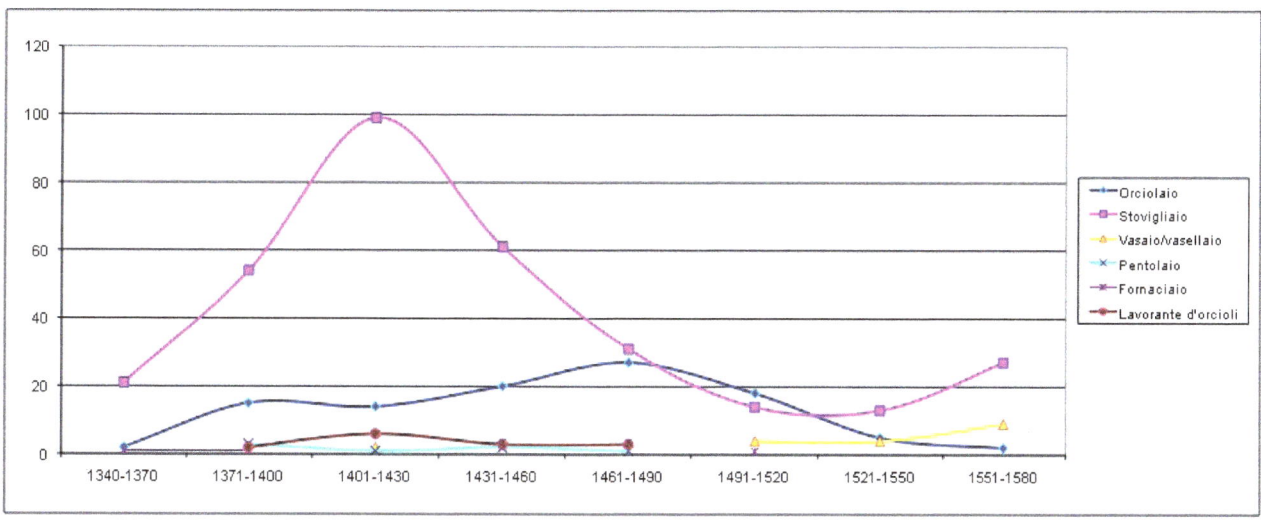

FIGURE 3 – CERAMIC PRODUCTION AND RETAIL IN FLORENCE. AS NAMED IN THE ORIGINAL DOCUMENTS: *ORCIOLAIO* = POTTERS AS CRAFTSMEN; *STOVIGLIAIO* = PEOPLE SELLING POTTERY AND SOMETIMES OTHER KINDS OF TABLEWARE; *VASAIO* = SAME MEANING AS *ORCIOLAIO* BUT IT IS REPLACED BY THE LATTER DURING THE MID 15TH CENTURY; *PENTOLAIO* = SOMEONE SPECIFICALLY MAKING COOKING POTS; *FORNACIAIO* = CRAFTSMEN MAKING BRICK AND LIME; *LAVORANTE D'ORCIOLI* = SOMEONE WORKING ON AN OCCASIONAL BASIS IN SOMEONE ELSE'S WORKSHOP.

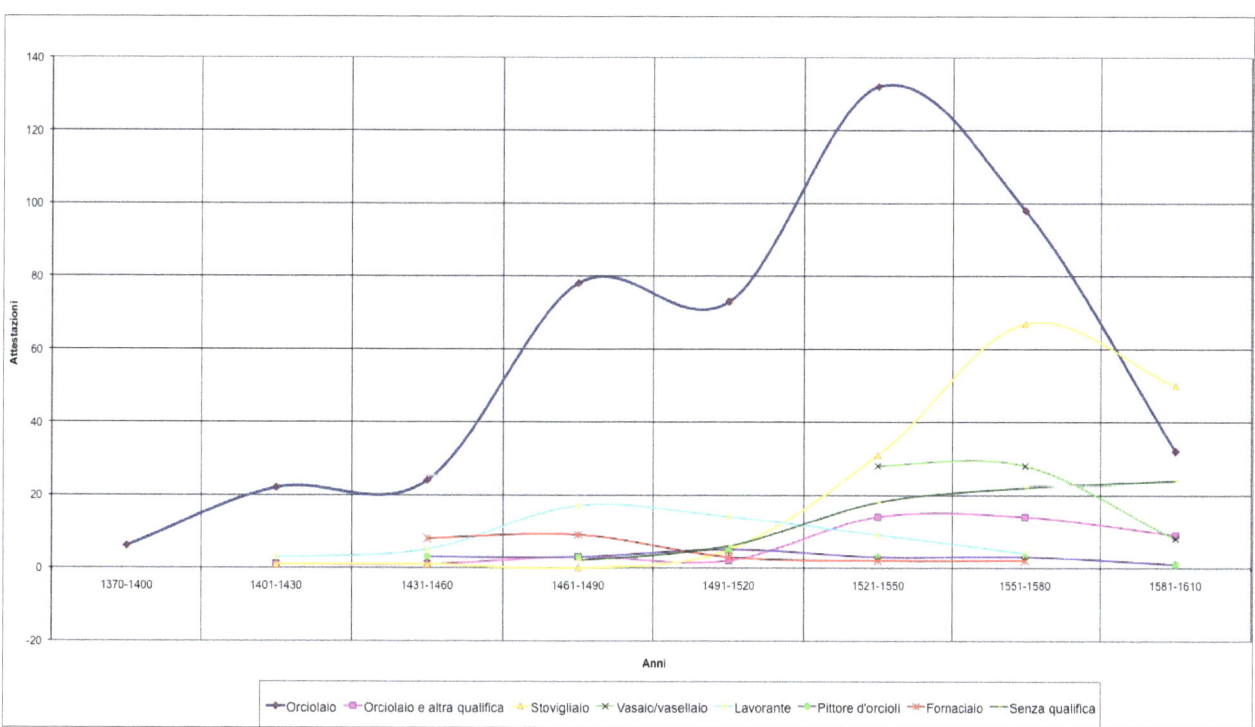

FIGURE 4 – CERAMIC PRODUCTION AND RETAIL IN MONTELUPO. IN THE COUNTRYSIDE POTTERS ARE NAMED THE SAME WAY AS IN TOWN, BUT THE CONTEXT SUGGESTS THAT THERE WAS A DIFFERENCE IN WHAT *ORCIOLAIO* MEANT. IN MONTELUPO, AS IN THE REST OF THE FLORENTINE COUNTRYSIDE *ORCIOLAIO* WERE BOTH PRODUCING (THEY HAD A KILN) AND SELLING DIRECTLY THE POTTERY THEY MADE; *ORCIOLAIO E ALTRA QUALICA* = POTTERS PRODUCING AND SELLING POTTERY, COMBINED WITH FURTHER SPECIFICATION ABOUT HIS ACTIVITY; *STOVIGLIAIO, VASAIO, FORNACIAO, LAVORANTE* = AS IN CAPTION FIGURE 3; *PITTORE D'ORCIOLI* = TIN-GLAZED POTTERY PAINTER; *SENZA QUALIFICA* = NOT SPECIFIED

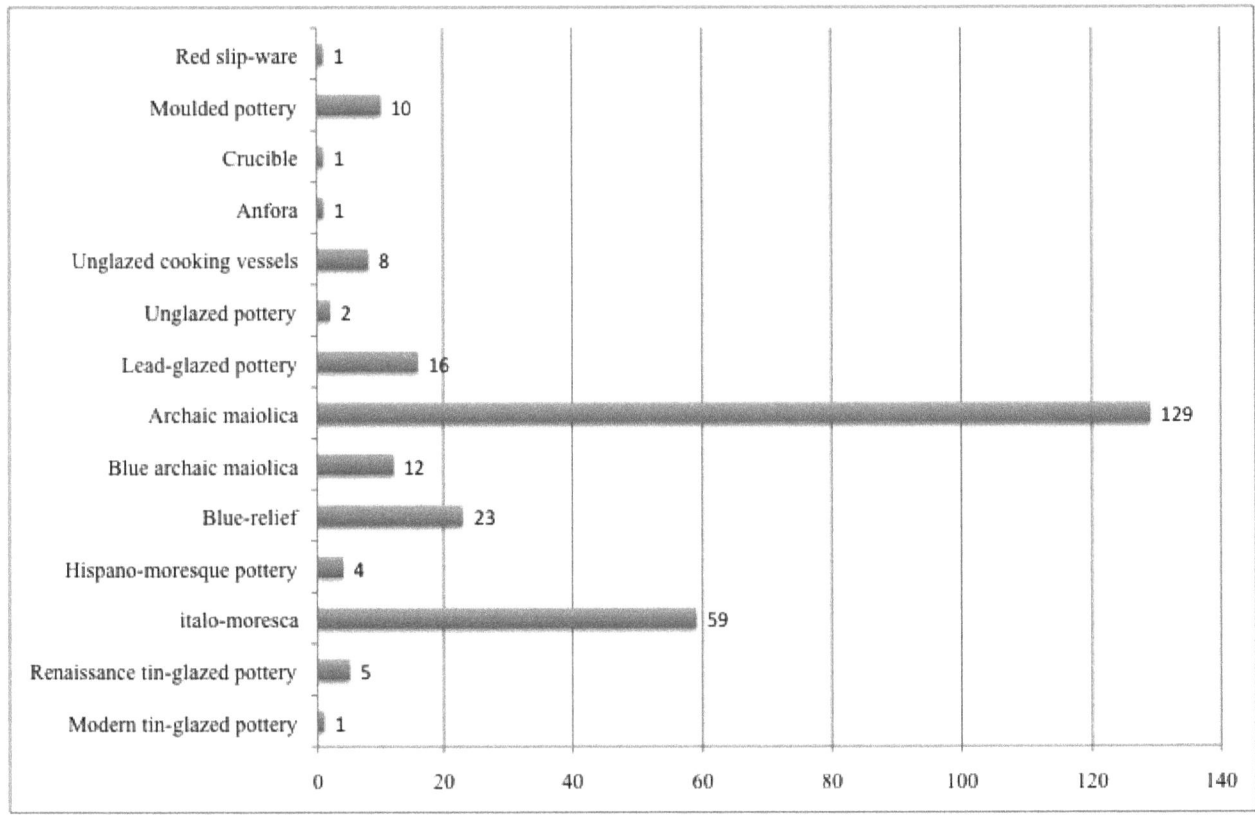

FIGURE 5 – FBM. MINIMUM VESSEL NUMBERS AND PERCENTAGE OF CERAMIC CLASSES FROM THE LATE 14TH CENTURY.

the same time being shipped to be sold abroad on a larger scale. As a consequence of the high number of kilns located in Montelupo, this village had a central role in pottery making on a national and international scale.

Wider research undertaken on ceramic production in central Tuscany has shown that, in addition to major production centres, there were many smaller centres producing cheaper, lead-glazed tableware and coarseware (Milanese 2006). According to the data published so far, these smaller centres can be divided into two groups: those located far away from major routes and from the river Arno, and those just next to the river. The first ones, made objects for the local market; the latter, produced ceramics (usually of lower quality) to be shipped into long-distance trade (Milanese 2006). Concerning pottery produced for the local market, it is worth pointing out that both archaeological evidence and written records have shown that products of diverse qualities (first and second choice pottery) coexisted during the same period and were sold at different prices. In fact, the production and retailing systems, from the late 15th century onwards tended to operate differently with regard to extremely high quality or second choice objects (Bojani 1992). As a consequence, the role of economic circumstances in determining the success of a certain production became more relevant (Wilson 1996).

If we consider the excavations undertaken in central Florence at two different sites (via de' Castellani – FVC, and Biblioteca Magliabechiana – FBM), the tin-glazed pottery recovered dating between the late 14th and the mid 15th century can be divided into three major groups.[3] The first group includes a variety of tin-glazed classes that we can define as belonging to the local tradition, and that can be identified with 'blue archaic maiolica' and 'blue relief maiolica' (Caroscio 2007a), produced within the district we have defined above. The second group can be identified with imports from the Mediterranean area, in this case uniquely from Spain and specifically from the Valencian area (Caroscio 2007b). These imports had an influence on local production and represented the fashionable models that local potters wished to imitate. Thus, Valencian tin-glazed pottery had a deep influence on the earliest Renaissance production, i.e. what known as *italo moresca* tin-glazed pottery. The latter represents the third ceramics group we are discussing: it was made within the same production district, sometime by the same workshops that produced group one tin-glazed pottery. Whereas, during the first phase of its production *italo moresca* tin-glazed pottery imitated more closely models from the Iberian Peninsula, it shortly developed its own style and by the last decades of the 15th century it can be regarded as the first Italian Renaissance production.

If we turn to analyse the quality of the production and the percentage of sherds at FBM, one of the two sites excavated in central Florence, the increase in Renaissance

---
[3] We are going to discuss only Renaissance production and specifically tin-glazed pottery that can be regarded as transitional between the late Middle Ages and the Renaissance, with decorations that involve the use of cobalt blue. Archaic maiolica will be taken into account for the assemblage in FBM only.

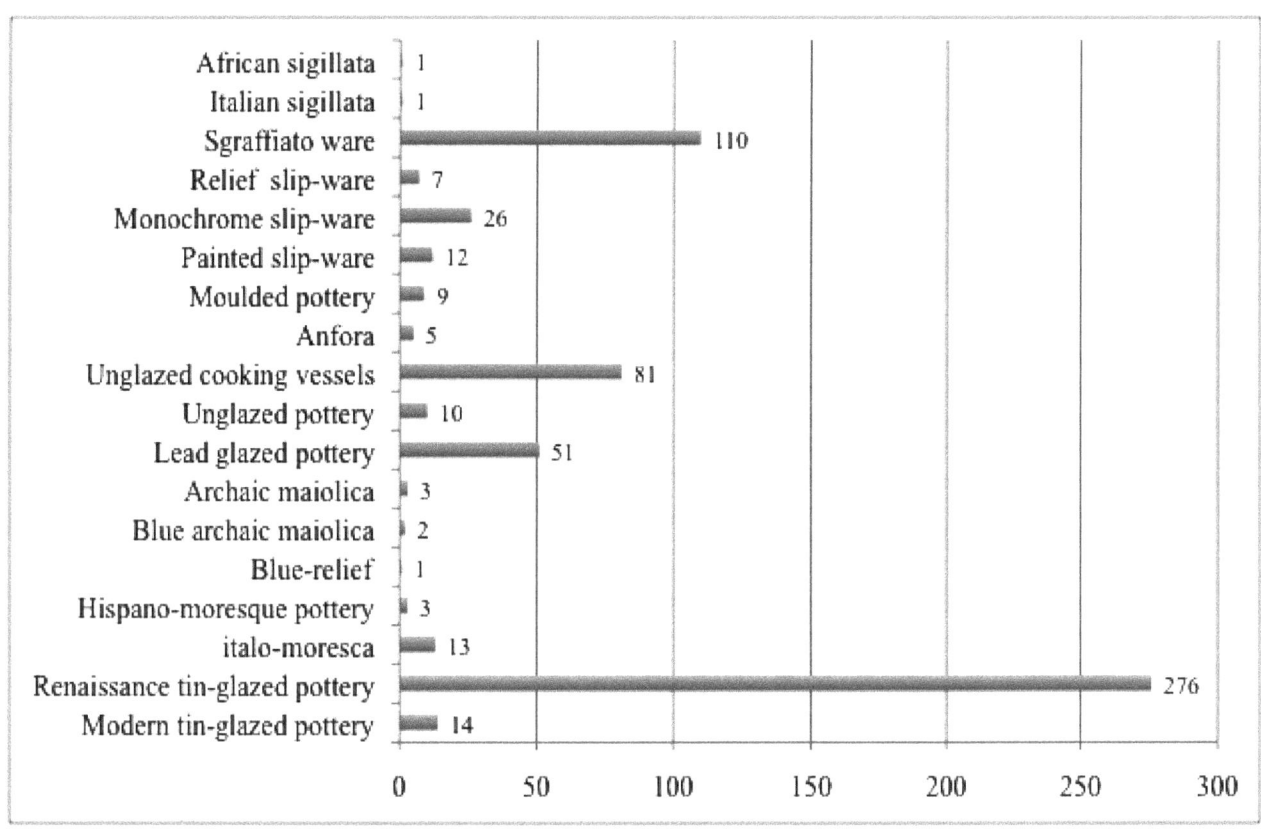

FIGURE 6 – FBM. MINIMUM VESSEL NUMBERS AND PERCENTAGE OF CERAMIC CLASSES FROM THE LATE 15TH CENTURY.

pottery and the decrease in imports from Spain and their local imitations during the span from the late 14th to the late 15th centuries, show up quite clearly (Figures 5-6).[4] In the last decades of the 14th century archaic maiolica is still widely spread and it represents the vast majority of tin-glazed pottery. Archaic maiolica, a production that can be regarded as fully medieval, is associated with blue relief and archaic blue maiolica (two kinds of tin-glazed pottery representing the 'transitional productions' (group one) towards the Renaissance), as well as with the first Renaissance tin-glazed pottery (*italo moresca*, group three). Even though the number of imports does not reach 2%, their presence should not be regarded as residual (Figure 5). One century later the situation proves to be quite different (Figure 6). Objects imported from the Mediterranean area, can now be considered residual together with archaic blue, blue relief maiolica, and archaic maiolica too. It is worth noting that nearly all the Renaissance pottery is from Montelupo.

The quality of tin-glazed pottery is generally high. Whereas the percentage of high standard objects was greaterer within the aristocratic areas of the town, at least one piece of ceramic that could be regarded as a "luxury object" was almost always present in all contexts. During the 15th century, imported tin-glazed tableware was regarded as a luxury good. Even though considered of higher standard than locally produced ceramics, this type of tableware was rather widespread and accessible (Spallanzani 2001, 2006). Thus, from the mid 15th century onwards we can generally talk about Renaissance *maiolica*, as Spanish models were replaced by new ones. This production and group three coexisted during the first half of the 15th century (Caroscio 2007c). Actually, tin-glazed pottery produced in Montelupo became the most common ceramic diffused within the area analysed. The objects produced in Montelupo were then the new fashionable models to look up to, and they also started to influence production abroad (Figure 7).

As pointed out above, during the 16th century the vast majority of tin-glazed pottery present in the context analysed in central Florence was from Montelupo and, as the analysis of the assemblage in via de' Castellani has shown, during the second half of the 16th century, a limited amount of pottery was also imported from outside the region, from Faenza or from Liguria (Figure 8). Only from the beginning of the 17th century onwards, did the presence of imported tin-glazed pottery from a different regional area (i.e. Faenza) become more substantial. As will be discussed at the end of this paper, according to written sources, at least in monastic environments, wooden tablewares were the most common vessels on the table during the 15th century and up to the mid 16th century, when they started to be replaced by tin and pewter vessels.

---

[4] The phases we are talking about and that are illustrated in Figures 5-6 refer to a sample of layers and not to the whole site, whose analysis is still in progress.

FIGURE 7 – JAR FROM MONTELUPO RECOVERED IN FBM.
BEGINNING OF THE 16TH CENTURY.

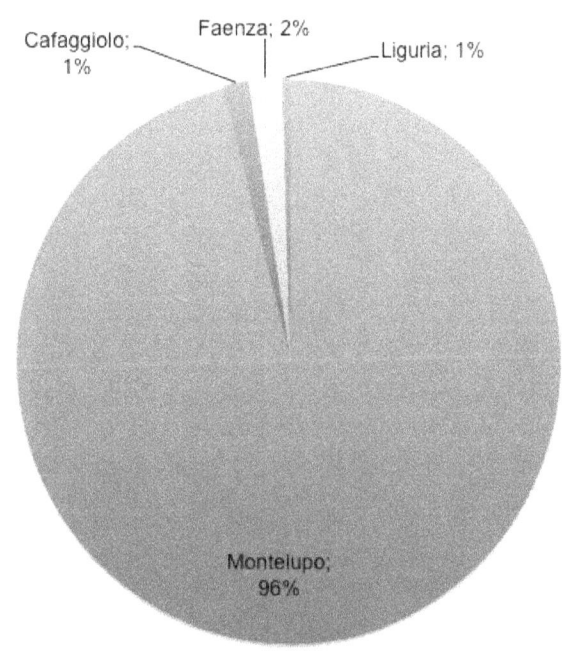

FIGURE 8 – MINIMUM VESSEL NUMBERS OF TIN-GLAZED
POTTERY FROM DIFFERENT PRODUCTION CENTRES IN FLORENCE
DURING THE SECOND HALF OF THE 16TH CENTURY.

Minor settlements

Turning to the discussion of minor settlements under the political control of Florence, the assemblages recovered in San Giovanni Valdarno will now be our focus. *Palazzo di Arnolfo*, formerly *Palazzo del Podestà*, was the mansion of the local governor there, who was appointed in Florence. The amount, provenience and quality of the sherds recovered there are comparable to the ceramic assemblages excavated in central Florence. The main difference between the two contexts is that goods imported on a long-distance basis, such as tin-glazed pottery from the Valencian area, are missing, while Italian tin-glazed pottery manufactured within the production district, and mainly in Montelupo, is quite common. The analysis of the ceramic bodies has shown that some objects were also locally produced, probably in the town itself or in its environs. The features of these products show the clear intent of imitating the objects made in Montelupo and in Florence. Even if not present in these layers, imports from the Western Mediterranean are known in other assemblages in San Giovanni Valdarno and in several excavation-samples undertaken in the environs of the Palace, in areas that might have been used as garbage places (Caroscio 2009a). These contexts have not been taken into account for this research because of their low stratigraphic reliability. Nevertheless, it is clear that imported goods from the Valencian area, and possibly from Malaga, were present in lower amounts than in Florence, the regional centre. On the one hand, this shows the wide circulation of these goods; on the other hand, it makes clear that they were more common in the regional urban focus (Figure 9).

We should now consider if there is any difference between a context like Palazzo di Arnolfo, whose connection with the centre of political and economic control is quite obvious, and the houses of ordinary people. Archaeological excavations have shown that the quantity and quality of the

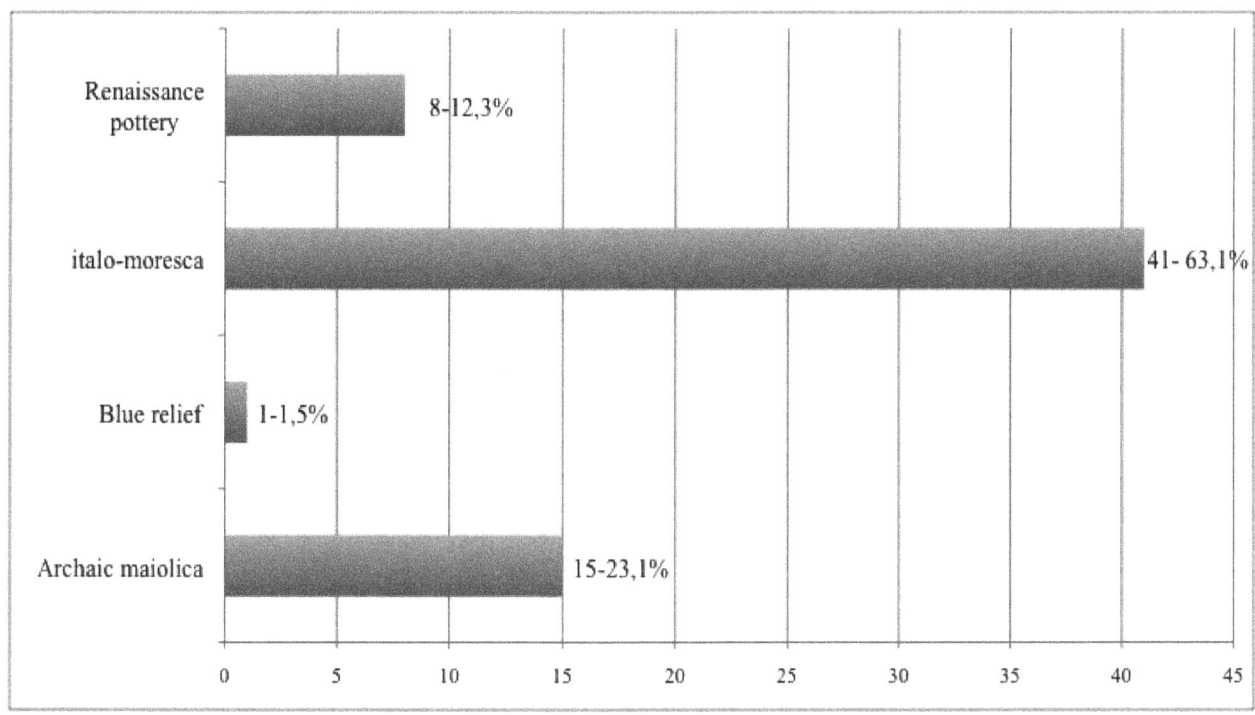

FIGURE 9 – MINIMUM VESSEL NUMBERS FOR FORMS AND PERCENTAGE OF TIN-GLAZED POTTERY IN THE ASSEMBLAGES DATING TO THE LATE 14TH AND THE BEGINNING OF THE 15TH CENTURIES INVESTIGATED IN A PUBLIC BUILDING (PALAZZO DI ARNOLFO, SAN GIOVANNI VALDARNO).

tableware present in the two contexts is similar, pointing to the same response to fashion and to the accessibility of these goods at different social levels (Figure 10). As marks and features clearly show, high quality jars made in Montelupo were common in San Giovanni Valdarno (Figure 11) and, generally, the objects circulating there were made within the overall production district.

Let us now turn to a fortified settlement under gentry control, Rocca Ricciarda, far away from the major trade routes and from the river Arno as well, where the situation is quite different. The vast majority of sherds are local products from central and southern Tuscany, including objects manufactured in Montelupo (Figure 12). In this case luxury products can be identified with imports from

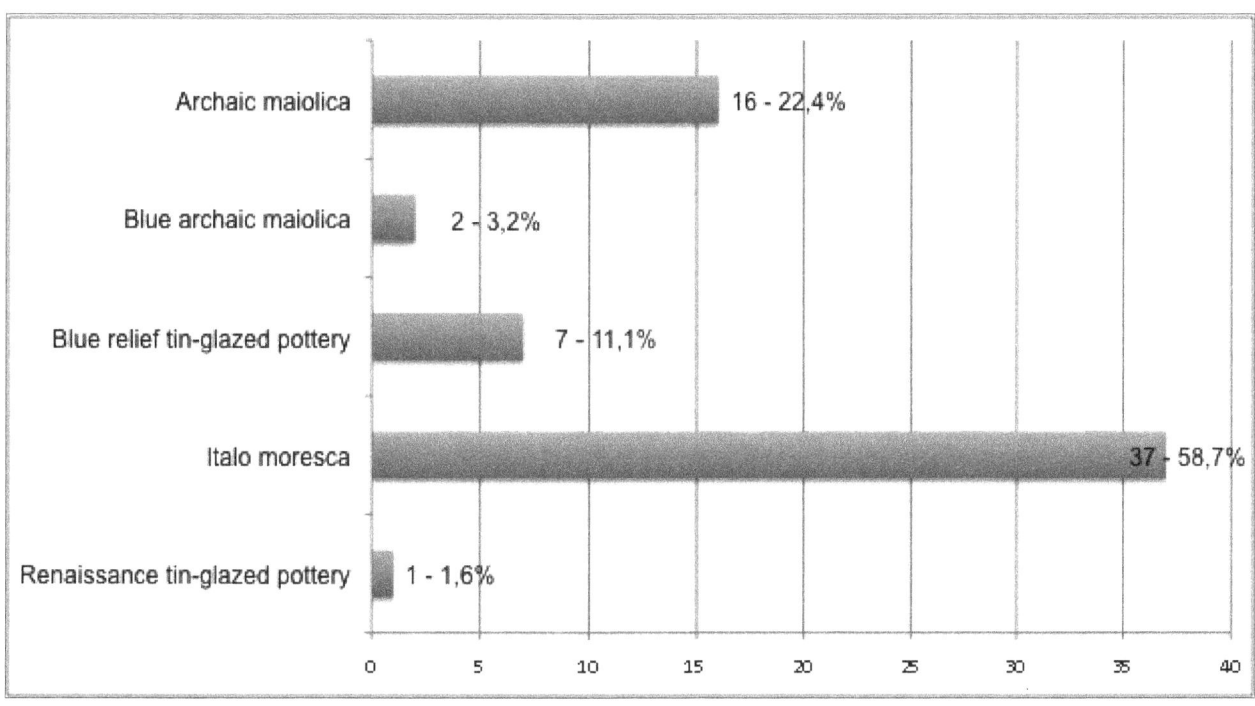

FIGURE 10 – MINIMUM VESSEL NUMBERS AND PERCENTAGE OF TIN-GLAZED POTTERY IN THE ASSEMBLAGES DATING TO THE LATE 14TH CENTURY INVESTIGATED IN A PRIVATE CONTEXT (CORSO ITALIA, SAN GIOVANNI VALDARNO).

FIGURE 11 – MARKED JAR MADE IN MONTELUPO RECOVERED IN SAN GIOVANNI VALDARNO. MID 15TH CENTURY.

FIGURE 12 – JAR MADE IN MONTELUPO FROM ROCCA RICCIARDA. FIRST HALF OF THE 15TH CENTURY.

the regional area: pottery made in Florence, rather than imports from long-distance trade (Figure 13). Nevertheless, two imports, one from Malaga and the other one from Syria are present. Unfortunately, these two shards are residual, and they were recovered in layers dating to later phases.

Written sources

What can written sources tell us about the circulation and use of tableware? We are now going to analyse some monastic inventories dating from the late 14th to the mid 17th centuries. Two monastic institutions have been taken into account: the Ospedale di Santa Maria della Scala in Florence and the Badia di Fiesole. The inventories of the first institution date from 1374 up to 1449; those of the latter were recorded from 1602 onwards. In both cases, the objects present in the kitchen and in the dining hall are listed on quite a regular basis. Research into inventories dating to the 16th century is still ongoing and it will probably clarify the shift in the use of diverse materials which occurred at that time. Nevertheless, the change in the use of some materials, especially the shift from wood to tin and pewter, clearly shows up. Tin glazed-pottery, especially jars and basins, is extremely common for personal use (i. e. toilet) and it is always listed as part of the furniture of each bedroom between the first half of the 15th and the 17th century, regardless of whether tin-glazed tableware was used or not.

What do these inventories tell us about the actual use of pottery, especially tin-glazed and lead-glazed ceramics?

Written sources, and contracts dating to the 15th and 16th centuries in particular, show that pottery was acquired to be used as tableware in diverse context: in monasteries, by wealthy families, and by retailers who were then re-selling it. Archaeological evidence has confirmed the presence of these objects in diverse contexts and, in the terms discussed above, at different social levels. On the one hand, it is commonly assumed that inventories tend to list the most precious things, on the other hand, by studying the inventories of the institutions mentioned above, it clearly shows up that all goods were recorded, even broken objects and vessels in bad conditions. We aim to present here a few notes about the results achieved so far.

In the inventory of the Hospital of Santa Maria della Scala in Florence dating to 1373 the most precious things only are listed. Among those there are several objects made of tin: 7 bowls, 6 small tin bowls, two salt cellars. The cooking vessels listed are mainly made of copper. In Florence and generally speaking in central Italy, the replacement of pottery cooking vessels with metal ones had already started during the second half of the 13th century. Furthermore, cooking for a large number of people obviously requires bigger pans and cooking pots than those used in an ordinary house. For this reason, metal pots of large dimensions were already used at an earlier stage.

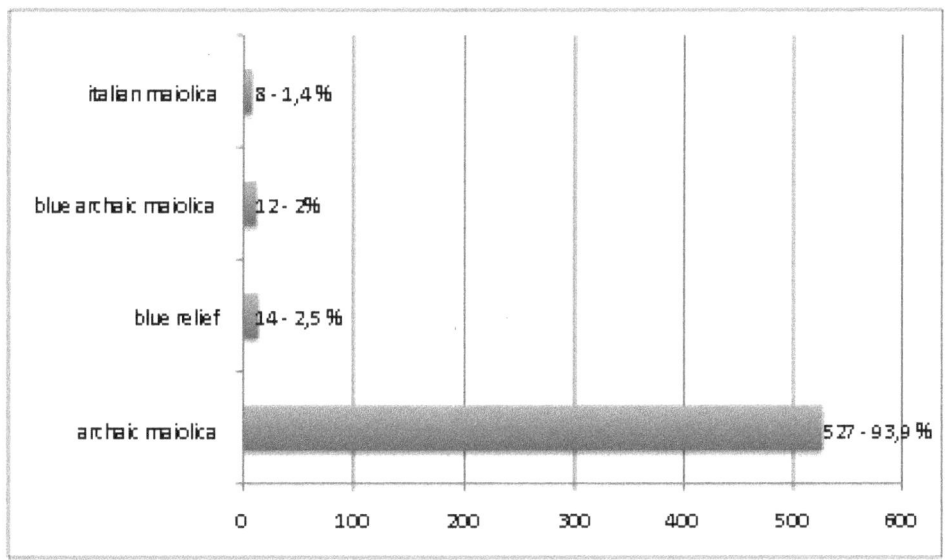

FIGURE 13 – MINIMUM VESSEL NUMBERS AND PERCENTAGE OF TIN-GLAZED POTTERY DATING TO THE LATE 14TH CENTURY AT ROCCA RICCIARDA.

In the inventories of the kitchen and of the dining hall of Santa Maria della Scala in Florence the number of tin objects is constant in the inventories dating to 1405 and 1409 (one big dish and either 6 or 8 bowls). In the inventory dating to 1405 there are 50 bowls defined as 'made of wood or clay' (*di legno e terra*), 60 'new trenchers' (*taglieri nuovi*) and 200 'old trenchers' (*taglieri vecchi*). Unfortunately we do not know what these trenchers were made of. In 1411 they are mentioned again as '150 trenchers and 50 bowls'. The inventory of the following year (1412) clarifies that they were wooden objects '150 wooden trenchers and 50 wooden bowls'. In the 1440s the number of trenchers and bowls is not specified, as they are mentioned as 'several', but tin objects have increased in number and are kept in a small room next to the dining hall: 'five dishes small and big' (*piattelli di stagno grandi e piccoli 5*) and '18 tin bowls and 14 small tin bowls' (*scodelle di stagno 18/ scodelline di stagno 14*) and a new object is listed: a small tin box for saffron (*bossolo di stagno per lo zafferano 1*).

The same register contains inventories of goods belonging to single people or families under diverse circumstances:

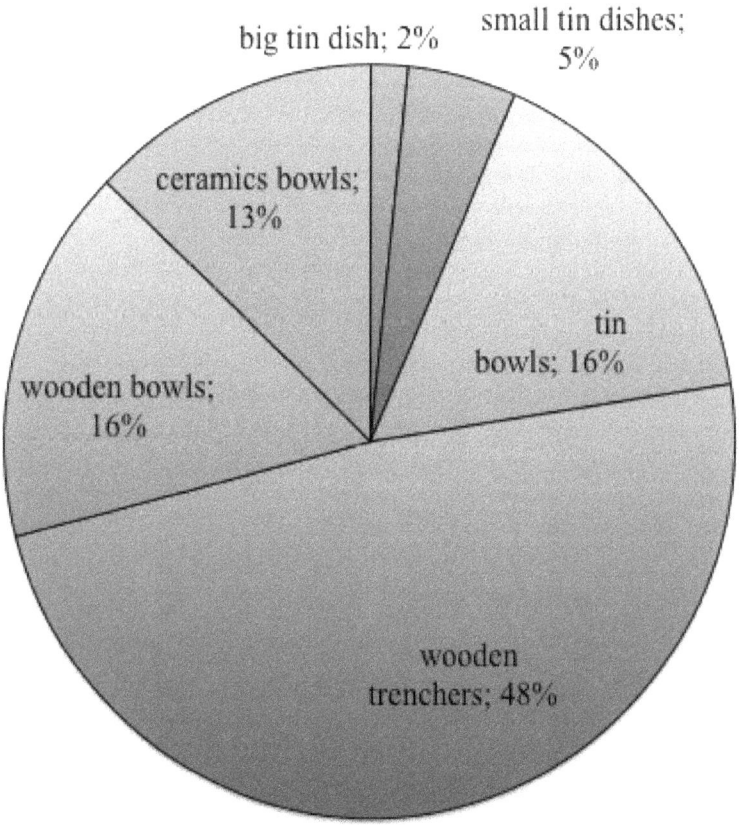

FIGURE 14 – PERCENTAGE OF OBJECTS MADE OF DIFFERENT MATERIALS LISTED IN AN INVENTORY OF GOODS DATING 1443 AND REFERRING TO A MONASTIC CONTEXT.

when entering the hospital; to make these goods available to a relative moving to the hospital as a friar; when goods were left to the institution in a testament, etc. One inventory dating to 1443 listed a variety of goods belonging to a barber, his wife and son. These objects range from pieces of furniture to items for personal use, including tableware: one big dish, three smaller ones and 10 bowls made of tin; 30 wooden trenchers and 7 bowls. Ceramic bowls, most likely tin-glazed and lead-glazed pottery are 8 in number. As shown in Figure 14, the majority of tableware (64%) is made of wood. Tin represents the remarkable amount of 23%, while ceramics are 13% of the objects. Unfortunately, the data about the kitchen and the dining hall of the hospital are not so detailed for the decade from 1440 to 1450 as for the first quarter of the century, when wood is present in even a larger amount.

Comparing the data of a 'private archive' with those recorded in the kitchen and in the dining room of the hospital during the same period, some differences show up. The most complete record is the one dating to 1405, when wood is the most common material. By the 17th century, as the inventories of the Badia Fiesolana show, tin is the most common material used as tableware and wooden trenchers have been completely replaced by tin and pewter dishes. In 1602 nearly all tableware but jars and saltcellars were made of tin. Only during the following decades will tin-glazed pottery start increasing in these records (Caroscio 2009b).

Conclusions

When studying tableware it is important to bear in mind that, as for most archaeological evidence, we are not dealing with the totality of objects present in the original context, but with what is preserved in an assemblage. Thus, perishables materials, especially wood, should be taken into account and an integrated use of archaeological and documentary records as well as of iconographic sources is needed. The actual use of tableware supposes the circulation of goods within a trading network that is the result of the political and economic influence over a certain area. Moreover, cultural issues both in terms of fashion and social behaviour plays an important role in the choice of certain goods or certain materials. Further research is needed on this topic, especially on archive sources related to private rather than to public contexts. This paper summarizes the results achieved so far and as raises debate on the impact and social meaning of goods regarded as luxuries according to the context within which they circulated.

Bibliography

Berti, F. 2001. *Storia della ceramica di Montelupo; uomini e fornaci in un centro di produzione dal XIV al XVII secolo, vol. IV (Una storia di uomini: le famiglie dei vasai)*. Montelupo Fiorentino, Aedo.

Berti, F. 1998. *Storia della ceramica di Montelupo; uomini e fornaci in un centro di produzione dal XIV al XVII secolo, vol. II (Le ceramiche da mensa dal 1480 alla fine del XVIII secolo)*. Montelupo Fiorentino, Aedo.

Bojani, G.C. (ed.) 1992. *Ceramica e araldica medicea*. Monte San Savino, Comune.

Caroscio, M. 2007a. *Dalle smaltate medievali al Rinascimeto*. In R. Francovich et al., *Firenze prima degli Uffizi. Lo scavo di via de' Castellani: contributi per un'archeologia urbana fra tardo antico ed età moderna*, 426-446. Firenze, All'Insegna del Giglio.

Caroscio, M. 2007b. *Smaltate di importazione*. In R. Francovich et al., *Firenze prima degli Uffizi. Lo scavo di via de' Castellani: contributi per un'archeologia urbana fra tardo antico ed età moderna*, 447-450. Firenze, All'Insegna del Giglio.

Caroscio, M. 2007c. *Maioliche del Rinascimento: tipologie e prime ipotesi sulla ricostruzione del mercato*. In R. Francovich et al., *Firenze prima degli Uffizi. Lo scavo di via de' Castellani: contributi per un'archeologia urbana fra tardo antico ed età moderna*, 451-470. Firenze, All'Insegna del Giglio.

Caroscio, M. 2009a. *La maiolica in Toscana fra Medioevo e Rinascimento. Il rapporto fra centri di produzione e di consumo nel periodo di transizione.* Firenze, All'Insegna del Giglio.

Caroscio, M. 2009b. *Suppellettili da mensa in legno e stagno in un contesto fiorentino fra XIV e XVII secolo alla luce delle fonti scritte e iconografiche. Note preliminari*. In P. Favia, G. Volpe (eds), *Atti del V Congresso Nazionale di Archeologia Medievale*, 688-693. Firenze, All'Insegna del Giglio.

Francovich, R., Cantini, F., Cianferoni, C., Scampoli, E., (eds) 2007. *Firenze prima degli Uffizi. Lo scavo di via de' Castellani: contributi per un'archeologia urbana fra tardo antico ed età moderna*. Firenze, All'Insegna del Giglio.

Milanese, M. 2006. *Da Pisa a Montelupo: aspetti e probemi della produzione ceramica nel Basso Valdarno (XV-XIX secolo), tra monolinguismo dell'ingobbio e serialità della tipologia*. In M. Baldassarri, G. Ciampoltrini (eds), *I maestri dell'argilla. L'edilizia in cotto, la produzione di laterizi e di vasellame nel Valdarno Inferiore tra Medioevo ed Età Moderna*, 89-104. Pisa, Felici.

Peacock, D. P. S. 1982. *Pottery in the Roman world: an ethnoarchaeological approach*. London, Longman.

Spallanzani, M. 2001. *Maioliche ispano-moresche a Firenze nei secoli XIV e XV*. In S. Cavaciocchi (ed.) *Atti delle Settimane di Studio e altri convegni N. 33. Economia e arte nei secoli XIII-XVIII (2000)*, 367-377. Istituto Internazionale di Storia Economica "F. Datini" – Prato. Firenze, Le Monnier.

Spallanzani, M. 2006. *Maioliche ispano-moresche a Firenze nel Rinascimento*. Firenze, S. P. E. S.

Wilson, T. H. 1996. *The Beginnings of Lustreware in Renaissance Italy*. In *The International Ceramics Fair and Seminar*, 35-43. London.

Rubbish and the Creation of Urban Landscape
A case study from Medieval Southampton, UK

Ben Jervis
English Heritage, 1 Waterhouse Square, 138-142 Holborn, London, EC1N 2ST
ben.jervis@english-heritage.org.uk

Abstract

I argue that our understanding and definition of 'rubbish' is far too limited. Analysis of two ceramic assemblages from sites in Medieval Southampton (UK) of different social status demonstrates that the way waste was treated and perceived is contextual. It is influenced by socio-economic factors and changed in response to developments in the social and economic landscape of the town. I propose that as waste, pottery occupies a transient position and an umbrella classification of 'rubbish' is too generalized. This paper explores how urban space is formed through processes of rubbish deposition. These processes also contribute to self-definition. The implications of this perspective for urban archaeology are considered, from interpretive and chronological viewpoints.

Key Words: Rubbish, Pottery, Medieval, Urban, Identity, Southampton, Order, Space, Waste

Introduction

Given that as archaeologists we deal with waste, little consideration has been given to the way rubbish was disposed of in Medieval towns (although see Bryant 2012). It is commonly assumed that most rubbish was deposited in pits, a theory which has recently been critiqued (Buteux and Jackson 2000). Whilst historical sources have been used to give insights into other ways rubbish was treated and its impact on the urban landscape (e.g. Keene 1982), we still understand little of how the deposition of domestic waste impacted upon household life and the development of the urban landscape. This is despite the fact that deposited rubbish is one of the principal sources used in archaeological interpretation.

The paper follows anthropological studies of rubbish in understanding waste management as an imposition of order (Douglas 1966; Edensor 2005). By studying the way rubbish was deposited in a Medieval town (Southampton, UK) it is demonstrated that order was created in different ways, and sometimes was not achieved. The transient nature of rubbish is also considered; that the meanings of objects change, both through use and stages of the depositional process. The meaning of waste is deemed highly situational and open to the influence of human agents. In taking such a standpoint, this paper challenges existing archaeological interpretations of Medieval rubbish deposits, to generate a more contextual and theoretically developed understanding of Medieval urban waste disposal. Through the paper I will answer three questions:

- How was rubbish perceived or categorized?
- How did this relate to the emergence of categories of people?
- How did this lead to the definition of urban landscape?

The Nature of Urban Landscape

Ingold (1993, 154-6) defines landscape as 'a materialization of all which occurs in and through it'. We can take this to mean that space is shaped, in part, by human behaviour. I will take this further in two ways. Firstly, by being formed by behaviour, a socialized space then acts to constrain or enable particular activities as defined by social convention. Secondly, we can argue that the behaviour which shapes landscapes also simultaneously forms groups (or categories) of people and acts to place people within these groups (Blake 1999, 36).

It is not the intention of this paper to reopen debates on the nature of towns, but it is worth defining their key features. Towns were often sited on rivers, Southampton for example is located on a peninsula at the mouths of two rivers. Streets were typically laid out in a grid pattern, with a market being placed in the centre. The main area was often bounded by a rampart or wall, however suburbs may have expanded outside of this area. The landscape of towns was typically dominated by the castle. Towns often had at least one religious house, in Southampton a Franciscan friary was founded in the 13th century. Tenement plots were densely packed with timber or stone buildings, which tended to index the socio-economic status of their inhabitants. A range of crafts took place within towns, including leather and textile working, metal working and pottery manufacture. Towns were also centres of trade, with ports such as Southampton having a community of merchants from England and elsewhere in Europe (Schofield and Vince 2003). The urban landscape had a varied population, engaging in a range of activities, leading to it being a vibrant materialization of human behaviour.

A Case Study: Medieval Southampton

The data presented here to explore these issues comes from the Medieval port of Southampton, specifically from 13th and 14th century deposits (the High Medieval period). Southampton has a large and well studied ceramic assemblage (Platt and Coleman Smith 1975; Brown 2002; Jervis 2009). This makes it a suitable case study. Pottery will provide the main body of evidence discussed in this

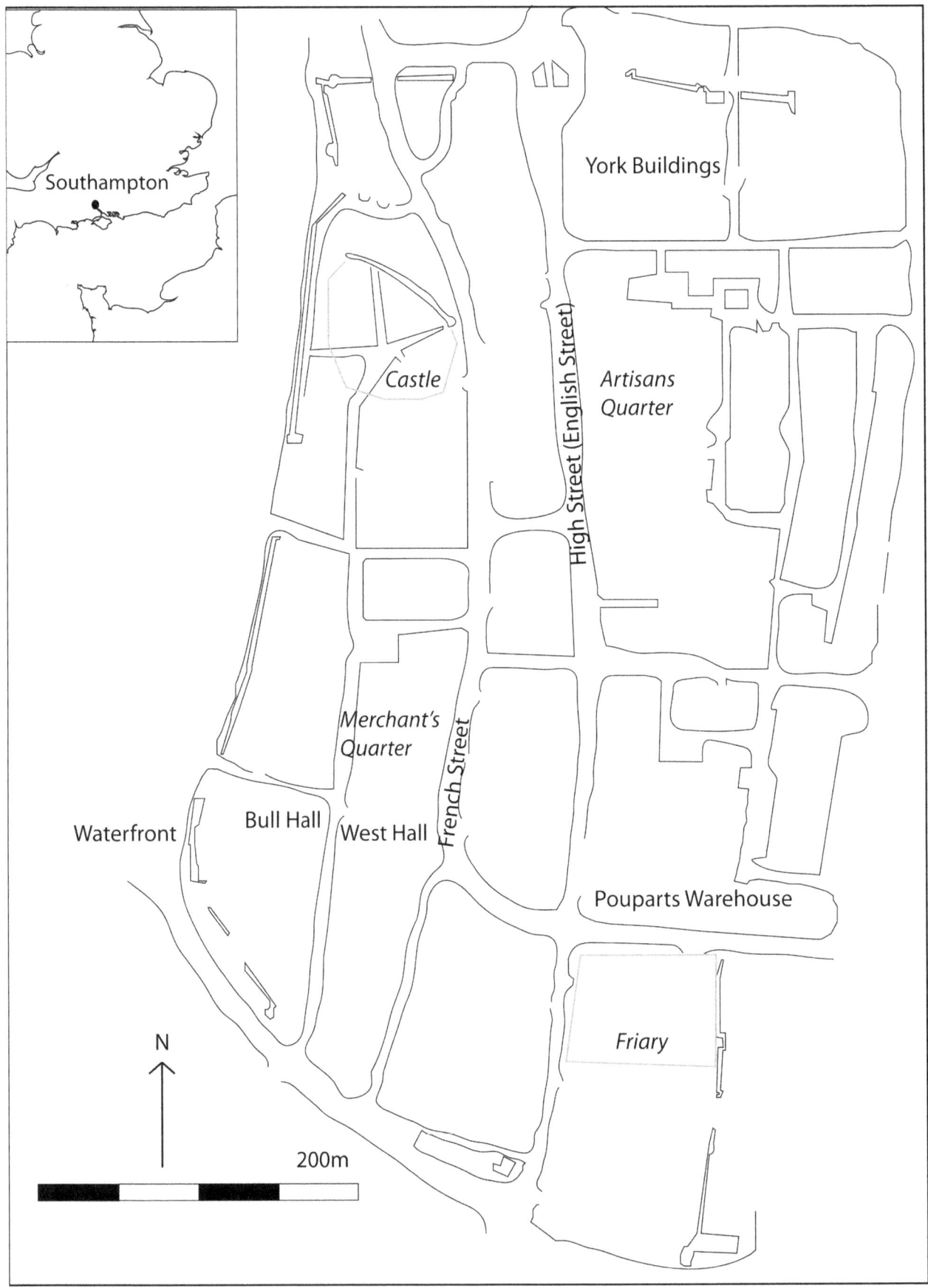

FIGURE 1 – THE LOCATION OF SITES IN SOUTHAMPTON MENTIONED IN THE TEXT, SHOWING HYPOTHETICAL MERCHANTS AND ARTISANS QUARTERS. SOURCE: AUTHOR.

paper. This is due to it being a sensitive indicator both of chronology and site formation processes. It also provides information about the processes in which waste was created (through use) and the social role of the consumers. Two sites, York Buildings and Bull Hall will be compared in depth as these provide two contrasting patterns of waste deposition (Figure 1). These will be placed in the wider context of Southampton as a whole and of some other Medieval towns. It is necessary to briefly review the ceramic evidence from Southampton and to introduce the sites which will be discussed in detail.

The Pottery From Southampton

As an important Medieval port, Southampton boasts a wide array of imported pottery as well as a variety of local wares (Figure 2a-b). The most common local ware is Southampton Coarseware, a wheelthrown coarse sandy ware. Typical forms are jars/cooking pots, although a small number of other vessel forms are present including curfews and bowls/dishes. For the purposes of this paper, these will be grouped with other minority coarsewares as local coarsewares. Sandy wares were also produced in or near to Southampton. Southampton Sandy Ware is a wheelthrown sandy ware, present as jugs and jars, some of which are glazed. Glazed jugs and other kitchen vessels are also present in South Hampshire Redware, which is known from sites in Portsmouth and Winchester (Brown 2002, 14; Jervis 2012), suggesting it was produced outside of Southampton. Jugs are the most common form, with simple glazed decoration. The final main locally produced sandy ware is Southampton Whiteware. The main vessel form is the jug, usually with a deep green glaze. A number of other wares are present, generally as glazed jugs. Throughout this paper these will generally be referred to together as local sandy wares.

The most abundant non-local wares are from Dorset and are present as jars, jugs and bowls (Brown 2002, 16). Products of the Laverstock kiln near Salisbury are known. A small number of sherds have been identified from further afield, including fragments of Scarborough ware knight jugs and sherds of Midlands, Ham Green and Cornish wares (Brown 2002, 17).

The majority of imports are from France, the most common being Saintonge Whiteware jugs. Other Saintonge types are known, the most common being Saintonge bright-green glazed ware and Saintonge Polychrome ware jugs. Other imported wares are generally from northern France, primarily the Paris and Rouen areas and include highly decorated zoomorphic jugs. Only one cooking vessel is known, a Ceramique Onctueuse jar from Bull Hall.

The Sites

Southampton can be roughly divided into four quarters (Figure 1). The south west of the town, close to the waterfront, was occupied by merchants. These were both of English and foreign (principally French) nationality and were wealthy and influential members of the town's community (Platt 1973, 69). To the north of this area was the Norman castle, into which were built the King's wine stores. The south east of the town was occupied by the Friary whilst the north east appears to have been inhabited by craftsmen. Evidence has been found for metalworking and pottery manufacture in this period.

Excavations at Bull Hall (SOU 25; Figure 1) in 1979 (Blackman, unpublished), investigated a large area of a Medieval tenement plot in the mercantile south west of the city. The tenement was owned by the English merchant Thomas le Halveknight, although it is suggested that he rented this property to another member of the mercantile community, possibly of Gascon origin (Brown 2002, 165). The High Medieval features consist of a yard area into which a number of pits, a limekiln and a garderobe were dug. Most pottery was recovered from pits (Figure 3). Analysis of the animal bone assemblage (Driver, unpublished) suggests kitchen waste was focussed on those pits closer to the house, whereas the pits further away were characterized by the presence of butchery waste. Pottery was deposited in most of these features. The High Medieval pottery assemblage consists of local coarseware jars, local sandy ware jugs and jars and a fine array of imported jugs, including vessels from northern France and the Saintonge (Brown 2002, 142-3).

The second site is York Buildings (SOU 175; Figure 1), excavated from 1983-9 (Kavanagh, unpublished). York Buildings is located in the north-east quadrant of the town, an area believed to have been occupied by craftsmen throughout the Medieval period (Platt 1973, 52). The excavations investigated the area behind several tenements, including a yard area identified as that of 4 High Street. This was a gravelled area into which a number of pits and a ditch, deemed to be a property boundary, were dug. The area behind this yard is characterized by a build up of garden soils suggesting that it was cultivated from as early as the twelfth century. Most of the High Medieval pottery was recovered from the garden soil layers, with very little actually being excavated from the pits in the yard area (Figure 4). Whilst these garden layers can be taken to be related to the tenements, it is unclear whether they represent a communal area or bounded gardens related to specific homes. Therefore they will be considered here as a whole. The town defences, the rampart and rampier, were also investigated. These areas appear to have been kept clear of waste in the High Medieval period, but waste started to be dumped in the rampier (an open space behind the rampart) during the 14th century. The High Medieval pottery assemblage is characterized by a relative lack of imported wares (Jervis 2009).

Depositional practices at other sites appear to follow the general patterns outlined above. At West Hall (SOU 110; see Figure 1), the main residence of Thomas le Halveknight, yard surfaces appear to have been kept clear, as at Bull Hall (unpublished site archive). In the east of the town, at the Pouparts warehouse site (SOU 934, 997),

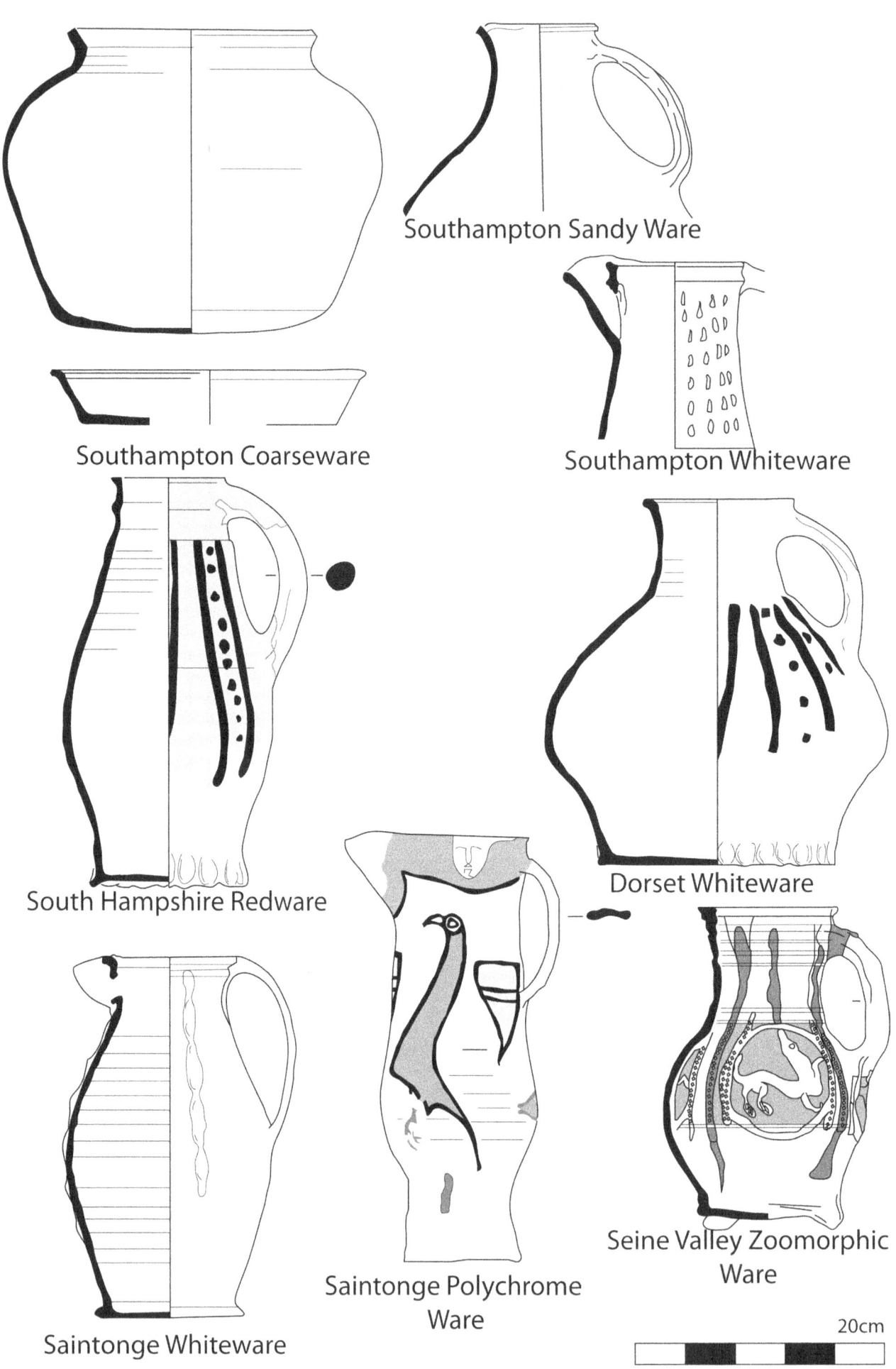

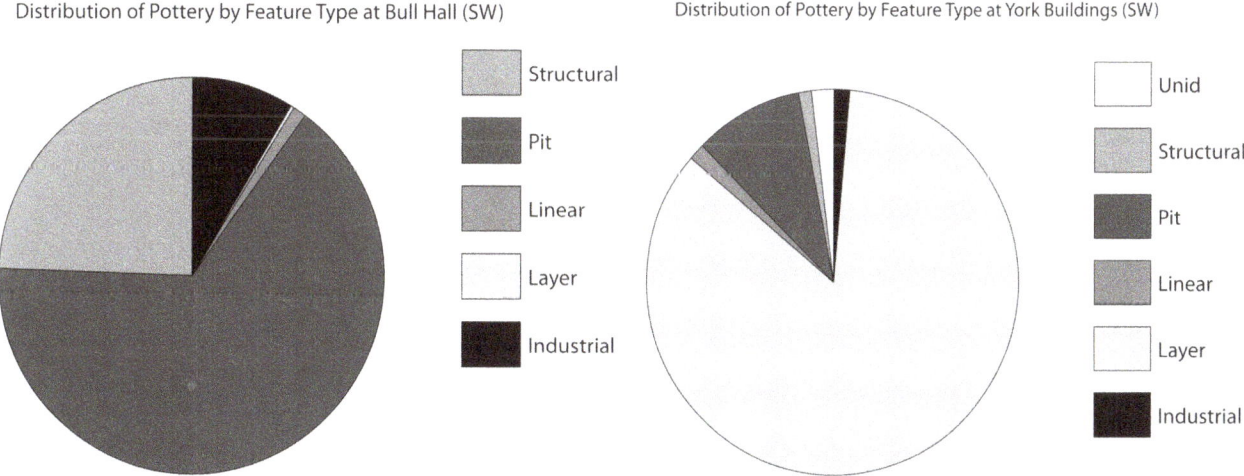

FIGURE 2A (PAGE 60)-B – SOME TYPICAL HIGH MEDIEVAL POTTERY FROM SOUTHAMPTON. COURTESY OF DUNCAN BROWN.

FIGURE 3 – PIE CHART ILLUSTRATING THE HIGH MEDIEVAL CONTEXTS FROM WHICH HIGH MEDIEVAL POTTERY WAS RECOVERED AT BULL HALL. SOURCE: AUTHOR (DATA COURTESY OF DUNCAN BROWN).

FIGURE 4 – PIE CHART ILLUSTRATING THE HIGH MEDIEVAL CONTEXTS FROM WHICH HIGH MEDIEVAL POTTERY WAS RECOVERED AT YORK BUILDINGS. SOURCE: AUTHOR.

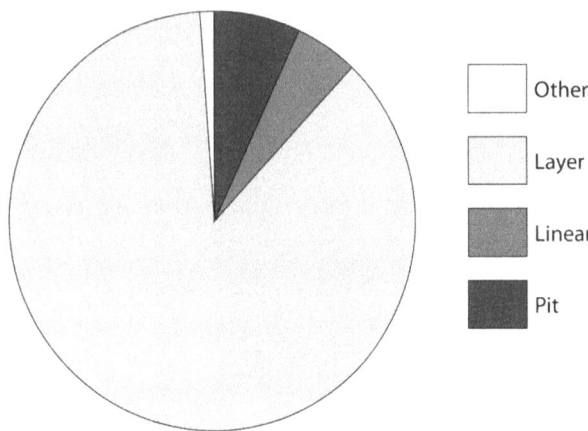

FIGURE 5 – PIE CHART ILLUSTRATING THE HIGH MEDIEVAL CONTEXTS FROM WHICH HIGH MEDIEVAL POTTERY WAS RECOVERED AT POUPARTS WAREHOUSE. SOURCE: AUTHOR.

in a small excavation of a tenement in the east of the town, rubbish was primarily recovered from layers, with only a small quantity recovered from pits, following the pattern identified at York Buildings (Figure 5; see Jervis unpublished a). Only fragmentary Medieval material was recovered from Southampton Friary (SOU 154, 199, 1355; see Jervis, forthcoming) and Winkle Street (SOU 162; see Jervis, unpublished b) which are close to the southern shoreline (Figure 1) and it is possible that much of the waste from these sites was deposited directly into the sea.

Rubbish and the Creation of Household Order

Waste can be seen as opposed to order; it is a by-product of activity, something of no use which has no set place in the world. The deposition of rubbish is designed to create order out of this disorder, the archaeological features in which waste is deposited are a medium through which this can be achieved (see Gardner 2002, 326; Edensor 2005,

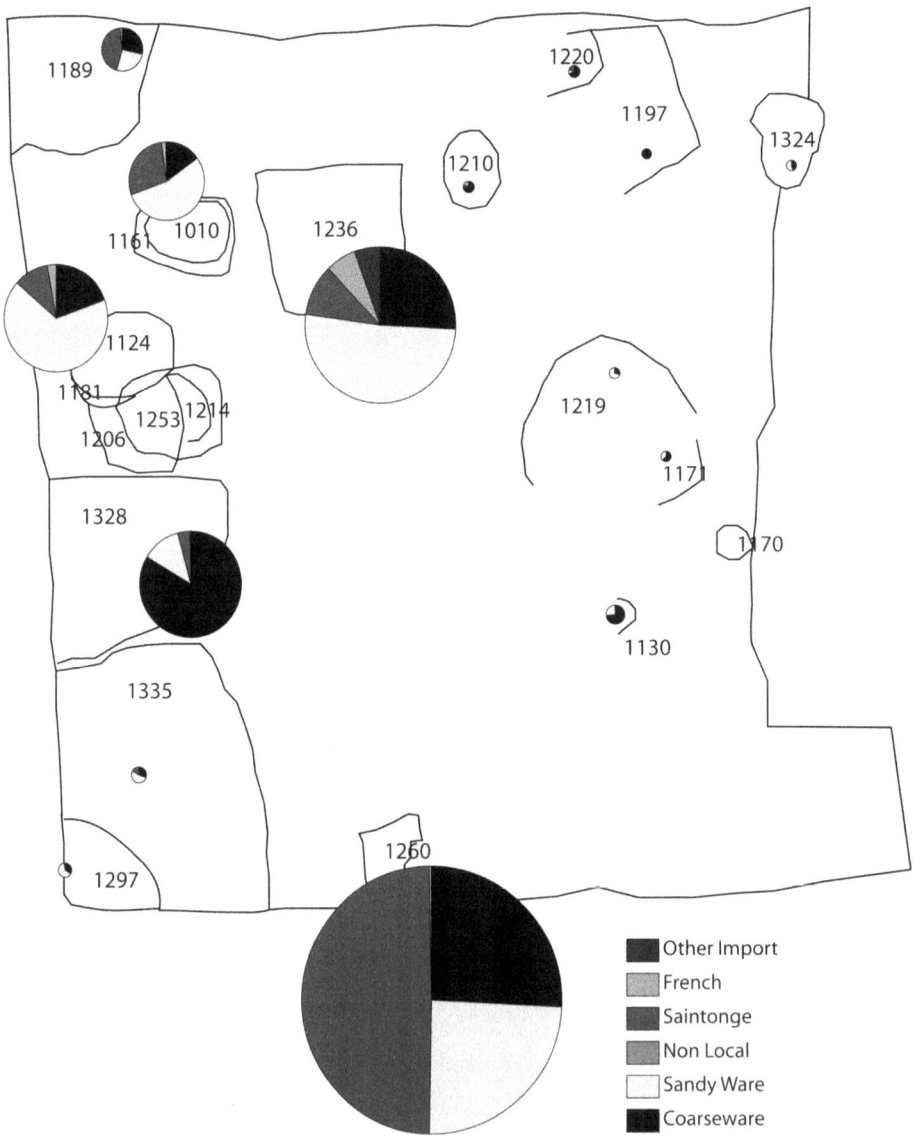

FIGURE 6 – PLAN AND PIE CHARTS ILLUSTRATING THE COMPOSITION OF HIGH MEDIEVAL JUG ASSEMBLAGES FROM FEATURES AT BULL HALL. WEIGHTS ARE THE TOTAL WEIGHT OF JUGS FROM EACH FEATURE. SIZE OF PIE CHART REPRESENTS ASSEMBLAGE SIZE. SOURCE: AUTHOR.

312). Where order is created it can be seen as related to the means through which the waste is generated. For example, in the yard at Bull Hall a number of pits have primary waste deposits within them. These cluster around a feature interpreted as a hearth. The ceramics deposited within these pits are primarily jugs of various fabrics (Figures 6, 11). These vessels appear to represent deposits of kitchen waste or waste from food consumption. The garderobe is characterized by a particularly high quantity of imported jugs, perhaps suggesting this waste represents that from food consumption (Figure 6). The yard space around these pits became a platform on which order was created (see Needham and Spence 1997, 85). The pits dug into this yard are ordering containers for the waste products of these activities. The layout of the yard served to organize these activities, placing them in a specific location where they occurred habitually, generating waste in a structured manner. A similar observation can be made at York Buildings. Here, the distribution of some sandy wares, generally interpreted as drinking vessels, is skewed towards the yard directly behind the house (Figures 7, 8, 12). The distribution of coarsewares (primarily cooking pots) and non-drinking jugs is more focussed on the garden. This suggests that some jugs may have been broken close to the yard, whilst the coarsewares and remaining sandy wares were deposited further away in the garden, possibly with the organic kitchen waste which was used as compost. Vessels associated with drinking appear to have been used to close some deposits where appropriate. One cess pit contained the complete profile of a Laverstock-type Ware jug for example. In contrast, kitchen waste was spread over the garden area, often mixed with these drinking vessels. It is noticeable that the average sherd weight of some jug types is considerably higher in the yard than the garden, suggesting some primary deposition (Figures 7-8). This distinction is less marked in what are interpreted as kitchen wares. The distribution of bone has a similar pattern, with it being spread fairly evenly through

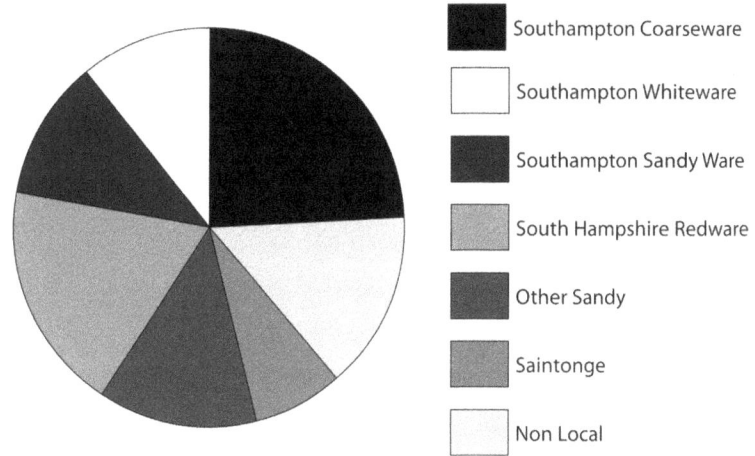

FIGURE 7 – PIE CHARTS WITH THE COMPOSITION OF HIGH MEDIEVAL FEATURES FROM THE YARD AT YORK BUILDINGS. SOURCE: AUTHOR.

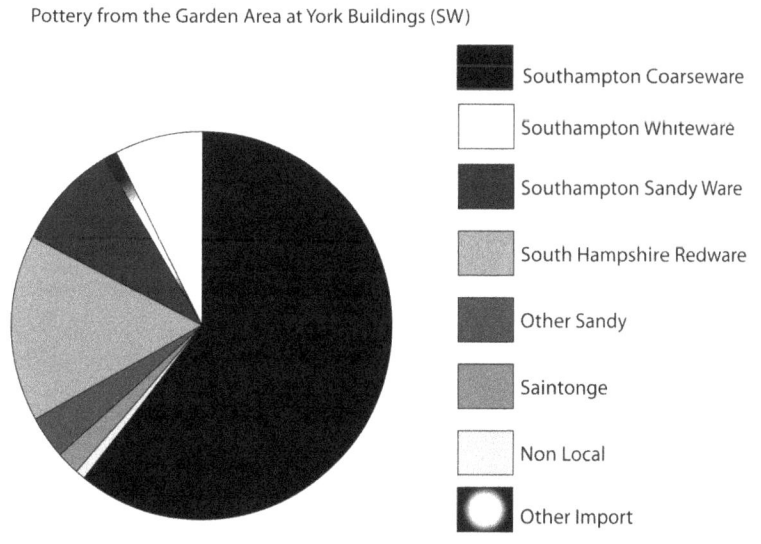

FIGURE 8 – PIE CHARTS WITH THE COMPOSITION OF HIGH MEDIEVAL FEATURES FROM THE GARDEN AT YORK BUILDINGS. SOURCE: AUTHOR.

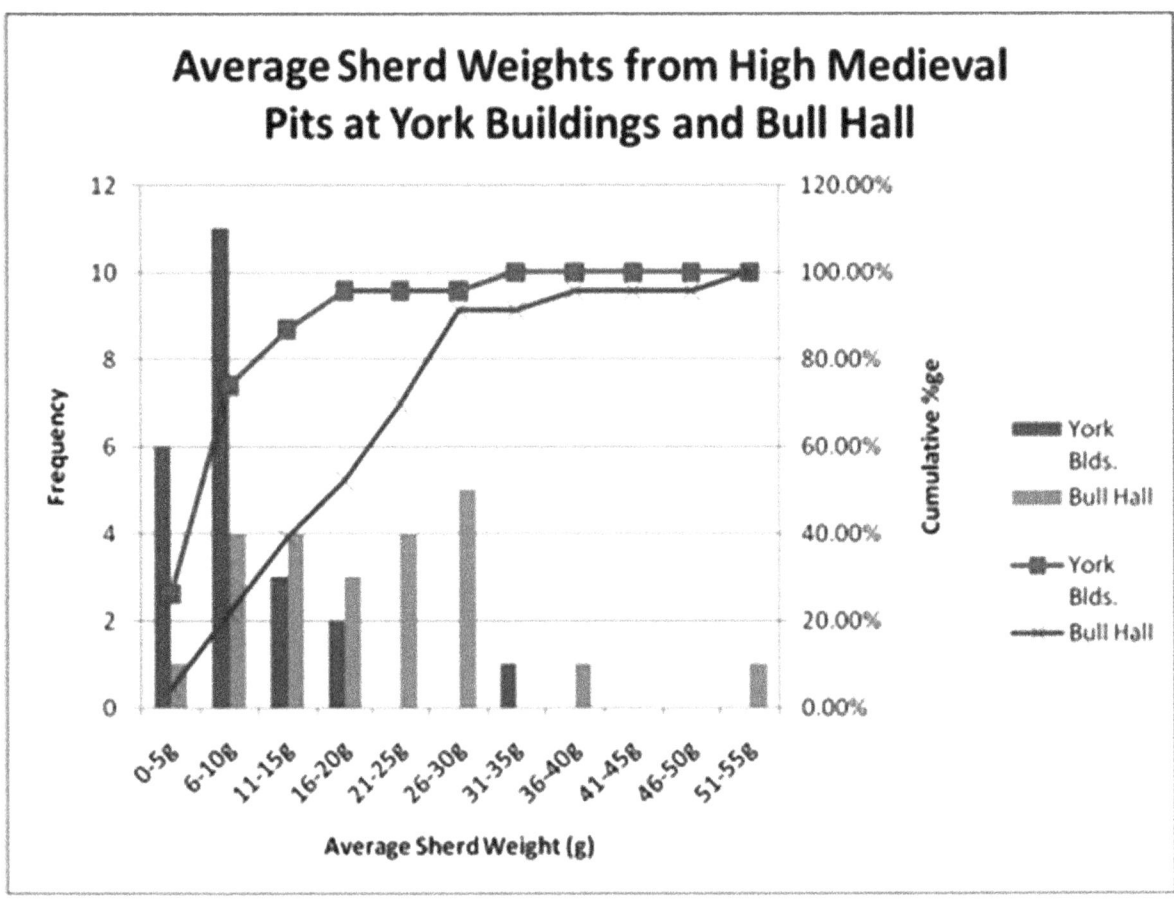

FIGURE 9 – BAR CHART AND CUMULATIVE PERCENTAGE GRAPH COMPARING THE AVERAGE SHERD WEIGHT OF HIGH MEDIEVAL POTTERY FROM HIGH MEDIEVAL PITS AT YORK BUILDINGS AND BULL HALL. SOURCE: AUTHOR.

the tenement plot, although no analysis of the Medieval faunal remains has taken place. In contrast, the waste from metal working, such as slag, an activity which occurred in the yard area, is very much focussed on the gravel yard surface and the pits which were dug into it.

The small sherd size in pits at York Buildings suggests that they were regularly cleared out (Figures 9, 13). The organic waste deposited in these pits may have been spread over the cultivated area to the rear of the tenements as compost, with pottery being incorporated within this waste as it had no useful function following its breakage, although it may have served to aerate the decomposing organic matter (Duncan Brown, personal communication). The pottery remaining in the pits represents a residual element, or the final infilling of the pit once it went out of use. The emptying of pits is supported by them often being lined with wood, suggesting they were designed to contain waste in an accessible manner. The pits at Bull Hall appear unlined, perhaps suggesting they were more bins than middens (see Atkin and Evans 2002), although there was limited organic preservation at this site. This is supported by sherds generally being larger in pits at Bull Hall (Figures 9, 14). As a general rule however, at both sites kitchen waste is treated as a homogenous whole, the distinctions between artefacts of different materials being blurred by those disposing of waste.

The treatment of waste varies between tenements. At Bull Hall kitchen waste was typically deposited in pits, whereas at York Buildings, a significant quantity of material was spread over the area at the back of the tenement used as gardens, presumably to act as a fertilizer, possibly after initial storage in pits. These different ways of disposing of waste relate to the households functioning in different ways. Bull Hall was occupied by a rich, merchant's household whereas York Buildings was inhabited by poorer craftsmen, who it is more likely had to grow their own food (Dyer 1994, 129). This patterning may also be related to the size of the tenements. with the smaller tenement at Bull Hall having more ordered deposition. Waste took up a lower percentage of the surface area of this tenement (Dyer 1994; see Arnold 1990, 930 for a contemporary example). The larger tenements at York Buildings are reflective of the undesirability of this area, away from the town centre, meaning that the tenements at York Buildings were large enough to include a garden area (Dyer 1994). At both sites order was created out of disorder, either through the deposition of waste in discrete pits, or by putting waste to a secondary use. The meaning of the waste clearly changed, from it being food and the associated material culture, to it being disposable waste at Bull Hall and useful fertilizer at York Buildings (see Beck and Hill 2004, 305; Edensor 2005, 319). It is important to note that even those objects such as pottery and bone, with no nutritional value are treated the same in deposition as organic kitchen waste at York Buildings.

The spreading of waste at York Buildings appears common on equivalent sites in other towns. At sites in Norwich (Atkin, Carter and Evans 1985) and Hereford (Shoesmith 1985) for example, the area inside the rampart was occupied by metalworkers, with some cultivation and rubbish spread across tenement plots, rather than being deposited in features. At St. Thomas Street, Oxford, a similar spread of garden soil occurred at the rear of a tenement believed to be of low status, consisting of a similar mixture of contemporary and residual sherds (Underwood-Keevil 1997, 249-50). The wealthier site at Westwick, Norwich, boasts a comparable pottery assemblage to that from Bull Hall, with a high quantity of imports. The tenement is also smaller in size than these peripheral tenements. As at Bull Hall, waste appears to have been more intensively managed than at poorer sites in the town, with it being deposited in pits or removed from the site (Jennings 2002, 143).

Differences in depositional practices relate to variability in the domestic practices through which households are formed and maintained as social entities. Waste practices can be seen as affective in this regard. The effective management of waste served to enhance and strengthen personal relationships with those occupying the neighbouring tenements (Dyer 1989, 189). For example, the property boundary ditch excavated at York Buildings was kept clear of waste, which was deposited discretely within tenement plots. The presence of this feature, rather than a row of rubbish pits, suggests that these yards were separated, unlike at equivalent plots in Norwich, for example, where a line of rubbish pits separated the tenements, suggesting a more communal yard space (Atkin 2002, 242). This created ordered space both within and between tenements. Secondly, differences in the relationship formed with waste by members of a household served to make durable the internal structures of these households, as different individuals dealt with waste within different networks of socio-economic interaction. At Bull Hall it was likely to be servants who used the yard and generated the ordered space. At York Buildings it is likely to have been the tenants. In both tenements it would have been desirable to dispose of waste in the most efficient way possible; at York Buildings this would be through gaining the maximum utility from all of the resources brought into the household. At Bull Hall the focus appears to have been more on disposing of the waste in such a way that the tenement remained relatively clean. Both the social and physical structure of the household can therefore be seen to have been a determining factor behind waste practices, but were also re-formed by them.

The disposal of waste created through household activity served to order space and time within and between tenements, occurring in conjunction with other activities. This was the result of repetitive embedded practices,

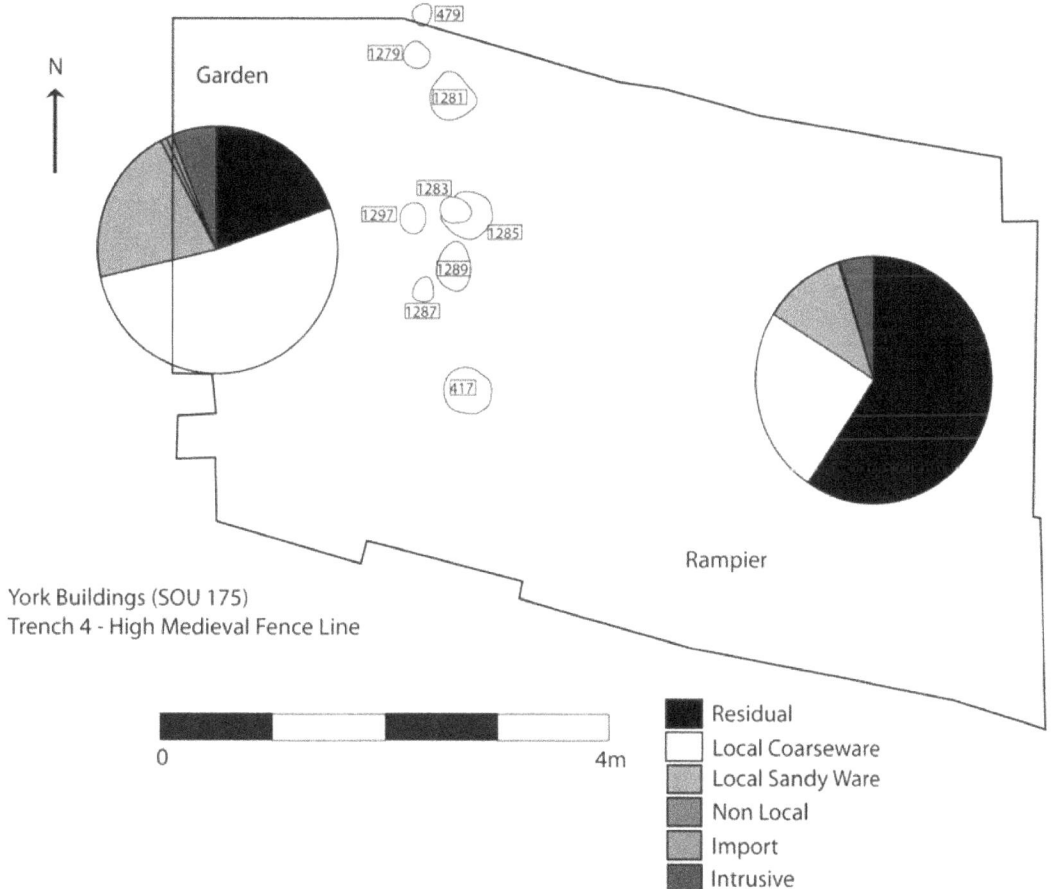

FIGURE 10 – PLAN AND PIE CHARTS ILLUSTRATING THE COMPOSITION OF POTTERY ASSEMBLAGES FROM LAYERS INSIDE THE TENEMENT PLOT AND THE RAMPIER AT YORK BUILDINGS.

Ware Type	Feature: Form	1124 SC	1124 SW	1130 SC	1130 SW	1161 SC	1161 SW	1189 SC	1189 SW	1206 SC	1206 SW	1210 SC	1210 SW	1214 SC	1214 SW	1220 SC	1220 SW	1236 SC	1236 SW	1253 SC	1253 SW	1260 SC	1260 SW	1285 SC	1285 SW	1297 SC	1297 SW	1328 SC	1328 SW	1335 SC	1335 SW
Coarseware	Cooking Pot	6	89	1	58	31	535	30	500	13	391			11	340	5	80	200	3411	2	29	55	1057	2	31	3	49	146	3593	6	84
	Bowl																					1	10					1	45		
	Curfew	1	23	8	302					2	97													2	37			8	646		
	Lantern																					109	2407					1	11		
	Pipkin																											1	100		
	Misc.	3	27			2	29	3	17	1	6	7	62					7	109	3	32	30	196	6	56	2	30	3	26	3	15
	Coarseware Total	10	139	9	360	33	564	33	517	16	494	7	62	11	340	5	80	207	3520	5	61	195	3670	10	124	5	79	160	4421	9	99
Sandy Ware	Cooking Pot					7	31											11	224			3	48								
	Jug	11	286	2	40	55	1441	8	219	32	959			5	144			271	6173	7	578	83	2883			1	31			1	21
	Curfew	1	56																												
	Dripping Pan									2	231																				
	Lamp																			4	42										
	Pitcher			1	42					17	737																				
	Pipkin																														
	Misc.	15	271	3	45	43	579	15	231	3	62			1	8	2	14	17	134	8	94	75	542	0	0	13	117	13	595	22	151
	Sandy Ware Total	27	613	6	127	105	2051	23	450	54	1989			6	152	2	14	299	6531	19	714	161	3473	0	0	14	148	14	602	23	172
Non Local	Jug	1	12					1	3									16	370	1	23							1	44		
	Misc.	3	40					2	20											2	39	1	12								
	Non Local Total	4	52					3	23									16	370	3	62	1	12					1	44		
Import	Cooking Pot																	2	48												
	Jug	5	74			49	1081	21	714	43	557	1	6					100	2869	9	72	151	1650	2	111	1	2	8	209	1	3
	Mortar							1	33									1	19			9	1841							1	41
	Pitcher							3	63									1	52			26	3478								
	Misc.			1	3	6	63	3	17			2	18			3	23	6	84	1	3	16	50			1	3	1	5	2	9
	Import Total	5	74	1	3	55	1144	28	827	43	557	3	24			3	23	110	3072	10	75	202	7019	2	111	2	5	9	214	4	53
	Total	46	878	16	490	193	3759	87	1817	113	3040	10	86	17	492	10	117	632	13493	37	912	559	14174	12	235	21	232	184	5281	36	324

Figure 11 – Composition of the High Medieval ceramic assemblages from selected features at Bull Hall by ware type and vessel form (sherd count (sc) and sherd weight (sw) in g). Data courtesy of Duncan Brown.

	Trench	Coarseware		South Hampshire Redware		Southampton Sandy Ware		Southampton Whiteware		Other Sandy Ware		Non Local		Saintonge		Other Import	
		SC	SW	SC	SW	SC	SW	SC	SW	SC	SW	SC	SW	SC	SW	SC	SW
Frontage/ Yard	3	18	297	6	51	19	230	3	9	18	151	6	105	6	46	1	4
	7	176	6639	186	5405	66	1320	30	334	63	4741	60	1207	49	733	5	90
	21	24	681	14	255	15	338	7	297	6	137	8	185	7	93	0	0
Frontage/ Yard Total		218	7617	206	5711	100	1888	40	640	87	5029	74	1497	62	872	6	94
Garden	4	145	6127	84	1368	59	810	39	541	44	617	9	88	28	188	12	72
	5	105	3515	81	1644	52	773	33	523	12	232	34	743	30	251	12	79
	18	42	1285	51	1047	23	508	16	330	9	129	9	207	12	91	3	19
Garden Total		292	10927	216	4059	134	2091	88	1394	65	978	52	1038	70	530	27	170

FIGURE 12 – COMPOSITION OF THE HIGH MEDIEVAL POTTERY ASSEMBLAGE FROM HIGH MEDIEVAL FEATURES IN THE GARDEN AND YARD AREAS AT YORK BUILDINGS (SHERD WEIGHT IN G).

Pit	Average Sherd Weight
168	10
191	4
1852	1
4051	18
4357	2
5464	6
5521	16
5552	12
5574	5
5593	5
5652	6
5998	8
6082	5
6830	7
7232	7
7237	14
7286	7
8035	11
8658	8
8755	7
9031	32
9856	4
9886	7

FIGURE 13 – MEAN AVERAGE SHERD WEIGHT (G) OF HIGH MEDIEVAL WARES BY HIGH MEDIEVAL PIT AT YORK BUILDINGS.

Pit	Average Sherd Weight
F1124	18
F1130	39
F1161	19
F1170	2
F1171	11
F1181	5
F1185	27
F1189	19
F1206	26
F1210	24
F1214	29
F1219	8
F1220	13
F1236	21
F1253	23
F1297	10
F1335	12

FIGURE 14 – MEAN AVERAGE SHERD WEIGHT (G) OF HIGH MEDIEVAL WARES BY HIGH MEDIEVAL PIT AT BULL HALL.

	Residual	Local Coarseware	Local Sandy Ware	Non Local	Import	Intrusive	Total
Underlying Fence Line	5567	652	463	51	51	88	6872
Inside Tenement	547	1441	580	26	26	163	2783
Outside Tenement	1401	571	259		11	106	2348
Overlies Fence Line	494	419	422		26	8	1378

FIGURE 15 – COMPOSITION OF THE POTTERY ASSEMBLAGES FROM LAYERS IN THE GARDEN AND RAMPIER AT YORK BUILDINGS (TRENCH 4) BY PHASE WITH A STRATIGRAPHIC RELATIONSHIP TO THE FENCE LINE. SHERD (WEIGHT IN G).

which led to waste being contained in a managed way, either through secondary use as compost or by containing it in pits or other features, with surfaces being deliberately cleared of waste. The way waste was categorized changed through these activities, with individual classes of artefact being broken down and deposited based more on the practices in which they were instigated. For example, the deposition of waste related to yard activities (such as metal working) in separate deposits to the bulk of kitchen and household waste at York Buildings. This is significant in terms of how we study these objects in use, considering that they were used together and not as discrete entities.

Rubbish and the Wider Urban Landscape

Elements of the wider urban landscape can be understood to have been created and maintained through rubbish disposal. An example of this is the enforcement of boundaries and of physical features in the urban landscape. One such feature is the rampier. At York Buildings a fence line was constructed marking the boundary between the rear of the tenements and the rampier. The rampart itself appears to have generally been kept clear of waste during its main period of use. A contrast exists in the composition of the layers between these two areas. Inside this fence line, the pottery assemblage is typical of High Medieval pottery from the site as a whole, composed primarily of local coarse and sandy wares. Several layers were deemed to have built up. Outside of the fence line a more homogenous layer was excavated consisting primarily of residual material (Figures 10, 15). This demonstrates that the presence of the fence line and the rampart imposed upon depositional activity on the site, and also the cleaner nature of this area marked it as different to the cultivated tenement plot. The presence of layers overlying this fence line suggests that during the 14th century this boundary was no longer enforced. During this period the defences at the east of the town were in a poor state of repair (Platt 1973, 122) and the rebuild in stone during the 14th and 15th centuries was poor in quality (Platt 1973, 122). This suggests that unlike in the earlier phases of the defence of the town, the area was not so heavily managed and rubbish may have been allowed to build up in the rampier, either through neglect or through changes in the way that the area was used. In contrast, the castle ditch was kept relatively clear of rubbish during the High Medieval period, demonstrating a deliberate policy of waste management, intended to enforce the influence of the royal authorities and to clearly mark functional and administrative differences between areas of the town. As the castle and royal interests in Southampton declined in the early 14th century (Oxley 1986, 111), rubbish began to be deposited in the ditch, before being cleared in the late 14th century as works on the castle restarted following the threat of invasion (Platt 1973, 128). The build up of rubbish in these defensive features can therefore be seen as indexical of the interests of, and power exerted by, different authorities in the town.

Once features went out of use, they were typically filled with rubbish. Limekilns at Bull Hall and York Buildings, associated with the strengthening of the town defences in the 14th century, are filled with kitchen waste, primarily a mixture of pottery and bone. This activity demonstrates the closing of redundant features and led to these themselves being waste, with the action of filling causing them to be forgotten. The original domestic order was restored to the yard or garden areas into which these temporary industrial features were dug. Such filling also served to impose order in domesticating a space. Whilst no other examples can be cited from Southampton, in Norwich, for example, gravel pits were filled with domestic waste prior to late Medieval occupation on the sites (Atkin and Evans 2002).

So far only rubbish that remains within or close to tenements has been dealt with, be it through intentional final deposition in pits or in a reused (or potentially reusable) state as compost or build up in redundant areas. Large quantities of rubbish may have been removed from the town. In the 15th century a workman was paid to clean the High Street and to carry waste to the sea (Platt 1973, 171). This represents a different kind of deposition to that in layers in redundant areas of the town. The sea represents a 'point of no return' (Lindenlauf 2003). Once rubbish has been deposited in the sea it is completely out of circulation, it cannot be reused or encountered as residual material in the digging of future features. This cannot be seen as reusable and it was not desirable for it to be deposited within the tenement. Why rubbish at Bull Hall and other similar sites was deposited within the tenement remains unclear, it may simply have been more convenient to dump household waste in the yard. It is likely the material deposited within the tenement reflects only selected depositional events, possibly the closing of features such as pits dug for other functions, the garderobe and the limekiln. In an attempt to retain order in the urban landscape, to prevent this waste building up in public areas such as roads, the material had to be removed, with the sea, in this instance, being a perfect location for this deposition. It is likely that this practice stretches as far back as at least the High Medieval period. For example, at Winkle Street, which lies only a few meters from the shoreline, little High Medieval pottery was recovered, despite the presence of High Medieval occupation (Jervis unpublished b; Platt and Coleman-Smith 1975). This may also explain the absence of large rubbish deposits in the area of Southampton Friary (Jervis forthcoming). It is also possible some was carted out of the town, as is suggested for towns away from the coast (Atkin and Evans 2002; Dyer 1989; Keene 1982). Accumulations of Medieval pottery at Cook Street (SOU 254; see Jervis unpublished c) and other sites to the east of the Medieval town, an area used for cultivation in the period (Dyer 1994), demonstrate that this is likely to have happened in Southampton. By removing the pottery from the walled town it can be argued that it is leaving the towns consciousness and is not expected to be encountered again. When carted to the countryside it may have been used as manure, but this was not experienced by town dwellers. This created a contrast between rubbish as refuse and rubbish as a resource and ended the period of transience between usefulness and uselessness.

As within tenements, the deposition of rubbish was highly managed to maintain order in the urban landscape. In the late 13th century for example, the rampier and castle bailey areas were kept clear of rubbish as there was a strong sense of a need for civil defence. In the 14th century the defences were not maintained to such a high standard and during this period these areas acted as a focus for waste deposition. This perhaps ceased periodically as the defences became more important following events such as a French raid in 1338. A contrast can be drawn between the ordered deposition within bounded tenements and the disorder created by the reuse of redundant features (such as the rampier) as dumping grounds. Similarly, rubbish removed from the town altogether is demonstrative of a desire to keep public areas of the town clear of waste, probably due to it providing obstructions rather than any public health concern (Keane 1982, 26; Dyer 198, 191).

Discussion

How Was Rubbish Categorized?

A distinction can be drawn between the two sites. At Bull Hall it appears to have been undesirable waste, large quantities may have been removed entirely, perhaps dumped into the sea. There are a number of primary deposits, and in the case of the lime kiln at least, we can argue that rubbish's only utility was to quickly fill redundant features. Its removal from the site or fast burying acted to impose order upon the tenement plot, creating a flat yard, with few surface deposits, in which household activities could take place. The rubbish from York Buildings was categorized in a much more transitory manner. Household waste was dumped into pits, but rather than acting as filling material, this was a period of renegotiation. Rubbish from household activities became mixed over time, fragmenting categories formed during consumption. Some of this material was spread over the garden area at the back of the plot, where the pottery sherds were perhaps re-encountered during horticultural activity. Other material may have been disposed of elsewhere or remained in the pits as a residual presence. Here, waste was much more integral to life in the settlement. Rather than being an unwanted and disordering presence it was central to the economic life of the tenement, having a role in food production and ensuring that the full potential of resources was extracted.

On this note we can ask to what extent do we actually recover material deemed as rubbish? This discussion has demonstrated that surface deposits, be they dumps of material or the build up of garden soil were open to reinterpretation. These deposits are often disturbed through related gardening activity, scavenging or attempts to clear dumps, interpreted as waste by later generations. It is only those pits containing primary waste and the in-filled redundant features at Bull Hall and of course the material dumped into the sea, which can be viewed as true rubbish. Even material dumped in pits at York Buildings can be seen as transient. They contain few objects and were emptied, either for deposition elsewhere, or for use as compost, with the few objects in these pits being residual. The issue of human agency in the decision to deposit waste and how this should occur is central to the biography of any object, although the utility and nature of the artefacts themselves may influence the depositional method (Gosden 2005). To see its classification as rubbish, as the end of an objects 'life' is therefore debatable. Instead this is dependable on the nature of deposition and whether it enters a deposit in which its meaning can become transient. Within this context it can be argued therefore, that whilst we only recover a sample of material deposited by a household on an archaeological site, the proportion of this considered rubbish in the true sense of the term is smaller still. It is only with the exception of significant deposits, such as the build up of material on the London waterfront (Vince 1985, 26-8), that we can recover this permanent waste in the urban setting in any great quantity.

How Did This Behaviour Create Categories of People?

The treatment of rubbish appears related to socio-economic status. By treating rubbish as a resource at York Buildings, people served to categorize themselves as different to those who occupied Bull Hall. Clearly, this was embedded in other economic and household activities. It was behaviours of preparing (or rather having food prepared) and consuming food and drink which created the accumulations of material comprising the primary deposits at Bull Hall. Similarly, a greater engagement with food (through horticulture) and a different means of preparing and consuming it (for example less use of tableware jugs) at York Buildings, created the process of transition that resulted in the spreading of accumulations of waste over the rear of the tenement plot (Jervis 2009, 81-3). Processes of self and group definition occurred through behaviour throughout the use-life of any given vessel, from the moment it entered the household to its deposition. Depositional practice is just one part of this behavioural sequence which allowed people to be marked as different or similar through practice (Blinkhorn 1997, 123; Dellino-Musgrave 2005, 221).

Categories of people emerged through behaviour. This behaviour was the result of choosing how to dispose of waste within a particular socio-economic context. All decisions regarding how to dispose of rubbish were rooted in wider, contextual concerns. This situated behaviour caused categories of material culture to accumulate and fragment, fracturing along lines drawn by socially embedded action.

We can also question the level to which an urban identity occurred, through the town defences. If, as Martin Hall (2006, 189) states, 'urban landscapes are an expression of identity and also shape the identity of those who live in them' we can expect behaviour in relation to these features to be both reflective and constitutive of an urban identity. Changes in the use of the rampier may index a shift in a feeling of urban identity or of control over the community, with people perhaps feeling less connected at the end of the period. Town defences did not necessarily mark a boundary between town and country and also were not a defining characteristic of a Medieval town (Creighton 2007). Walls were not even a communal enterprise, instead walls embodied the ambitions and fortunes of elites within a town (Creighton 2007, 56). Any unified urban identity may then have been marked in a different way, with behaviour bringing about a different sense of belonging (Blake 1999, 47; Hall 2006: 204). The carting of waste out of town to the countryside also served to create a distinction between urban and rural communities. This relationship was reciprocal however, embedded in the process of provisioning the town. What becomes clear, is that different elements of depositional practice can be used to identify groupings of people, some of which intersect at different levels.

How did this lead to the definition of urban landscape?

Within tenements, rubbish deposition can be seen as a materialization of cycles of household activity. At York Buildings processes of waste accumulation and their subsequent fragmentation through the gardens enabled the continuation of this activity. This specific treatment of waste brought about order in that it enabled people to continue to live in the manner in which they were socialized. Such activity at Bull Hall, I contend, would have been disordering. Here, rubbish deposition created a different sense of order. The infilling of redundant features created a working, socialized space. This process served a dual purpose of removing disordering waste and closing these features.

In this way, at a tenement by tenement level, depositional activity served to create a patchwork of materialized human behaviour. This served to create a varied landscape with divisions between groups of people emerging through a variety of factors including, perhaps, economic activity, social status and ethnicity. The landscape also indexes wider social and political relationships. The example of the town defences shows how, at various times, the urban landscape became a materialization of a fear of attack and at others a nonchalance which, ironically, led to the town being devastated by a French raid in 1338. The town can be seen as a complex indexical network (Jones 2003), with all choices and actions indexing those in other areas of life. To return to Ingold's (1993) definition of landscape, rubbish deposits are one materialization of this network of activities, choices and ways of life within this space, which led to the creation of a uniquely urban landscape.

Implications

This discussion of waste disposal in Medieval Southampton has posed a number of issues which are of direct relevance to the way we excavate and interpret rubbish deposits. The nature of the rubbish pit has come under question in recent years (e.g. Buteux and Jackson 2000). Here it has been demonstrated that other deposits are equally complex. Conceptually, the transient nature of rubbish poses a problem. For too long, deposits have been seen as the final resting place of waste, and most material that is recovered in the archaeological record was perceived as rubbish. This research has demonstrated that it is fairly rare to excavate such deposits, in Southampton at least. Instead, a series of deposits have been identified which played distinct roles in the defining of the urban landscape, the rubbish in which was open to reinterpretation, some of which was reused. The exceptions are those disused features, themselves waste, which are in-filled with rubbish deposits and the primary deposits associated with particular craft or household activities. At the household level the treatment of waste was entwined within other household practices, being determined in part by the social structure of the household, but also having an effect in the maintenance and re-formation of the household as a social entity.

Whilst such deposits are broadly dateable, the use of ceramics to spot-date layers appears misguided, at least in some circumstances. For example, the layers divided by the fence line at York Buildings have different ceramic compositions. The layers inside the fence are datable to the High Medieval period, with those outside being dated to the Anglo-Norman (eleventh and twelfth centuries) period, despite them being contemporary on stratigraphic grounds. Where layers are built up for a particular purpose, be it a floor or the rampart, they consist of few items of rubbish. Pits at York Buildings appear to have been regularly emptied, with their contents spread elsewhere, again bringing into question the dating evidence provided by the small quantity of pottery which they contain. Every feature must be considered on its own merits, its depositional history and its function considered in order to fully understand its role in ordering or disordering; constructing or deconstructing, the household or urban landscape (see also Morris and Jervis 2011).

Conclusions

The management of rubbish played an important role in the creation of household space and the generation and maintenance of the urban landscape as a whole. The ordering of these practices brought about changes in the way waste was identified and hence its treatment in deposition. We need to adapt our methodologies to understand these identifications, to recognize whether we are actually dealing with rubbish in the true sense, or something more transient. Topographical factors influenced the treatment of rubbish and this can be seen as a metaphor for the imposition of civil authority and its subsequent decline in the late 14th century, as deposits accumulated. These conclusions are matched in other towns, where topography as well as social status appears to have played roles in how rubbish was deposited. The definition of Medieval rubbish can be brought into question, with the way it was produced and the means of deposition determining whether waste exited circulation completely or re-entered the social consciousness. The disposability of waste appears to vary temporally and spatially within Southampton. Similar patterns can tentatively be observed in other towns such as Norwich, Oxford and Hereford, where dumps of rubbish occur in the poorer areas and differences have been observed in the types of material recovered from pits. Such issues pose methodological concerns about how we treat rubbish deposits. We need to acknowledge that these deposits as highly contextual, emerging from distinct sets of household practice and having differing effects depending upon the context created through these networks of action.

Acknowledgements

Most of this research was carried out whilst working on an Institute for Archaeologists funded workplace bursary at Southampton Museum. This placement was supported by the Medieval Pottery Research Group. The research has continued as part of an Arts and Humanities Research Council funded PhD project at the University of Southampton. I would like to thank my supervisors, Dr. Andrew Jones, Dr. David Williams and Professor David Hinton for their support throughout the project. Thanks also go to Duncan Brown for commenting on drafts of this paper, sharing his data and all of his support during and after my time at Southampton Museum.

Bibliography

Atkin, M., Carter, A. and Evans, D. 1985. *Excavations in Norwich 1971-78 Part II*. Norwich, East Anglian Archaeology Report 26.

Atkin, M. and Evans, D. 2002. *Excavations in Norwich 1971-1978 Part III*. Norwich, East Anglian Archaeology Report 100.

Arnold, P. 1990. The Organization of Refuse Disposal and Ceramic Production within Contemporary Mexican Houselots. *American Anthropologist* 92, 915-32.

Beck, M. and Hill Jr., M. 2004. Rubbish, Relatives and Residence: The Family use of Middens. *Journal of Archaeological Method and Theory* 11(3), 297-333.

Blackman, P. Unpublished. *SOU 25 Site Archive Report*. Southampton City Museum.

Blake, E. 1999. Identity-Mapping in the Sardinian Bronze Age. *European Journal of Archaeology* 21(1), 35-55.

Blinkhorn, P. 1997. Habitus, Social Identity and Anglo-Saxon Pottery. In P. Blinkhorn and C. Cumberpatch (eds), *Not so Much a Pot, More a Way of Life*, 113-24. Oxford, Oxbow.

Brown, D. 2002. *Pottery in Medieval Southampton c1066-1510*. York, CBA Research Report 133.

Bryant, V. 2012. The Mystery of the Missing Miskins. Rubbish disposal and dispersal in a medieval urban context. *Medieval Ceramics* 32, 1-8.

Buteux, V. and Jackson, R. 2000. Rethinking the Rubbish Pit in Medieval Worcester. In S. Roskams (ed.), *Interpreting Stratigraphy: Site evaluation, recording procedures and stratigraphic analysis*: 193-6. Oxford: British Archaeological Reports (International Series 910).

Creighton, O. 2007. Town Defences and the Making of Urban Landscapes. In M. Gardiner and S. Rippon (eds), *Medieval Landscapes,* 43-56. Macclesfield, Windgather Press.

Dellino-Musgrave, V. 2005. British Identity Through Pottery in Praxis. *Journal of Material Culture* 10(3), 219-43.

Douglas, M. 1966. *Purity and Danger*. London, Routledge.

Driver, J. Unpublished. *Mammalian and Avian Fauna, Period IIB, SOU 25*. Southampton City Museum.

Dyer, C. 1989. *Standards of Living in the Later Middle Ages*. Cambridge, Cambridge University Press.

Dyer, C. 1994. Gardens and Orchards in Medieval England. In C. Dyer (ed.), *Everyday Life in Medieval England*, 113-32. London, Hambledon Press.

Edensor, T. 2005. Waste Matter – The Debris of Industrial Ruins and the Disordering of the Material World. *Journal of Material Culture* 10(3), 311-32.

Gardner, A. 2002. Social Identity and the Duality of Structure in Late Roman-Period Britain. *Journal of Social Archaeology* 2(3), 323-51.

Gosden, C. 2005. What do Objects Want? *Journal of Archaeological Method and Theory* 12(3), 193-211.

Hall, M. 2006. Identity, Memory and Countermemory: The archaeology of urban landscape. *Journal or Material Culture* 11(1/2), 189-209.

Ingold, T. 1993. The Temporality of Landscape. *World Archaeology* 25(2), 152-174.

Jennings, S. 2002. The Pottery. In M. Atkins and D. Evans, Excavations in Westwick. In M. Atkins and D. Evans, (eds), *Excavations in Norwich 1971-1978 Part III*: 134-45. Norwich, East Anglian Archaeology Report 100.

Jervis, B. 2009. For Richer, For Poorer: A synthesis and discussion of Medieval Pottery from eastern Southampton in the context of the High and Late Medieval Towns. *Medieval Ceramics* 30, 73-94.

Jervis, B. 2012. Medieval Pottery in East Hampshire: A preliminary study. *Medieval Ceramics* **32**, 35-53.

Jervis, B. Forthcoming. The Pottery from Telephone House (SOU 1355) in J. Russel (ed.), *Excavations at Telephone House (SOU 1355)*.

Jervis, B. Unpublished a. *The Pottery from Pouparts Warehouse (SOUs 934 and 997)*. Southampton City Museum.

Jervis, B. Unpublished b. *Medieval and Post-Medieval Pottery from Winkle St (SOU 162)*. Southampton City Museum.

Jervis, B. Unpublished c. *Medieval and Post-Medieval Pottery from Cook Street (SOU 254)*. Southampton City Museum.

Jones, A. 2007. *Memory and Material Culture*. Cambridge, Cambridge University Press.

Kavanagh, H. Unpublished. *SOU 175 Site Archive Report*. Southampton City Museum.

Keene, D. 1982. Rubbish in Medieval Towns. In A. Hall and H. Kenward (eds), *Environmental Archaeology in the Urban Context*: 26-30. York, CBA Research Report 43.

Lindenlauf, A. 2003. The Sea as a Place of No Return in Ancient Greece. *World Archaeology* 35(3), 416-33.

Morris, J. and Jervis, B. 2011. What's so Special? A reinterpretation of Anglo-Saxon 'special deposits'. *Medieval Archaeology* 55, 66-81.

Needham, S. and Spence, T. 1997. Refuse and the Formation of Middens. *Antiquity* 71, 77-90.

Oxley, J. 1986, *Excavations at Southampton Castle*. Southampton, Southampton Archaeology Monograph 3.

Platt, C. 1973. *Medieval Southampton*. London, Routledge.

Platt, C. and Coleman-Smith, R. 1975. *Excavations in Medieval Southampton* (2 volumes), University of Leicester Press.

Schofield, J. and Vince, A. 2003. *Medieval Towns: The archaeology of British towns in their European setting*. London, Equinox.

Shoesmith, R. 1985. *Hereford City Excavations Volume 3: The Finds*. York, Council for British Archaeology Research Report 56.

Underwood-Keevil, C. 1997. Pottery. In A. Hardy, A Archaeological Excavations at 54-55 St. Thomas's Street, Oxford. *Oxoniensia* 61, 225-73.

Vince, A. 1985. Saxon and Medieval pottery in London: a review. *Medieval Archaeology* 29, 25-93.

Gone Fishing! New dating evidence for the fish trade in the North Sea

Derek Hall

with contributions by

Gordon Cook and Derek Hamilton

Abstract

The results of the Carbon 14 dating of carbonised deposits of Shelly-Sandy Ware pottery from Perth, London and Bergen is discussed and some consideration given to possible links with the stockfish trade across the North Sea. It is suggested that this dating technique could be usefully applied to other pottery fabrics whose provenance and date is not very well understood.

Key Words: Bayesian Analysis, Bergen, C14 dating, London, Perth, Stockfish

In recent years the reanalysis of the sizeable pottery assemblage from excavations at 75-96 High Street, Perth, Scotland has allowed for some proper consideration of the dating of the early phases of this site (Figures 1-2). Dug as a Manpower Services Scheme in the mid to late 1970's in advance of a major retail development in the core of the medieval burgh, this site produced a remarkable collection of preserved organic artefacts, timber buildings and 52,000 sherds of medieval pottery (Perry et al. 2011).

The earliest phases of this excavation produced a sizeable assemblage of a fabric known as Shelly Sandy Ware (Figure 3) which was identified as probably being manufactured in South Eastern England and of a date no earlier than AD 1150 (Figure 4; Blackmore and Pearce 2011). The dating of the fabric from London was based on the relationship between a series of dendrochronologically dated timbers from Thames waterfronts and deposits containing sherds of Shelly Sandy Ware. Ceramic researchers from Perth were unhappy with the suggested date as they were convinced that the early phases at Perth High Street ought to date before the burgh's foundation charter in the 1120's. The author collected 15 samples of carbonised Shelly-Sandy Ware that were associated with occupation and building floor levels at the High Street excavation and submitted them for dating. The results were remarkably consistent with an apparent cross over between AD 1020 and 1030, at least 100 years earlier than had been suggested by the London chronology. Concern was then expressed by colleagues in England about these early dates and it was suggested that it ought to be checked that the dated fabric was definitely of Southern English origin. Therefore as a next step chemical analysis (ICPS) was undertaken to confirm the suggested provenance and the results supplied to Dr Alan Vince for analysis. Dr Vince confirmed that the dated sherds were manufactured in the Thames Basin.

The author then contacted Alex Bayliss at English Heritage to discuss the possibility of dating samples from the Billingsgate excavations in London (the site where the original chronology had been defined; Figure 5). Permission and funding were granted and samples were selected specifically from the phases that had been dated in tandem with the dendro dates. Seven C14 dates

Figure 1 – Excavations at 75-96 High Street, Perth looking South East
(©Scottish Urban Archaeological Trust)

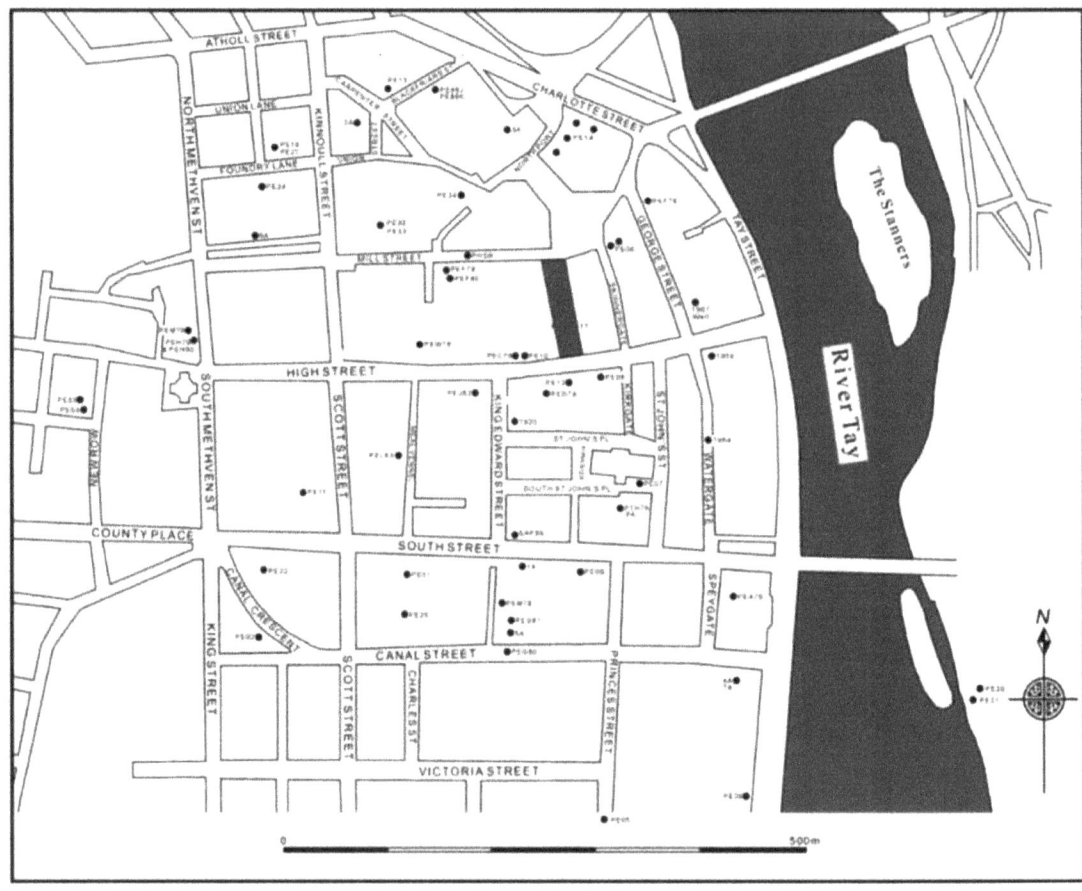

FIGURE 2 – LOCATION OF 75-96 HIGH STREET EXCAVATIONS (AFTER BOWLER, D P 2004, *PERTH THE ARCHAEOLOGY AND DEVELOPMENT OF A MEDIEVAL BURGH*)

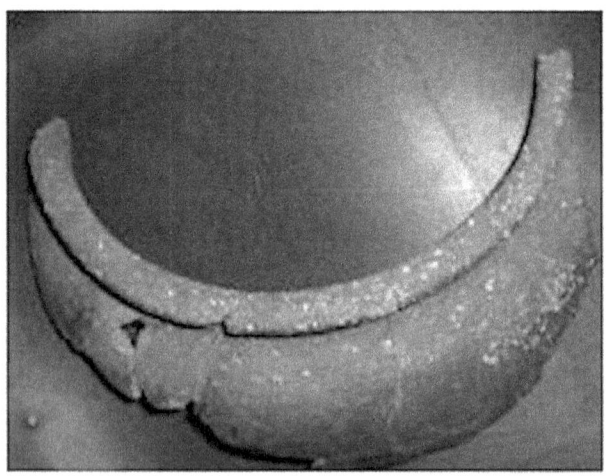

FIGURE 3 – SHELLY SANDY WARE RIMSHERD FROM 75-86 HIGH STREET EXCAVATIONS (©D HALL)

were received of a similar range to those that had been received for Perth. In an attempt to back up the dating results samples of leather from the early phases of the Perth excavations were also submitted for dating; these also produced results in a similar bracket. Intriguingly a similar C14 date had been received for the wattle lining of an early ditch directly across the High Street in excavations in the early 1990's.

With a combination of the dating results from both Perth and London we now had twenty six dates of the mid 11th century AD for the use of this pottery.

Norway was the next piece of the jigsaw, particularly the excavations on the Bryggen waterfront in Bergen, where sizeable quantities of Shelly Sandy Wares (Figure 6) had been identified by Lyn Blackmore and Alan Vince in 1994 (Blackmore and Vince 1994; Hansen 2005). The author visited the Bryggen museum in Bergen in early 2008 and sampled twelve sherds of carbonised Shelly Sandy Ware and submitted them for dating. Yet again the dates received were in the same mid 11th century date bracket as those from Perth and London.

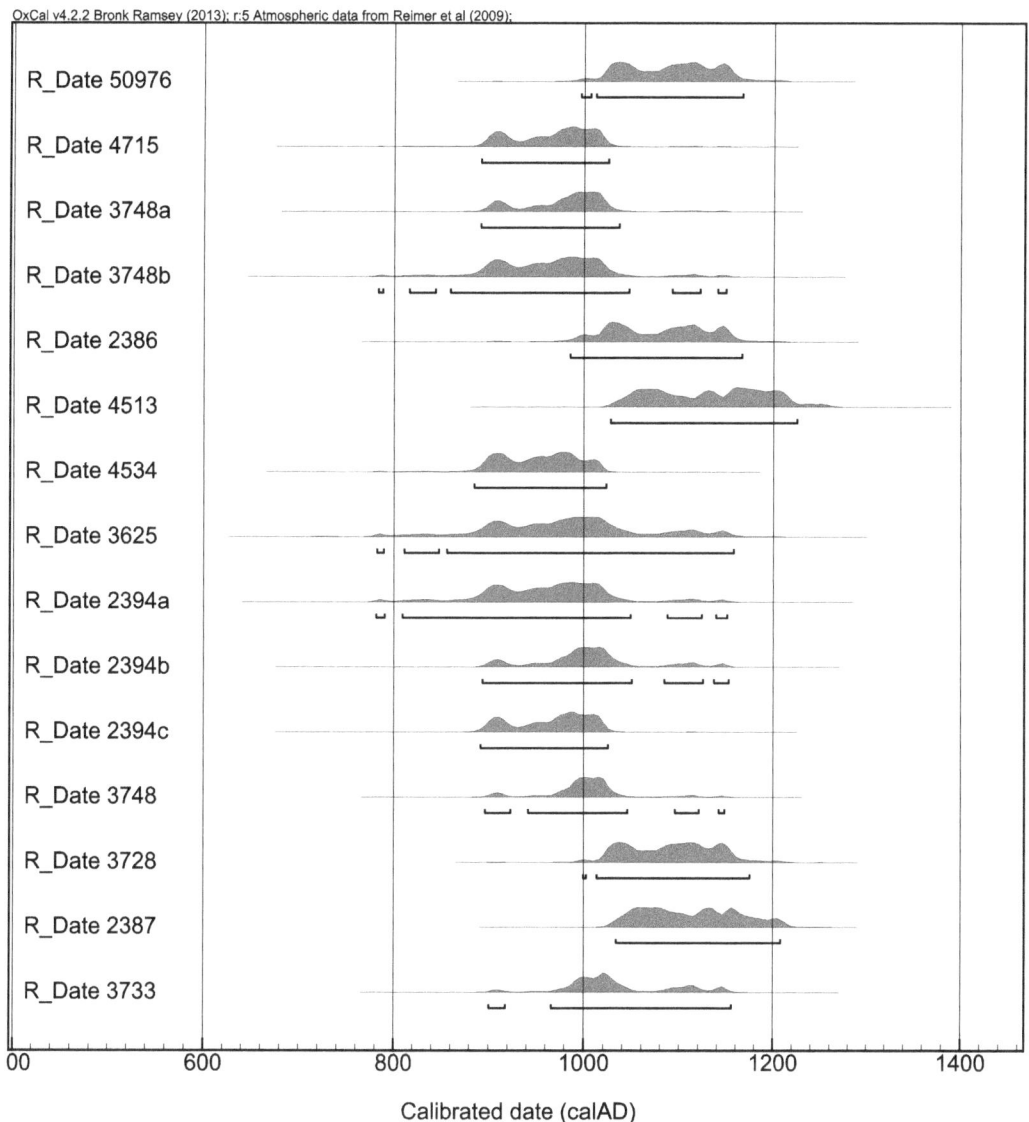

FIGURE 4 – CARBON DATES FROM 75-96 HIGH STREET, PERTH

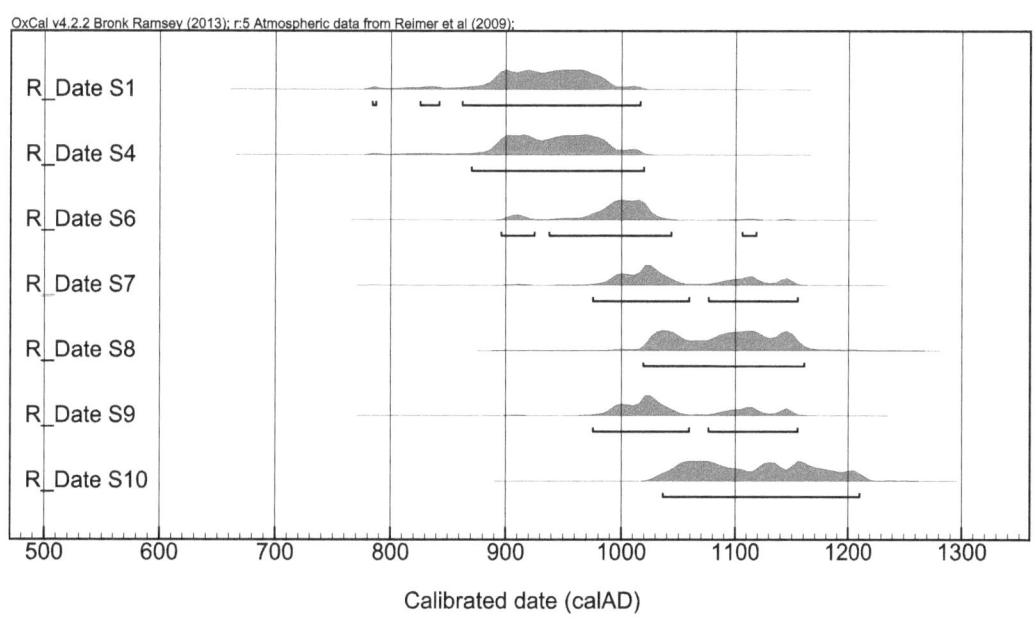

FIGURE 5 – SHELLY-SANDY WARES FROM BILLINGSGATE, LONDON (ENGLAND). CARBON DATES

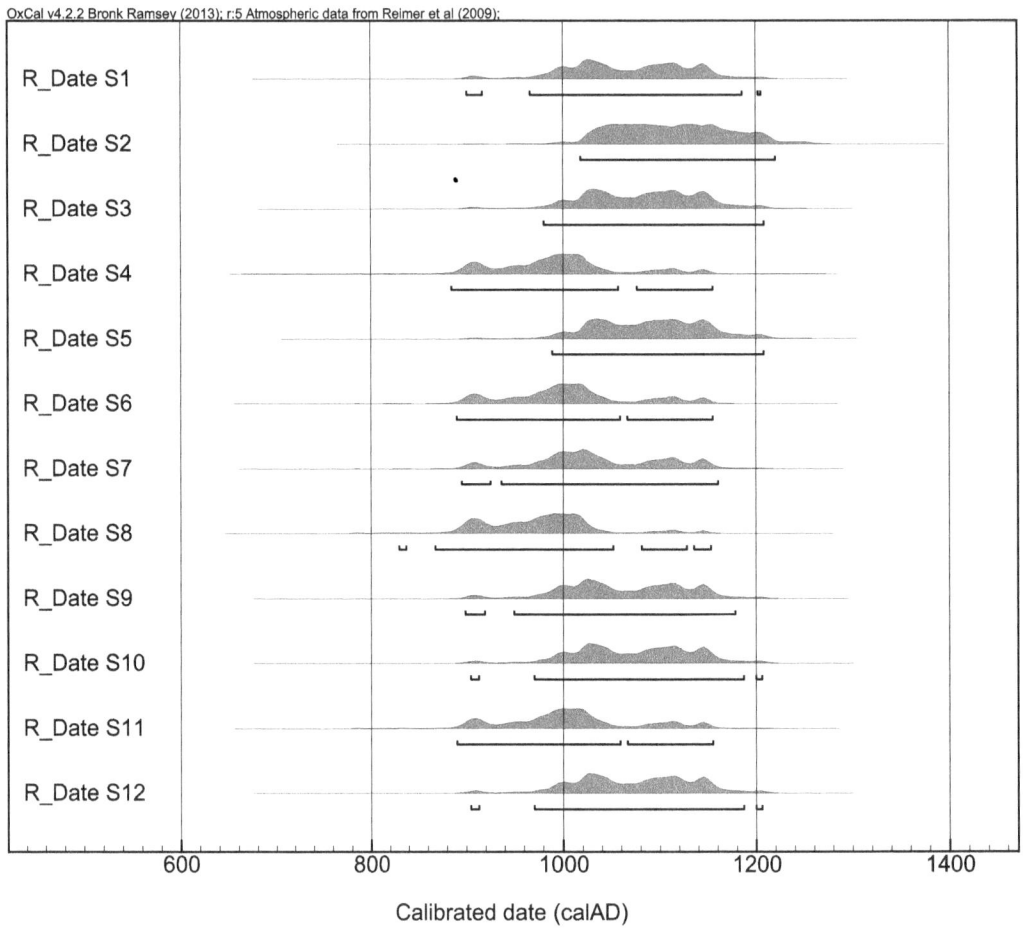

FIGURE 6 – SHELLY-SANDY WARES FROM BRYGGEN, BERGEN (NORWAY). CARBON DATES.

Summary and Conclusions (Figure 7)

In summary this now gave us 38 C14 dates from three different locations on the North Sea that all seemed to suggest dates at least a hundred years earlier than the published chronology for this pottery fabric (Blackmore and Pearce 2011). Bayesian analysis of the dates by Dr Derek Hamilton suggests that Shelly Sandy Ware comes into fashion in the order London-Perth-Bryggen and falls out of fashion in reverse order. The model supports this with an 89% probability that London precedes Perth and that Perth precedes Bryggen (98% probability London precedes Bryggen) for the introduction of this fabric type. Furthermore, there is a 79% probability that Shelly Sandy Ware falls out of fashion in Bryggen prior to Perth and an 80% probability that it falls out of fashion in Perth prior to London (Hall Cook and Hamilton 2010, 333).

If we now try and put these potential dates in context what can they tell us? From the point of view of pre charter settlement in Perth, research has suggested that St Johns Kirk (or at least its site) has probably always been the focus for early settlement. Indeed this part of the burgh has remained dry in any flooding episodes (Bowler 2004; Hall, Hall and Cook 2005). The dating from 75-96 High Street suggests that we could be looking at early settlement in the mid 11th century being focused on either side of the major routeway (later the High Street) down to the fording point across the River Tay. What about other material from similar deposits in Perth? Early groups of pottery also include quite a high proportion of greyware fabrics which were originally identified as being of Low Countries (Belgium, Holland) origin but their apparent date did not seem to match that identification. So samples of these fabrics were chemically sourced in comparison with samples from kiln sites in Jutland and East Anglia. At least one of the Perth samples is closely comparable with a sample from a production centre on Mors Island in Jutland. Other samples had good comparisons with a couple of the East Anglian kilns and a small group remains unidentified (Hall and Chenery 2004). There is good documentary evidence for the presence of merchants of East Anglian origin in Perth and this may be reflected in the ceramics. Interestingly enough a property owned by Thomas De Lynn was in close proximity to the site of the Horsecross excavations where we have our only sherds of Ely Type Ware, another East Anglian product (Hall 2009). The apparent Danish link is important because I feel it confirms that there is archaeological evidence for Baltic trade which may be going unrecognised. A recent comment that has been made to me on the remarkable collection of wooden vessels from the Perth High Street

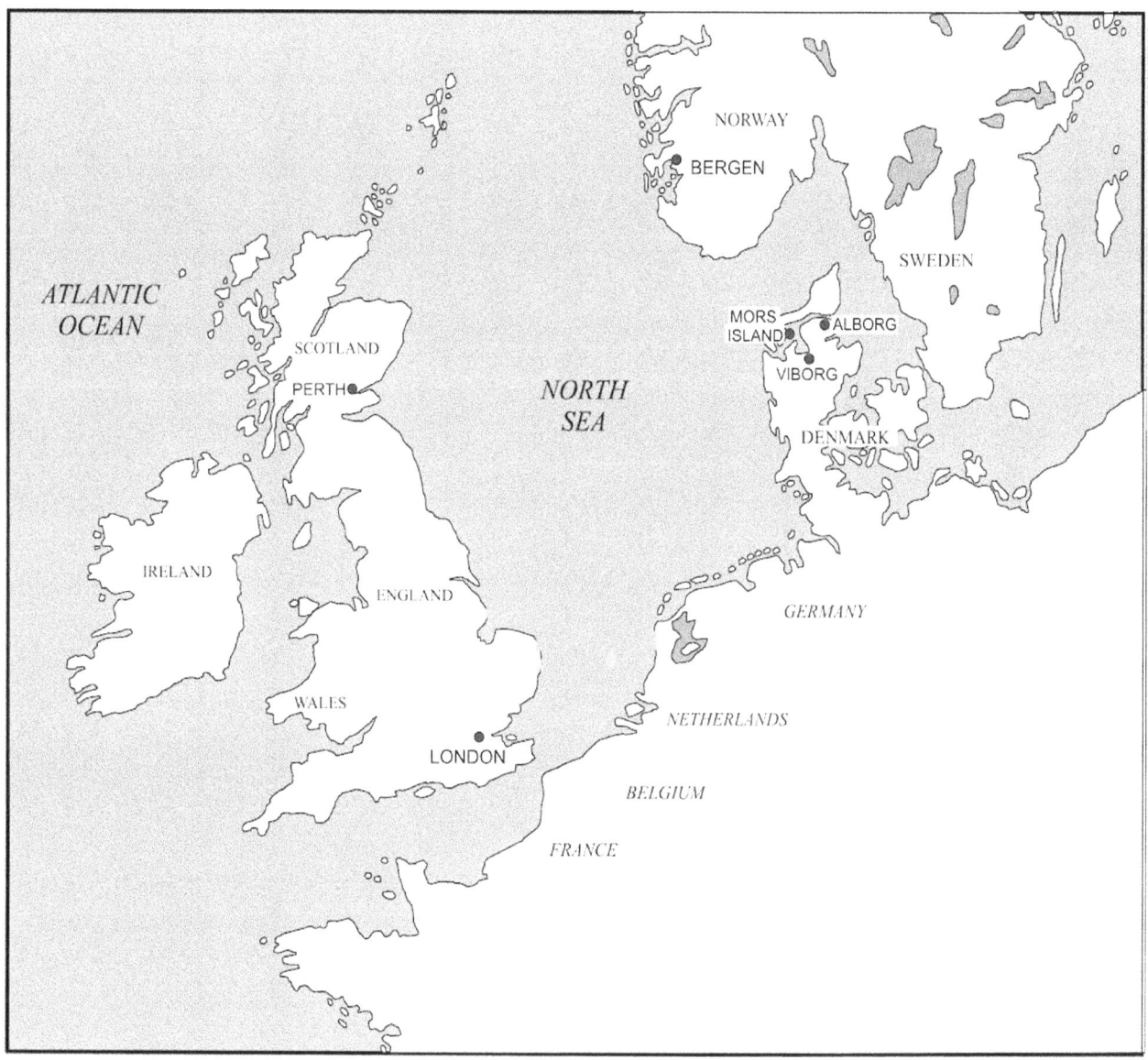

FIGURE 7 – MAP OF BRITAIN AND NORTHERN EUROPE SHOWING PLACES MENTIONED IN TEXT (©D HALL)

excavation has indicated what strong parallels there would seem to be with material from excavations in the Hanseatic port of Lübeck in Northern Germany.

When we combine our dating evidence from all three sites we are left with the intriguing question as to why this particular pottery type should be travelling around and across the North Sea in the 11th century? This is a subject that requires a great deal more research and study but is it possible that there is a connection with the trade in stockfish? Recent work by Dr James Barrett on fishbones from several sites on the North Sea littoral has produced carbon dates that are comparable to those that have been received for carbonised Shelly-Sandy Wares, and this has suggested an intensification of fishing in the North Sea in the 11th and 12th centuries (personal communication J. Barrett; Barrett *et al.* 2010).

Without a doubt the main question that a ceramicist is asked is 'OK, what date is it then?' With the improvements in the accuracy of AMS dating do we now have an answer to that question? Potentially the answer is yes but I cannot overstress the importance of the stratigraphic location of the samples. My Perth samples were all from stratified layers associated with first phase buildings on the site, so you can argue that the dates are absolute and do relate to the deposition of the sherds. Both Billingsgate and Bryggen produced samples of Shelly Sandy Ware that were from dumped layers, so the dates relate to the last use of the potsherd rather than the action of dumping. If my argument for the earlier dating of London Shelly-Sandy Ware is correct, then it would be sensible to try and date some well stratified samples from sites in London in the same manner. Put simply, the Bryggen excavations have been dated using the London chronology, and the time is nigh for the entire assemblage to be properly studied. We should all keep this dating technique in mind when we begin to process our excavated pottery!

Be careful with those toothbrushes....

Acknowledgements

The author would like to acknowledge the support and interest of Professor Gordon Cook and Dr Derek Hamilton at SUERC in East Kilbride, George Haggarty, Research Fellow, National Museums Scotland, Mark Hall, Perth Museum and Art Gallery, Scotland and Gitte Hansen, Bryggens Museum, Bergen, Norway. He would also like to acknowledge Historic Scotland and English Heritage for funding the Perth and London C14 dates and the Strathmartine Trust and Perth and Kinross Heritage Trust for other grant aid. Marta Carascio and John Bintliff are thanked for allowing the author to present this paper at the 2009 EAA conference in Riva del Garda, Italy. Finally Lyn Blackmore of MOLAS and the late Alan Vince are acknowledged for taking part in the debate on these dates. A full description of the methodology of the C14 dating technique used on these carbonised deposits is published in Hall, Cook and Hamilton 2010.

Bibliography

Barrett, J. H., Johnstone, C., Harland, J., Van Neer, W., Ervynck, A., Makowiecki, D., Heinrich, D., Hufthammer, A. K., Enghoff, I. B., Amundsen, C., Christiansen, J. S., Jones, A. K. G., Locker, A., Hamilton-Dyer, S., Jonsson, L., Lõugas, L., Roberts, C., and Richards, M. 2007. Detecting the medieval cod trade: A new method and first results. *Journal of Archaeological Science 35 (4), 850-861.*

Blackmore, L. and Pearce, J. 2011. *A dated type series of London medieval pottery: PART 5 Shelly-Sandy Ware and the greyware industries*, Museum of London Archaeology Monograph 49, London.

Blackmore, L. and Vince, A. 1994. Medieval pottery from south-east England found in the Bryggen excavations 1955-68. In *The Bryggen Papers Supplementary Series No 5*, 9-160.

Hall, D. 2007. The Pottery. In A. Cox, Excavations at the Horsecross, Perth, *Tayside Fife Archaeological Journal* 13, 147.

Hall, D. W. and Chenery, S. 2005. New evidence for early connections between Scotland and Denmark? The chemical analysis of medieval greyware pottery from Scotland, *Tayside and Fife Archaeological Journal* 11, 54-69.

Hall, D., Cook, G. and Hamilton, D. 2010, New dating evidence for North Sea Trade between England, Scotland and Norway in the 11th century AD, *Radiocarbon* 52 (2-3), 331-336.

Hall, M., Hall, D. and Cook, G. 2005. Whats Cooking? New radiocarbon dates from the earliest phases of the Perth High Street excavations and the question of Perth's early medieval origin, *Proceedings of the Society Antiquaries of Scotland* 135 (2005), 273-285.

Hansen, G. 2005. *Bergen c 800-c 1170: The Emergence of a Town* (Bryggen papers Main Series 6) 298. Bergen, Fagbokforlaget Vigmostad & Bjorke.

Perry, D. *et al.* 2011. *Perth High Street Archaeological Excavation 1975-77 The Excavations at 75-96 High Street, Perth and 5-10 Mill Street, Perth Fascicule 1*, Tayside and Fife Archaeological Committee, Perth.

French Imported Pottery in Scotland

George R. Haggarty
Research Associate National Museums Scotland

Abstract

Summary of French Medieval and Post Medieval pottery imported into Scotland, dates, distribution, socio-economic impact.

Key Words: Scotland, French Pottery, Trade.

After more than a quarter of a century, it would be interesting to know if many medieval historians still adhere to the view summarised by Davey and Hodges, in their introduction to the proceedings of the 1980 Hull Conference on Ceramics and Trade (Davey and Hodges 1983, 1-14); 'the study of ceramic trade is of great value for the early periods of our history when there is little documentation, but after 1200 its value is more doubtful'. Indeed, the historians Colin Platt and David Hinton had previously concluded that later medieval archaeology, particularly the study of later medieval pottery imports, was an expensive way of finding out what is known from the documents. Included in the same volume by Davey and Hodges is an important essay, which should be read by all who process medieval and later ceramics, in which they addressed the then current concerns of economic historians. First they highlighted much of the excellent work being carried out by medieval ceramicists, but at the same time drew attention to their many weaknesses. The most significant of these were the lack of scientific aids being employed and the absence of regional studies of production and distribution, which, they quite rightly said, would undoubtedly shed real light on the significance of archaeology in the historic period. Finally, they stated that we were strikingly ignorant about the marketing patterns implicit in the distribution of specific well-known ceramic products and that our analysis literally did not extend beyond plotting dots on maps.

Have we in Scotland addressed these criticisms over the last two decades? The answer must be both yes and no. My own research shows that, over the 20 years 1980-2000, a large number of different analytical and dating techniques were applied to Scottish medieval white gritty ware pottery, at a huge cost in both time and money. The results of all that expense and effort is a moderately good thin-section database, mainly created in his own time, by Eoin Cox, and a number of Thermo Luminescence dates of somewhat limited value (in some cases varying in date by as much as + or – 150 years). The failure of almost all other procedures was, I consider, due to the lack of monitoring by the funding bodies, poor or non existing research strategies and the quality of our national fabric type series; this despite a generally held view, and one subscribed to by English Heritage, that all processed pottery and scientific work should be related to such a sequence (Barclay 2001, 2). Moreover, 'the importance of a type-fabric/ware series cannot be overestimated as a way of reducing costs and increasing efficiency in processing and reporting' on pottery' (Fulford and Huddleston 1991, 46).

It was only with the commencement of a number of Historic Scotland funded, ICP-MS, inductively-coupled plasma mass spectroscopy, projects, (Chenery *et al.* 2003; Jones *et al.* 2006; Haggarty *et al.* 2010), initiated with the aim of working towards the construction of a medieval and post medieval fabric series, that those of us studying Scotland's wheel thrown ceramics, have begun to address Davey and Hodges' first criticism. As for work on marketing patterns and the distribution of specific ceramic types, it is fair to say that, apart from a publication in 1970 on the distribution of Scarborough type ware and facemask jugs in Scotland (Laing and Robertson 1970), work in that area has virtually stagnated.

It is unfortunate, that in comparison with many European countries, Scotland's early medieval documentary record is relatively poor, and I would contend, we require as much help as the analysis of traded ceramics can bring to the study of our social and economic history. In saying this, I am also aware that, with very few exceptions, we are still failing to retrieve enough information from our excavated ceramic assemblages; information crucial to those involved in the study of our past.

I am also aware that using the evidence, either physical or documentary, gained from the study of imported ceramics to make assumptions on trade can be contradictory. For instance, John Allan found no mention of trade from Italian ports in the Portsmouth port books, whereas the large assemblage of archaeologically derived Italian ceramics recovered from the town clearly implies a trade connection. It was not until Allan examined other types of documents, such as litigations, that a complete picture of the town's complicated trading network began to emerge (Allan and Barber 1992, 290). Not all areas traded their locally produced pottery, even when it was superior in quality, while other ceramic types were trans-shipped. This has been shown to good effect in Southampton, where the analysis of imported pottery is often at variance with the

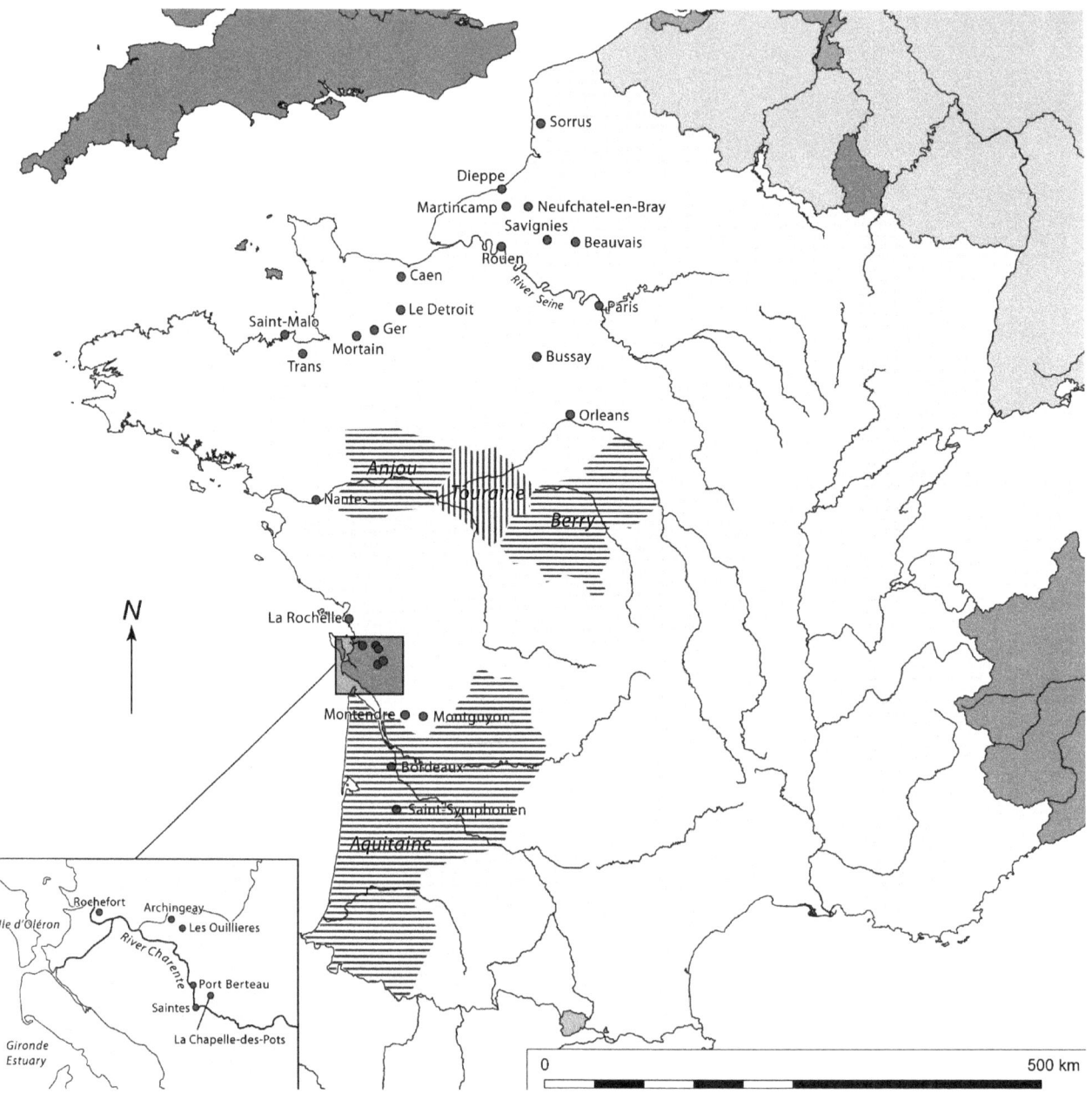

Figure 1 – France: Shows areas and towns from which different types of French pottery found in Scotland originated

historical trends in trade (Platt and Coleman-Smith 1975, vol 1, 36; Duncan Brown pers comm.).

There is no doubt that post-Roman Scotland was, at least in ceramic terms, on the periphery of medieval Europe and, as I have previously written (Haggarty 1984, 396), it is my view that there is as yet no good evidence for an indigenous medieval pottery industry in Scotland prior to c. 1125-50. This suggests that the introduction of wheel-thrown ceramic technology into Scotland sprang indirectly from King David I's policy of Normanisation and feudalisation, when he encouraged Normans, Bretons, Flemings and other Anglo-French supporters to settle here. He and his new nobles also advocated and supported the importation of monasticism from both England and France and it was this influx of merchants, craftsmen, monks, etc,

which led to a number of general, economic and social benefits, almost certainly including ceramic production and trade from France (Figure 1).

It is now generally accepted by those of us working with Scottish medieval ceramics, that it was the great abbeys, such as Kelso, which produced in the 12th century what was by far Scotland's finest pre-industrial pottery. These new abbeys were also involved in prospecting and mining for gold and other metals including lead (Cochran-Patrick 1878), which they used for roofing, glazing and plumbing, as well as glazing of pottery and tiles.

King David's capture of the northern English town of Carlisle and its Mint, along with local silver mines led to the establishment of a Scottish coinage, which with

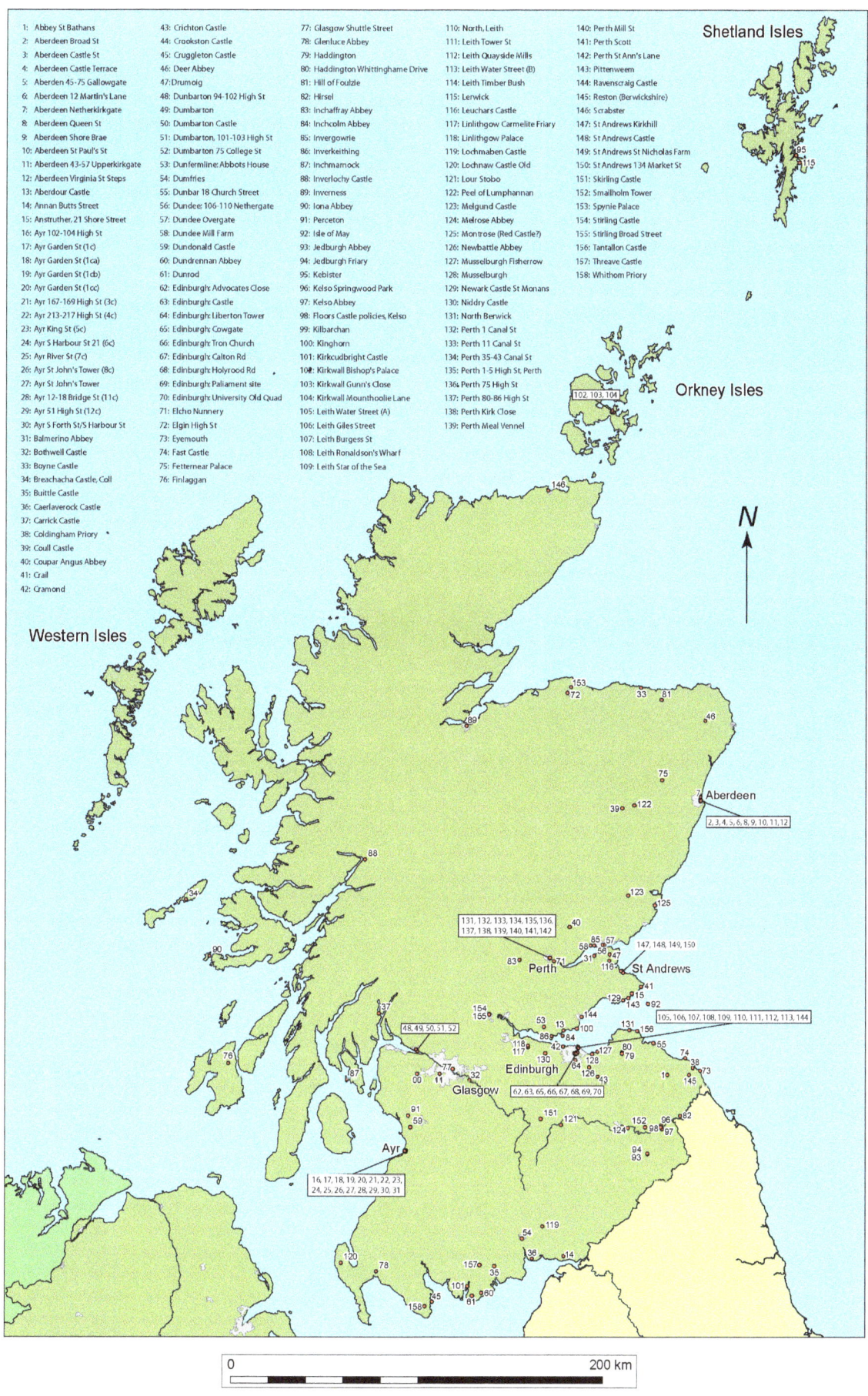

FIGURE 2 – SCOTLAND - ALL ARCHAEOLOGICAL AND FIELD WALKING SITES WHERE FRENCH POTTERY FROM
C. 1150 – C. 1650 HAS BEEN RECOVERED

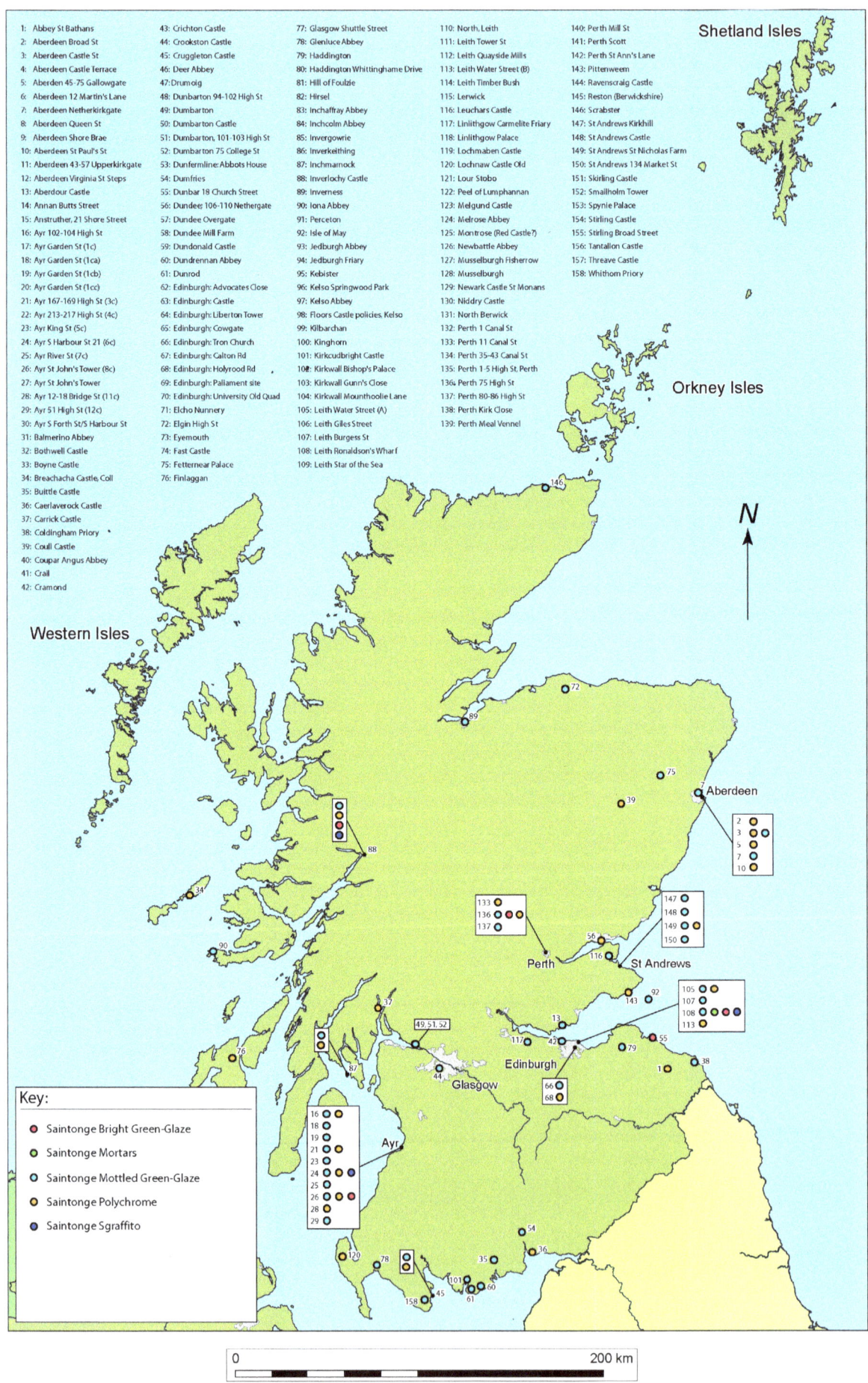

FIGURE 3 – SCOTLAND - THE DISTRIBUTION OF SAINTONGE POTTERY - MEDIEVAL TYPES

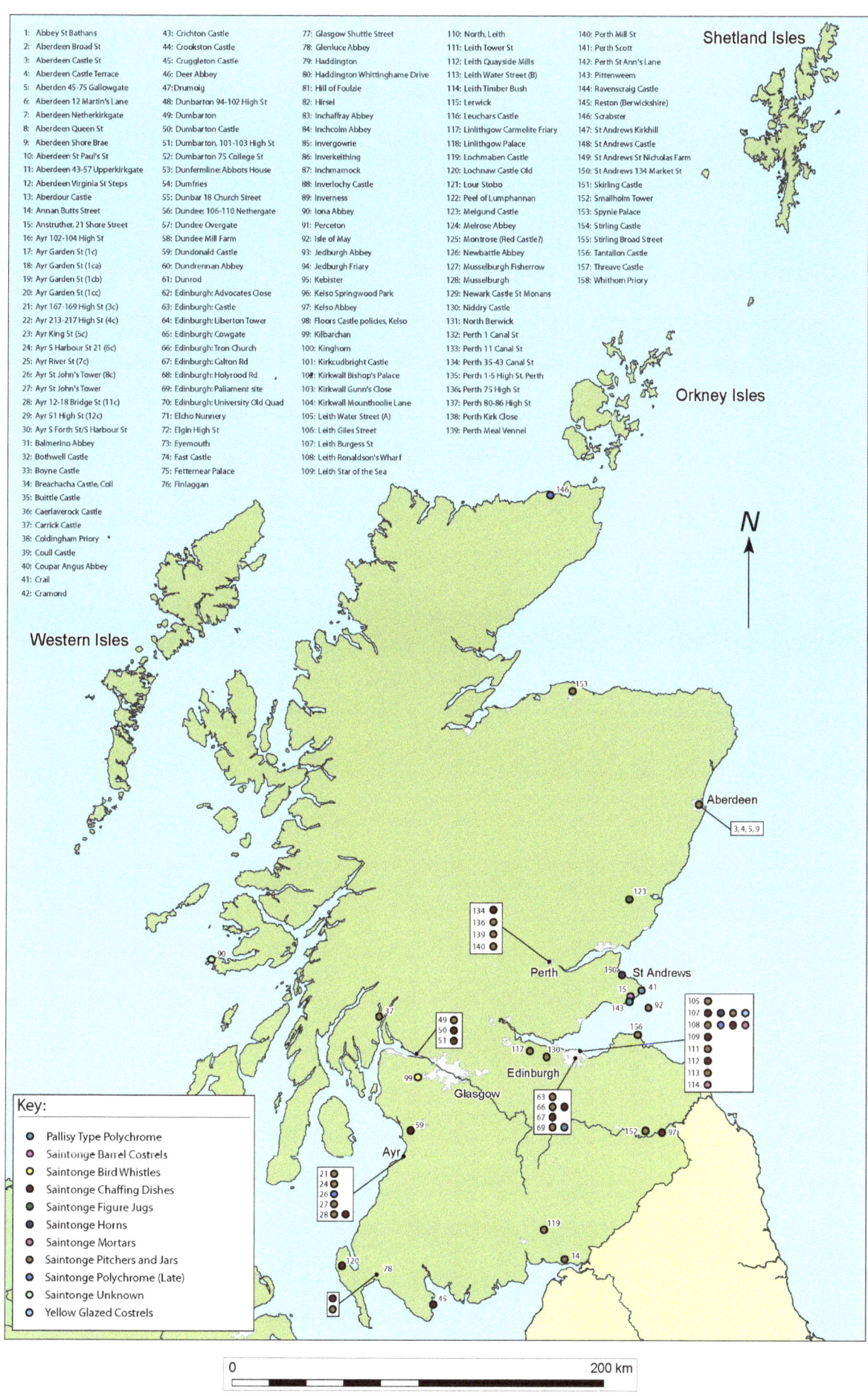

FIGURE 4 – SCOTLAND - THE DISTRIBUTION OF SAINTONGE POTTERY - LATER TYPES

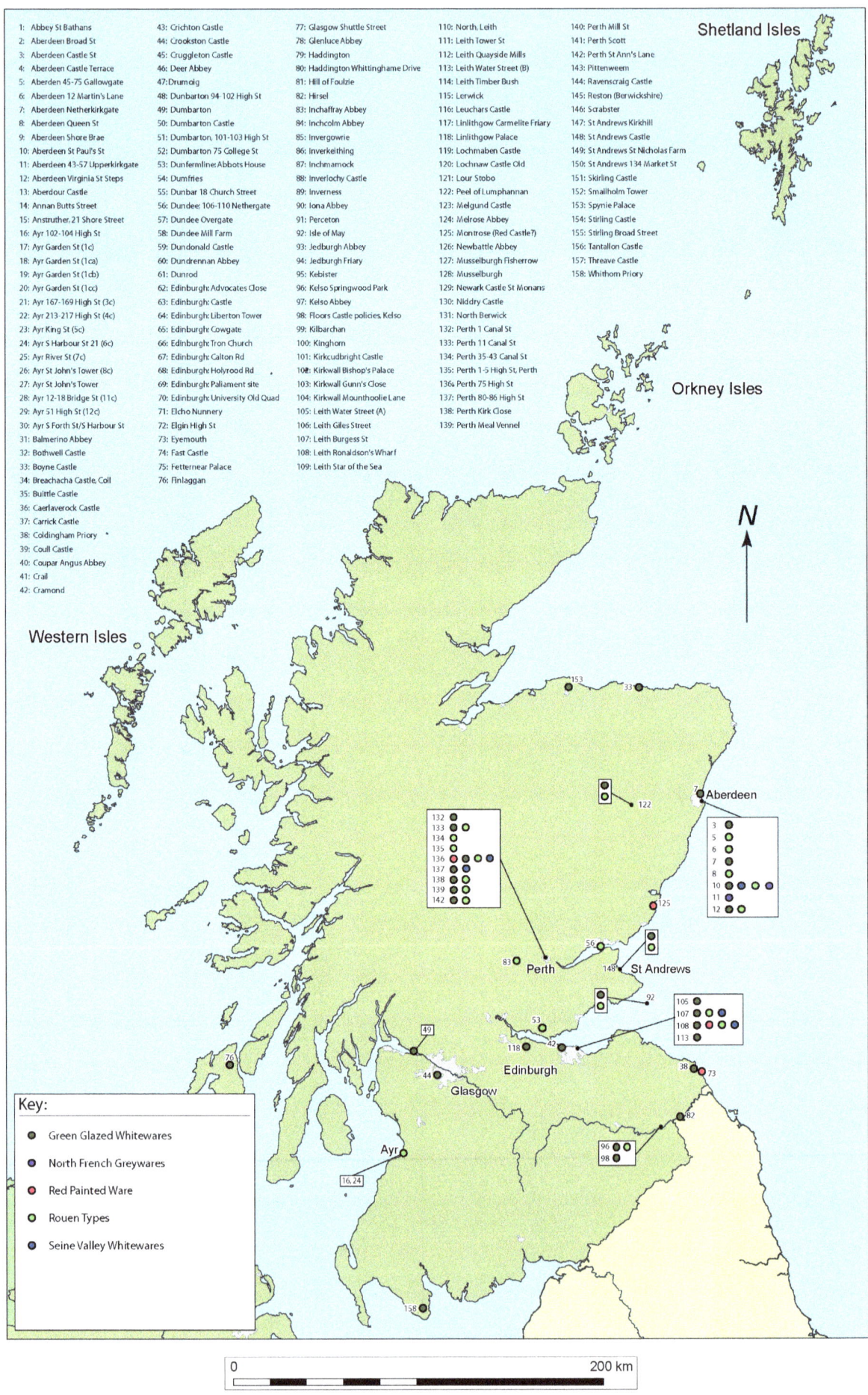

Figure 5 – Scotland - The distribution of North French pottery - medieval types

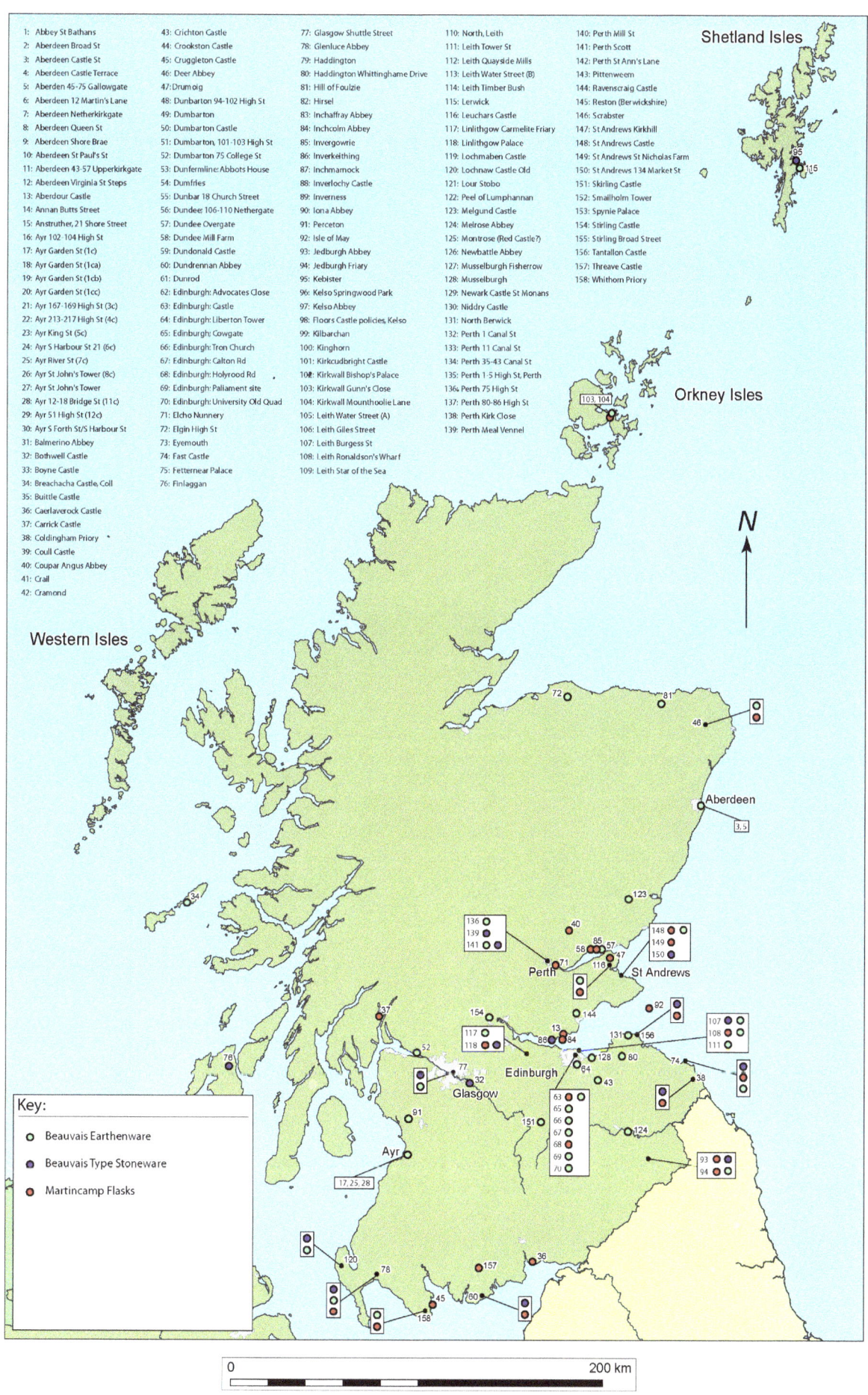

FIGURE 6 – SCOTLAND - THE DISTRIBUTION OF NORTH FRENCH POTTERY - LATER TYPES

his tight control of the newly founded trading burghs, contributed to a major upsurge in the Scottish economy (Claughton date not given). It was however the exports of wool from the new monasteries, principally through at that time the border town of Berwick upon Tweed, to the Low Countries which helped sustained the long and prolonged period of monastic building. It is interesting that this increase in trade was not reciprocated to any great extent with the importation of what was probably construed as high status, Low Countries, highly decorated pottery. This may suggest that locally well produced white gritty ware was dominating the market. The Scottish evidence is in stark contrast to that in Scandinavia and the Baltic regions, which at this period were importing large quantities of Low Countries pottery (Vince 2002, 137). Intriguingly, in the same paper, Vince also tells us that, although the evidence from kiln waste recovered in Bruges suggests that the twice fired Low Countries red wares were not matched for quality by most other European red earthenware industries, they are also remarkably scarce in eastern England. Vince also wondered if examples were not being recognised due to a similarity to English redwares. This certainly cannot be the answer for much of Scotland, including ports and towns like Leith, St Andrews, (Figure 14) and Edinburgh, where local pottery in use at the period came mainly from white firing clays, suggesting that white wares were the colour of choice and these were being imported from a number of areas including north France (Figure 5).

Until the Wars of Independence in the 14th century, there was an almost continuous expansion of the Scottish economy, with the development of a diverse international trade stretching from Norway to the north and Italy to the south. It seems likely that by the 1290s Scotland was, in contrast to England, substantially more prosperous than it has been since (Lynch and Strang 1996, 238-9). In the 14th century, however, Scotland's trade with the rest of Europe was substantially disrupted. The trade which did survive was mainly with Flanders and the Baltic, while the remaining links with France were extremely tenuous. The situation showed signs of improvement from the latter end of the 15th century, by which time there was a Scottish community in Dieppe, and it was this town which attracted the bulk of the increase in Scottish trade (Lynch and Strang 1996, 238-9). This was no doubt encouraged by privileged access, albeit of a rather indefinite nature, to some areas of France, although this concession did not seem to include Gascony or Bordeaux (Davidson and Grey 1909, 101). Nevertheless, for most of the 16th century, France continued to be one of Scotland's principal overseas markets. Certainly, acknowledged contact between Scotland and France developed at this period, and gradually began to supplant previous Flemish influences. An example of this can be seen in the form of words used by the Scottish Parliament when drawing up legislation on the jurisdiction of the Dean of Guild Court in 1593. 'According to the lovable forme of jugement usit in all gilds towns of France and Flanders quhair burses ar erected and constitute and speciallie in Paris Rowen Bordeaulx Rochel' (Davidson and Grey 1909, 6). The mid 16th century also saw what has been called the 'French colonial period' of Scottish architecture c. 1538-1601, which proclaimed the leaning of the Scots nobility towards France (McKean 2003, 13).

A charter of c. 1510 had given Scottish merchants exemption from all customs duty in Normandy, and this was repeatedly approved right into the 17th century and this is possibly why we start to see ceramics from that area in Scotland, (Figure 7). When the charter was ratified by Henry II in 1554 it was on condition that the Scottish merchants should declare an oath that the goods were their own and were to be shipped to Scotland (McKean 2003, 103).

On the marriage of Queen Mary and the Dauphin, in 1558, all Frenchmen in Scotland were naturalised and all Scotsmen received the same rights in France, no doubt bringing benefit to Scottish merchants at a time when commerce was hedged in by many national barriers (McKean 2003, 103). In a warrant of 1594, Henry IV commanded that Scottish merchants 'freelie traffique through all his kingdom without any trouble' while his successor, Louis XIII, confirmed, on more than one occasion, privileges to Scottish merchants in Normandy.

By the beginning of the 16th century Normandy had become an important recipient of Scottish fish, receiving 68% of the salmon and 99% of the herring exported from Leith. In 1510-11 and 1512-13 this was some 2,448 barrels in total (Ditchburn 2001, 146). Leith's importance was on the increase, so that by the 17th century, 35% of all French cargoes bound for Scotland docked there, against 20% in Glasgow. In 1692, 63% of French wine from Bordeaux entered Leith, accounting for £37,000 one third of the burghs income, with only 17% going to Glasgow. This however was partly offset by the large trade in imported French salt from La Rochelle, landing at Glasgow. This was almost certainly due to the fact that there were far fewer saltpans on the River Clyde than on the Forth (Lynch 1996, 281). At this period Dieppe and Rouen were the sources of most manufactured goods, which were of high value in relation to their bulk, entering Scotland (Lynch 1996, 281). Unfortunately there are no port books and little published documentation from Dieppe, as most of it was destroyed when the Dutch and British navies bombarded the town in 1694, and much of the Rouen material has yet to be worked on (Ickowicz 1993, 58).

It was the French ceramics recovered during the excavations at Kirkcudbright Castle between 1911 and 1913, which resulted in the published thesis, that it was Edward I's invasions of Scotland during the Wars of Independence, which resulted in good quality medieval Saintonge pottery finding its way north of the border (Cruden 1951, 180). Although a number of French troops from 'Gascoyne and off Almany and the duche of Bretayngny' are known to have entered Scotland with Edward II's army and fought at the battle of Bannockburn (Ditchburn 2001, 202). I would suggest there is now little to back Cruden's invasion thesis, as the distribution of Saintonge pottery in

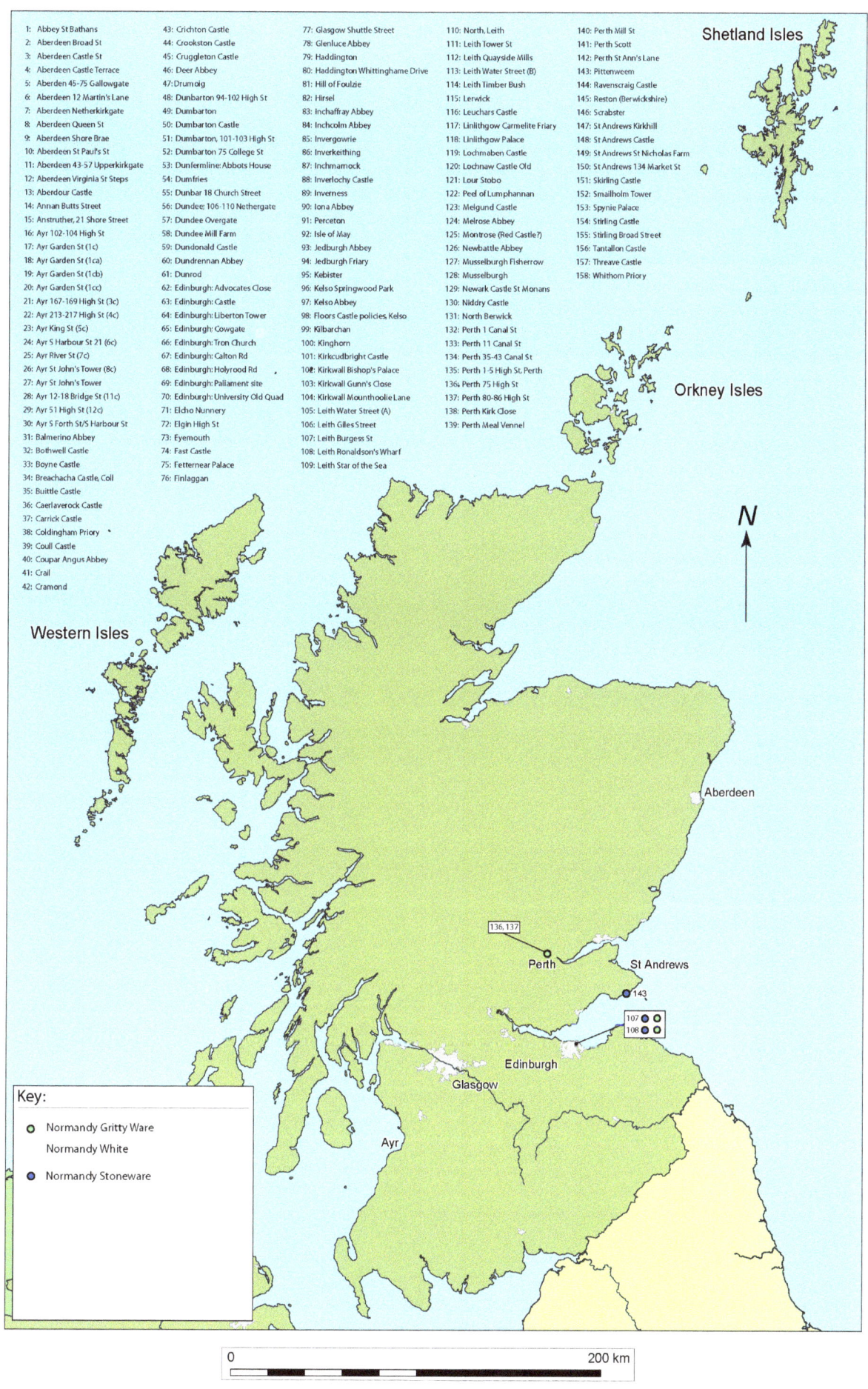

FIGURE 7 – SCOTLAND - THE DISTRIBUTION OF NORMANDY POTTERY

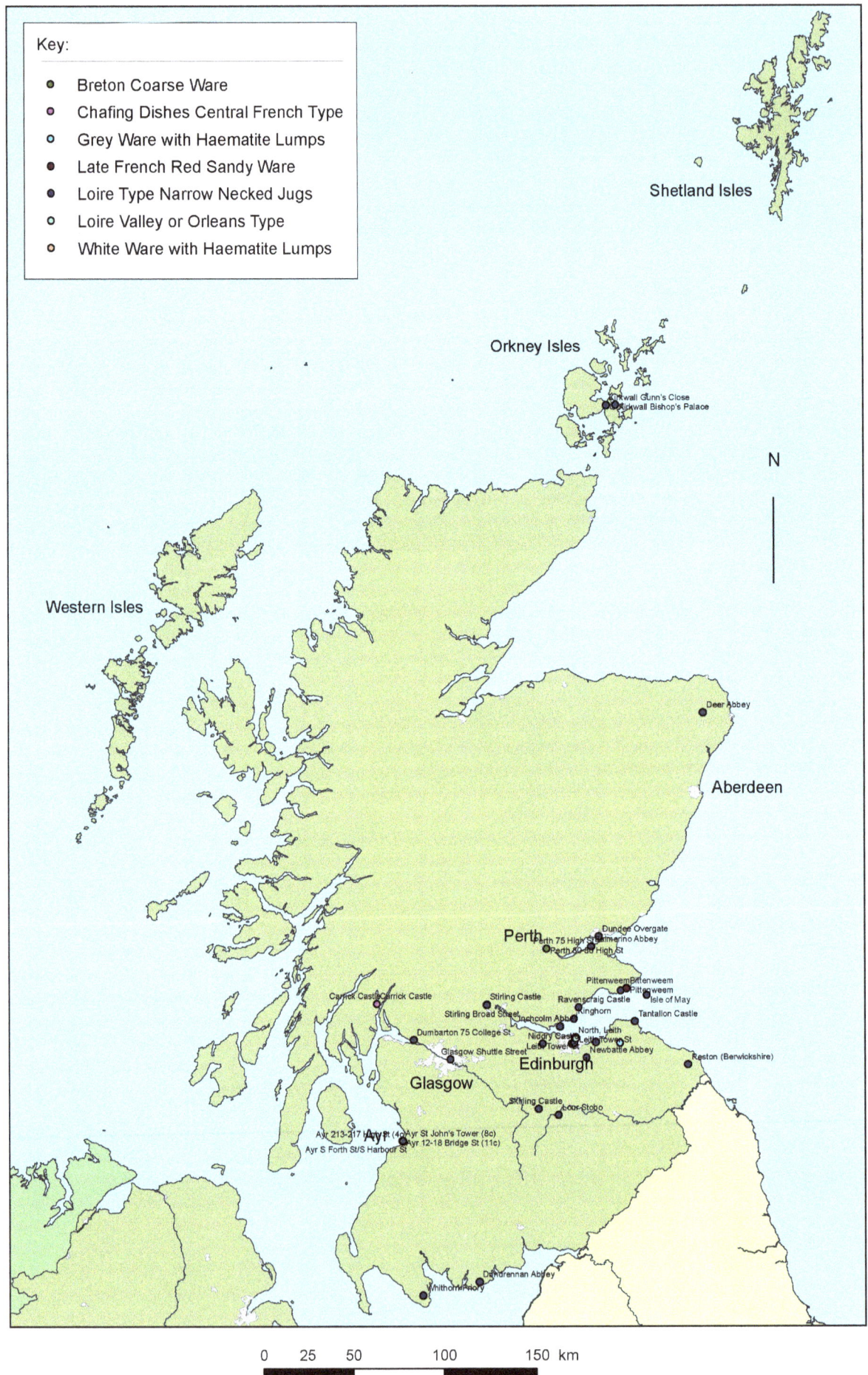

FIGURE 8 – SCOTLAND – THE DISTRIBUTION OF LOIRE AND BRETON POTTERY, PLUS UNKNOWN TYPES

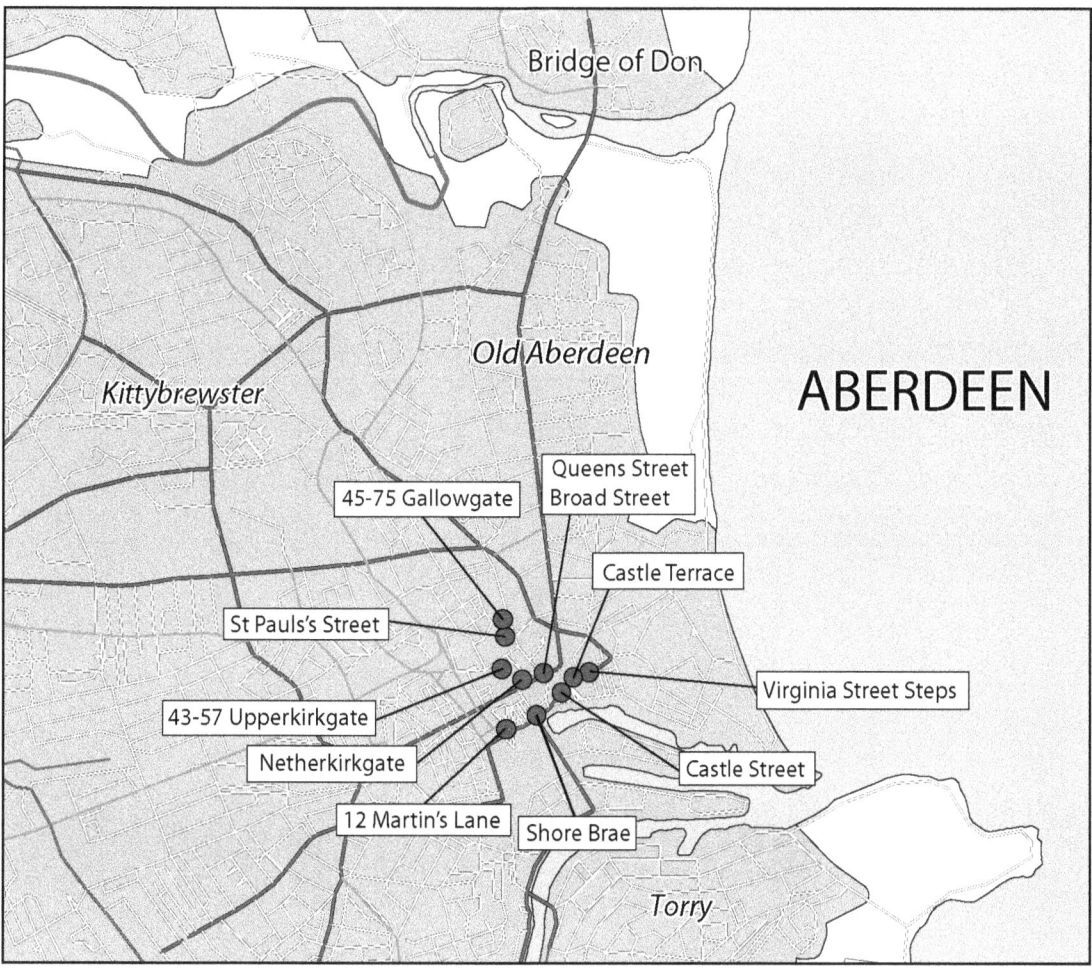

FIGURE 9 – ABERDEEN – THE DISTRIBUTION OF FRENCH POTTERY - ALL TYPES

Scotland is mainly coastal, (Figure 3). Shards have now been recovered from the east coast burghs of Edinburgh and Leith (Figure 12), Aberdeen (Figure 9), Perth (Figure 13), Dundee, Pittenweem and from a number of sites on the west coast, including the burgh of Ayr (Figure 10), Finlaggan on Islay, the castles of Inverlochy, Buittle, Carrick, Cruggleton, Caerlaverock, Kirkcudbright and the abbeys of Dundrennan, and Whithorn.

I would therefore suggest that the medieval Saintonge pottery which to-date has been recovered from sixty four sites in Scotland should at best be regarded as merchandise of medium to high status, which was entering the country as part of the milieu of North and Irish Sea trading patterns. What I do find significant, is that despite the concentration of large archaeological excavations in the large east coast burghs of Perth, Aberdeen, Edinburgh and Leith, it is from the west coast of Scotland, especially the burgh of Ayr, that the majority of medieval Saintonge pottery shards have to date been recovered.

The demand for wine in Scotland, for both religious and secular use, exploded with the Anglo-Normanisation of the country in the 12th century. Published documentary evidence shows that wine was being imported into a Scottish east coast burgh by at least the middle of that century (RRS 1, 278), exported from Normandy in the first quarter of the 13th century, and directly from Maine in 1226, (CDS 1, 331, 881 and 935). Merchants from Perth were trading in wine from Bordeaux before 1246 (CDS 1694). Meanwhile, on the Scottish west coast, Ayr, founded around 1198, was also importing large amounts of corn from Ireland (Duncan 1975, 505), while abbeys like Glenluce, Holmcoltram and Kilwinning, from 1220 to 1252, went directly to the Irish to purchase shiploads of corn and other victuals for their own use. (CDS 1, 765, 930, 933, 974, 982 and 1889). According to Barbour, when on the 29th June 1315 Edward Bruce captured Dundalk, a supply depot for the English campaigns in Scotland, he discovered an abundance of wine (McNamee 1997, 171).

However this east–west trade divide may not be that clear-cut. There is evidence for the exportation of fish in 1291 from the port of Aberdeen, in the north east of Scotland to the Irish town of Waterford, which at that time was an extremely important cog in the French wine trade (McEneaney 1979, 22). The fish in question was probably mackerel, since the document quoted from states, a different tax for imported salmon and herring. I have given only a few examples of what was almost certainly a very complicated trading network, which unquestionably

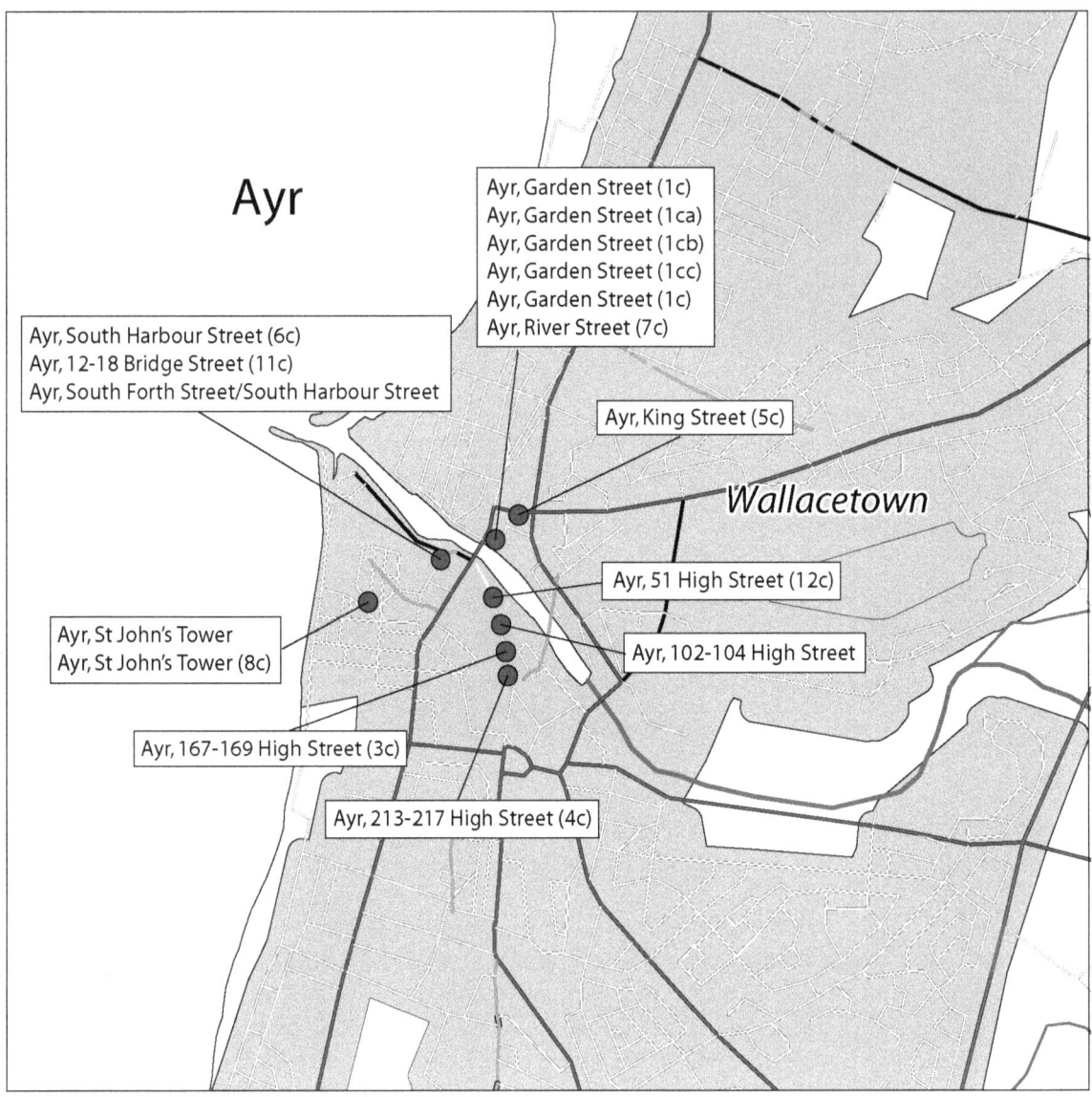

FIGURE 10 – AYR – THE DISTRIBUTION OF FRENCH POTTERY - ALL TYPES

allowed French-made ceramics to enter Scotland either directly or indirectly as an adjunct to sea-borne trade.

The evidence for the extension to the north of an Irish Sea dispersal of early Saintonge pottery adds weight to what was highlighted at the Medieval Pottery Research Group's Annual Conference in 1980 and later ably summed up by Patrick Wallace (1983, 225-30) in his paper on the pottery from Dublin. To quote, he states that 'Bristol, Exeter, the Welsh ports, and especially Dublin, overwhelmingly favoured French wares. This contrast in pottery recovered [from the east coast of Britain] is probably a general reflection of an overall medieval trading pattern most likely connected with sea-routes firmly entrenched in the mercantile experience of early historic southern Britain' (Wallace 1983, 227). This view has been reinforced by more recent work carried out on other Irish towns, which shows an analogous pattern (Hurst 1988, 242-44; Gahan et al. 1997, Table 4-1, 110; McCutcheon 1997, 82-3). Wales and the north east of England, in the main, show a similar coastal distribution pattern (Davey 1983, 209-218 and Papazian and Campbell 1992, 1-107).

Excavations at Finlaggan on Islay in the Inner Hebrides produced 15 shards of early Saintonge pottery from a midden on the edge of the island site of Eilean na Comhairle, which is substantially more than recovered from all the excavations in Edinburgh. Interestingly the geochemical analyses of loch sediments from the island, confirm that it had a longer history of lead mining than the earliest historical account of 1511-12 (Cressey 1995, 293). Given the potters' need for lead, I cannot but suggest that this may have been part of an Irish Sea trading link. It is hoped that this hypothesis can be tested in a programme of scientific lead glaze analysis, on medieval pottery and tiles.

Although not specifically included in this survey, but published by Marshall, there is a pottery rim shard from Little Dunagoil on the Isle of Bute, (1964, Plate 20, 4), which it has since been suggested may be from a ninth century Carolingian cooking pot, comparable with

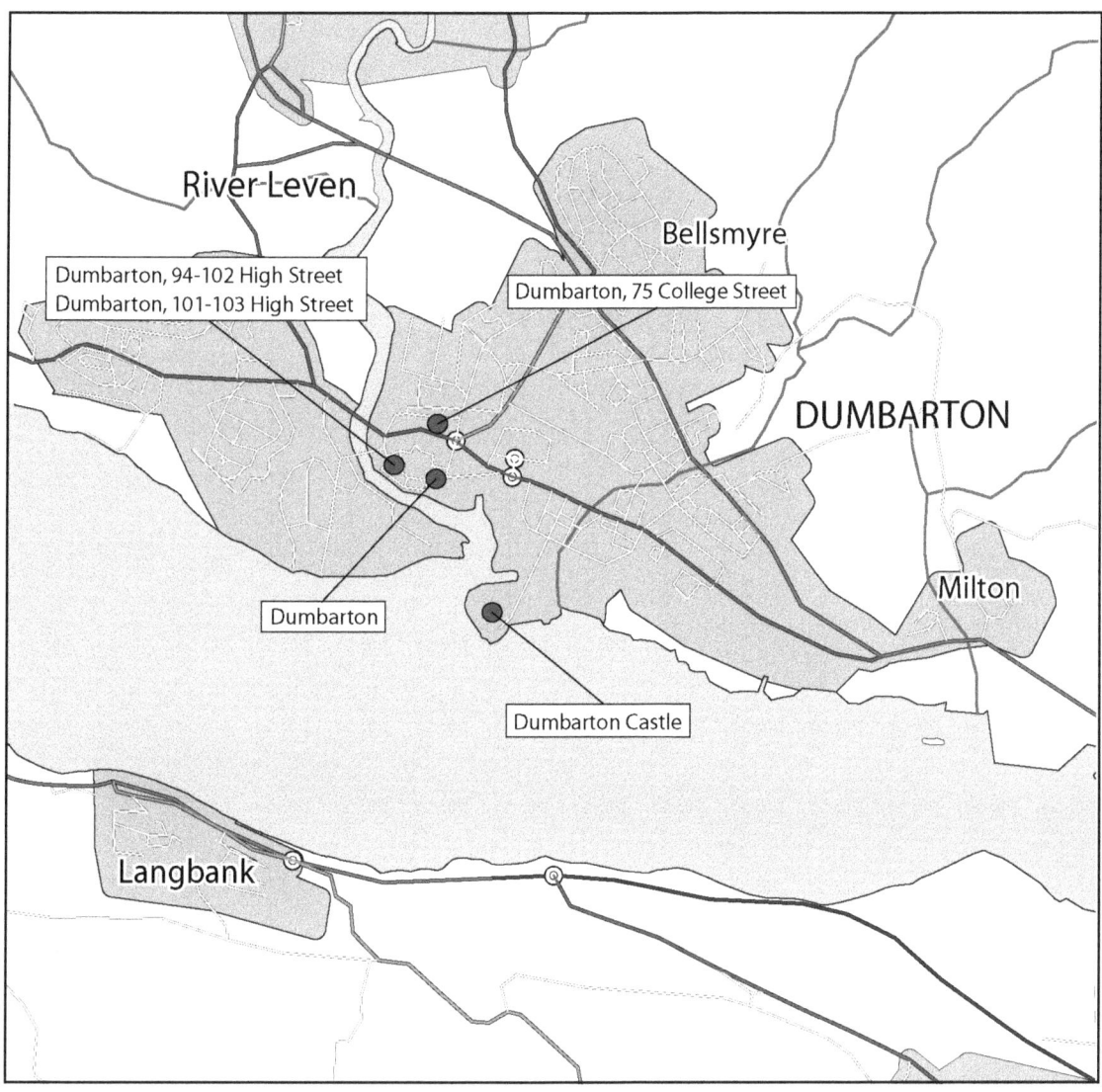

FIGURE 11 – DUMBARTON - THE DISTRIBUTION OF FRENCH POTTERY - ALL TYPES

published pottery from a kiln site at Saran, Loiret, (Laing *et al.* 1998, 559). If this source is correct, it could suggest, with what are said to be 8th to 10th century shards from a crannog at Lochspouts and Stranraer (Campbell 1996, 57), a tentative parallel between the trade in E-ware and other post-Roman imported pottery types and the later importation of high medieval French pottery into the west of Scotland. So far as I know, there is still no evidence for a Gallo-Roman ceramic production in this area of the Saintonge, which up to the 1970s has produced no pottery that could be dated earlier than the 12th century (Chapelot 1972, 75). However, petrographic analysis has led some authorities to consider an area of Aquitaine, lying to the south of Saintonge, to be the probable source of E-ware (Peacock and Thomson 1967, 35-46; Hodges 1977, 240).

The evidence from my survey shows that, despite significant contact between Scotland and South West France in the 15th century, there is significantly less Saintonge pottery of that date from Scottish sites, with the exception of the Port of Leith. The main contact with France at that period began in October 1419, when a large contingent of Scots mercenaries, possibly as many as 6000, entered the service of the French king. This was through the port of La Rochelle and they were present at a number of major engagements. They were however, probably only about a third of the total number of Scottish soldiers who were in France between 1419 and 1424. Professor Contamine suggests that at least 15,000 fought there under a number of prestigious leaders (1992, 16), and it has also been very cautiously estimated that this may have been as much as 2% of the Scottish population (Simpson 1992). Among French grants of land given, or promised, to prominent Scots around this time was the county of the Saintonge, gifted to James I in 1428, as part of an agreement about further military help. The grant however was never enacted, as the tide of war quickly moved in the French King's favour, and most of the Scots returned home (Watt 1996, 115). Many Scots however chose to stay in France, settling mainly in the areas of Berry, Touraine, Anjou Poitou and Saintonge, and in some numbers became the owners of houses, lands and fiefs (Contamine 1992, 21; Macdougall 2001, 4-5). Amongst a number of Scots who acted as bailiffs or seneschals for the French crown, was

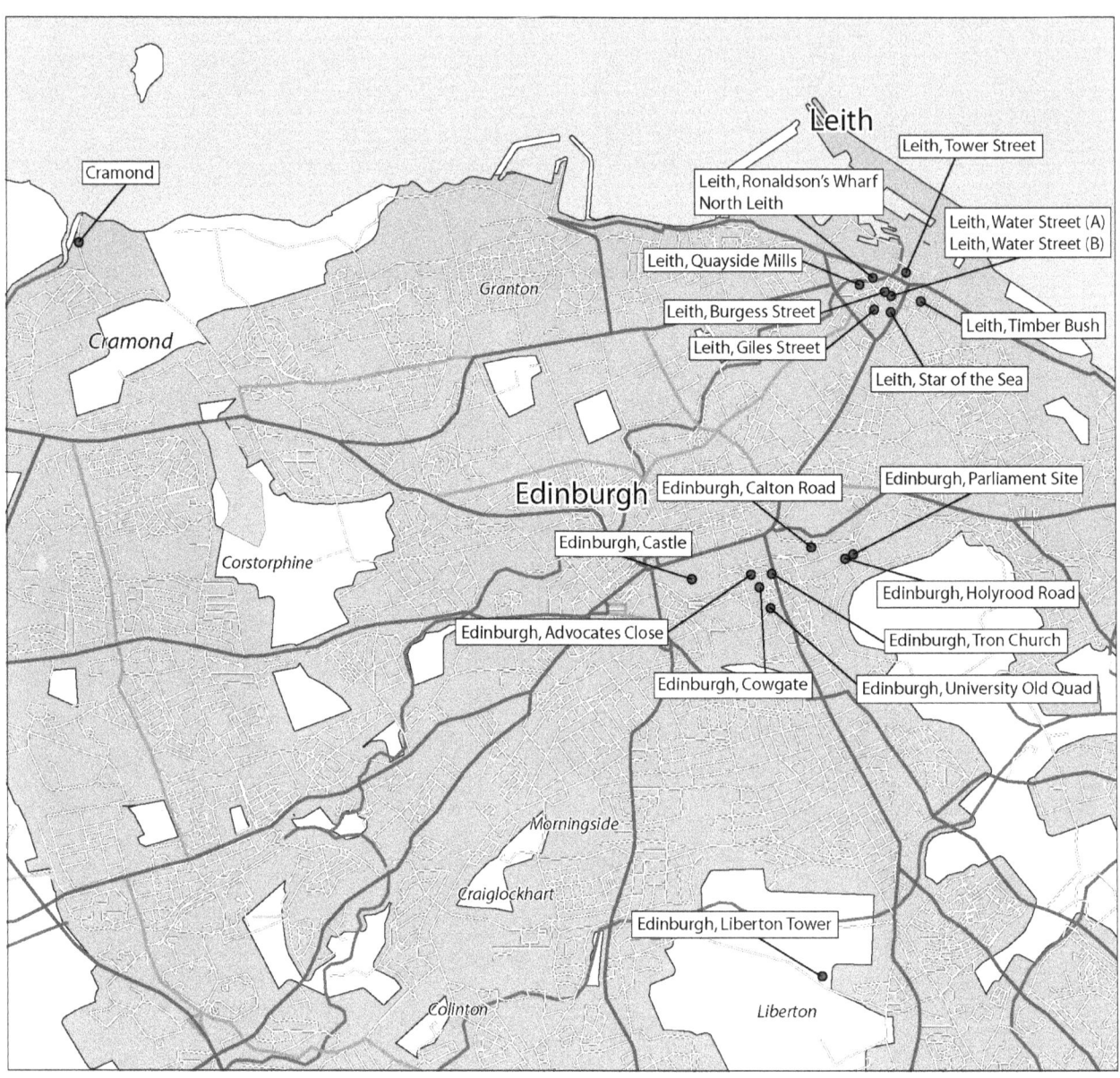

FIGURE 12 – EDINBURGH AND LEITH - THE DISTRIBUTION OF FRENCH POTTERY - ALL TYPES

one Patrick Folcart, who acted as seneschal of Saintonge for Charles of France from 1468 to 1472 and then for Louis XI in 1472-3 (Contamine 1992, 21).

Subsequent to the landing of a French force of 2500 men at Dumbarton on the 31 May 1545 and their removal in July 1560, we know, from the documents, where variations of troop numbers were mustered and stationed and also where places were fortified. Among these, and where one may be expected to find French material, are Roslin Muir, Haddington, Anguston, Perth, Kinghorn, Edinburgh, Dunbar, Montrose, (Blackness) Eyemouth and importantly Dumbarton (Figure 11). After the accession of Henry II on March 1547, French investment and commitment to Scotland was greater than at any previous time, while at least some of this movement in troops and provisions was through Dieppe (Bonner 1992, 31- 46).

1650s and 17th century sites have produced late Saintonge earthenware in Scotland, with fifteen find spots for Type I chafing dishes (Figure 4). This however is in sharp contrast to the distribution of 16th century ceramics such as Beauvais and Martincamp, which have now been recovered from seventy two Scottish sites and in some cases, in significant quantities (Figure 6). This may at least owe something to the Scottish community which by this time was residing in Dieppe, or perhaps it was just the sheer high quality of the white earthenware now being produced in the area around Beauvais. Whatever the reason, the pottery from the Saintonge seems to have lost its dominance in the Scottish market for imported ceramics.

As I have stated previously, it is possible that some of the changes and anomalies seen reflected in the ceramic record could be explained by examining relevant social documentation. For example, according to early Scottish

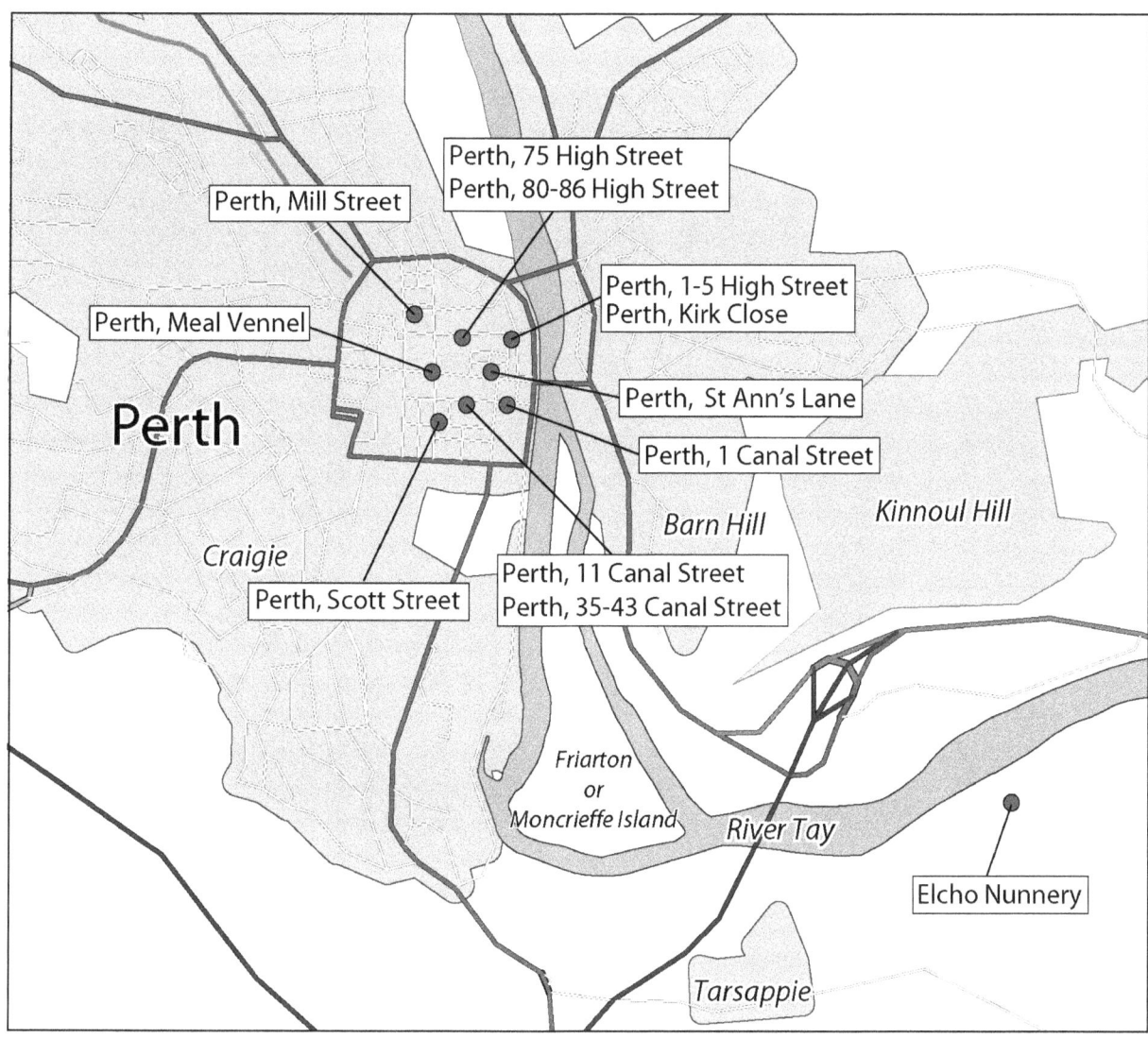

FIGURE 13 – PERTH - THE DISTRIBUTION OF FRENCH POTTERY - ALL TYPES

recipes it was traditional to begin the day in the kitchen by making a basic stock, a practice also firmly rooted in French cuisine. This practice probably developed from the ties between Scotland and France which went back to the 13th century and which are reflected in words such as 'gigot' a leg of mutton and 'ashet' a large meat plate, which have been absorbed into the Scots language (Brown 1996, 12-3).

During the fifteen century there were other important links with France, for example the purchase of the superb, fifteenth century, Paris-made medieval mace of St Salvator's College St Andrews, commissioned and donated by Bishop James Kennedy (d 1465). There is no doubt that St Salvator's mace, along with the French silver casket given to Mary, Queen of Scots by her first husband King François II of France, and now the property of the Hamilton family, are the two principle examples of late French medieval goldsmiths' work surviving in Britain. Fairly recently writing on the mace, Godfrey Evans,suggests that it demonstrates the strength and continuity of the 'Auld Alliance' (1994, 197).

It was not however until the 16th century that contacts between Scotland and France, reached a peak. No longer was it just about anti-English political intrigue and French soldiers based in Scotland giving support to Scottish troops in skirmishes with the English. There were now other influences. Following her marriage to James V, in 1538, Mary of Guise-Lorraine brought a large entourage of masons, servants and courtiers to Scotland, with over 100 French individuals in her substantial household being paid directly from France. Francophilia became evident in entertainment and in the Scottish mode of dress, which copied their extravagant doublets, puffed-out breeches, frilly shirts, flat bonnets, high hats and perfumed gloves (McKean 2003, 14). It was reported that the Scottish king had learned expensive tastes in France, with the result that his household expenses reached new heights, 'more superfluous and voluptuous' than the nation could sustain (Donaldson 1965, 58). After the death of her husband, James V, the French Queen Regent began to play a major role in Scottish politics, presiding over a French administration for almost 20 years (Macdougall 2001, 6).

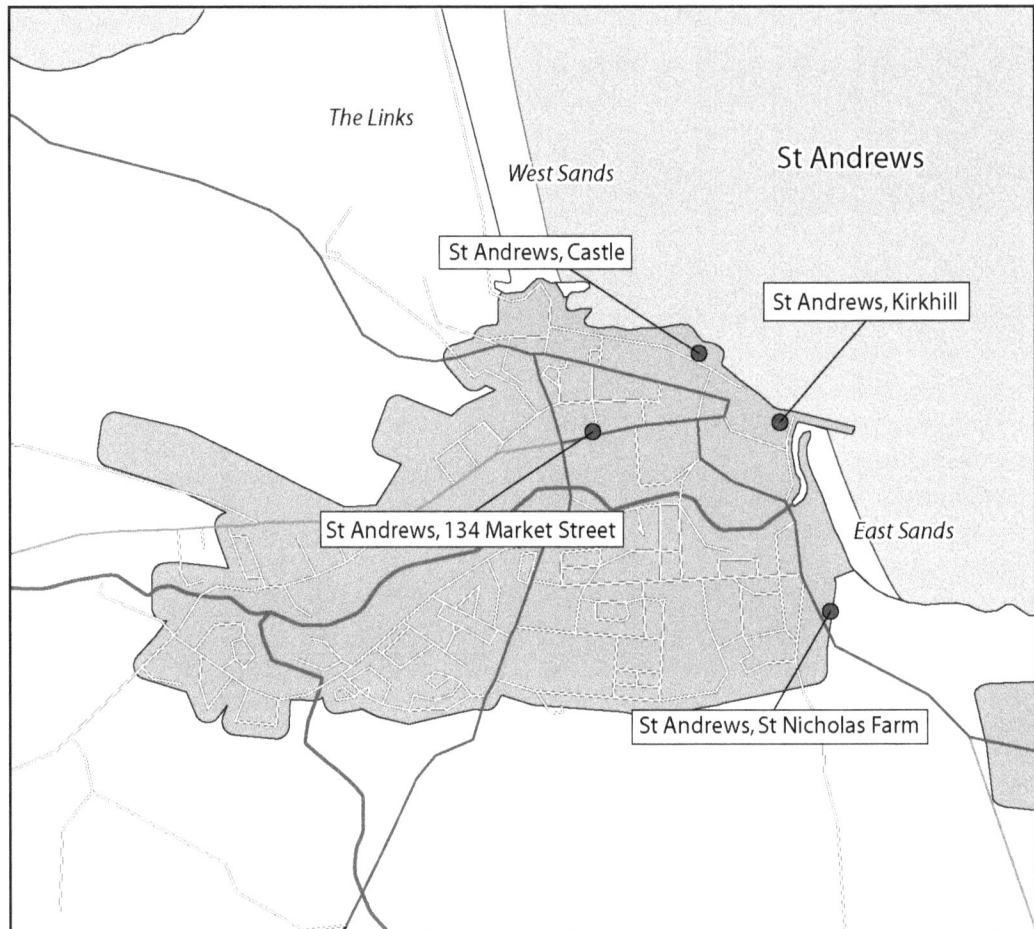

FIGURE 14 – ST ANDREWS - THE DISTRIBUTION OF FRENCH POTTERY - ALL TYPES

It was during this period that fashionable folk vied with one another in order to follow the Queen's lead, and to set the most lavish of tables in the French style. This new style of French entertaining intensified somewhat after 1561, with the return to Scotland of the young Queen Mary, who had been brought up at the French Court. Thereafter, everyone connected with the Scottish court hankered after a French chef and it was around this time that the French way of eating desserts in a separate room from the main fare was introduced (Warren 1979, 21). At first these new, more elaborate, trends were probably confined to Edinburgh and its environs, spreading only gradually to other parts of Scotland. This may in part be due to a slow acceptance by the conservative lairds, so consequently French customs did not become fashionable in many wealthy rural houses till the later 17th and early 18th centuries. By this time the Scottish dining room had become such a high status apartment that it invariably included a buffet for the display of plate or ceramic substitutes (Gow 1996, 129).

It is possible that it is in these cultural transformations, which dissipate somewhat after the unification of the Scottish and English parliaments in 1707, that we find the reason for the importation of the distinctive narrow necked Loire-type ceramic bottles which have been recovered from at least 26 sites (Figure 8). There are Scottish household accounts of that period which mention permanent supplies of, amongst other things, salad oil (Brown 1996, 10), and it is interesting that even today the French still call Loire-type narrow necked vessels 'oil bottles' (Hurst *et al.* 1986, 100). Assuming their purpose was to hold olive oil, it would be interesting to know if they were imported full or empty; if the latter, were they augmenting French taste, given the Scottish ceramic industry's reluctance to leave its medieval time warp. A late medieval date has been given to a couple of Loire–type jug shards from Scotland, and although olive oil is mentioned in England on a vellum roll, 'The Forme of Cury' allegedly written by the Master Chef of Richard II, published evidence from well stratified sites around Britain shows clearly that Loire-type long necked jugs, which come in different sizes, do not seem to occur in deposits of these dates.

As I have already noted, social changes were taking place in Scotland, and to a limited extent these are reflected in locally produced ceramics recovered from excavations. In the sixteenth and seventeenth centuries we do see a few new forms appearing in coarse earthenware. Mostly these are found along the east coast and are being copied from German Stoneware and Low Countries red earthenware, skillets, cauldrons and tripod pipkins. Shards from flanged dishes, a few with stamped decoration, have been recovered from Linlithgow Palace, Stirling Castle and a few other sites in the Forth littoral. However, evidence from the publication of the 17th and early 18th century pottery kiln site at Throsk (Caldwell and Dean 1992, 14-24) clearly demonstrates that what I wrote more than thirty years ago still holds good (Haggarty 1980, 38-9). This is that Scotland in the late medieval and post-medieval period had nothing to compare with the new ceramic technologies being developed and used in France, technologies which were also being imported into England, and which, it has been suggested, led to a number of new English fine ware industries developing (Barton 1992, 247). These new pottery types, which encompass the Tudor Green, Cistercian, Midland Black and Yellow ware industries, were firmly linked to the introduction of the earthenware cup and the large expansion in the pottery industry to meet the fundamental changes in English eating and drinking habits (Brears 1971, 13). This leads me to ask a question of Scottish cultural historians - why was this new ceramic culture, based on the cup, not embraced in Scotland? This lacuna is even more surprising when one considers that, between 1585 and 1590, 15,717 stone weight of lead was shipped for foreign destinations from the port of Leith, (Cressey 1995, 13), much of which was probably for the use of mainland Europe's fast developing pottery industries. Certainly this is the case by the second decade of the 18th century, as shown in the published account of Henry Kalmeter's *Travels in Scotland* 1719-1720 (Smout 1978, 29). 'In Rotterdam there is a company of merchants who by a contact with My Lord Hopetoun ship out all this lead ore at there own risk and expense from L[e]ith where it is ground up very fine, and used in the manufacture of all sorts of porcelain vessels and for that reason it is called potters ore'. Although hard paste porcelain was being produced by this time in Europe, initially at Meissen from 1708-9, the porcelain mentioned by Kalmeter would almost certainly have been Delft or Tin Glazed Earthenware, which is often referred to as Lame Purcelain in Scottish documents of the period (Forbes and Haggarty 2004, 4).

Conclusions

Because of the significant problems of trying to identify French whitewares, a major weakness in this paper stems from the author's inability, in a number of museums holding ceramic assemblages, to examine fabrics by use of a binocular microscope. In a few cases, it was almost imposable to lay material out and in one case the lighting was truly appalling. Personally I don't see any point in museums holding shard material if it is unavailable for academic study. Research time was also a limiting factor, as in a number of museums, little or no thought has been given to how to make material accessible, and in one case it took a whole day for a Scottish medievalist Derek Hall and myself with the help of staff to find and examine nine shards of pottery, despite the fact that they had previously been published, and we could give them site name, context and figure numbers.

To date nothing of any consequence has been published in Scotland on ceramic trade and there has also been little attempt to use the burgeoning archaeological data, both published and in the grey literature, to study the cultural and economic consequences of medieval or post-medieval imported ceramics. This paper, which is based primarily on archaeological evidence, suggests that at various times throughout the medieval and post medieval periods, French ceramics were arriving in Scotland but never in full-cargo quantities. During the later 13th and early 14th century this was mainly from the region of the Saintonge. Although the European-wide movement of 13th and 14th century Saintonge pottery has been the subject of much discussion (Clark 1983; Chapelot 1983; Deroeux and Dufournier 1991; Deroeux et al. 1994) I believe that what the Scottish evidence (Figure 3) suggests, is that it was nothing more than a minor trade for use in establishments of some status. Its distribution has also been linked to the wine trade through both primary and secondary contacts, but in Scotland it is just as likely to be mirroring the trade in fish, salt, grain, and the as yet only partly understood movement of other goods and people

The outcome of a discussion on early Saintonge wares at the 2004 Medieval Pottery conference, held at Winchester, was that 13th and 14th century Saintonge pottery in Britain was not a luxury commodity. This however is a generalisation that I would not necessarily subscribe too. What might have been the norm in the affluent South of England is unlikely to be true for much of Scotland. While it is obviously correct to suggest that because shards are recovered in high status sites they are not necessarily the property of the lord, in Scotland the number of shards recovered from rural contexts is negligible and they are also scarce in many of our major burghs.

Looking at the subject from a wider perspective, at present it is difficult to see any clear relationship between the excavated ceramic assemblages from Scotland's major east coast ports, with Aberdeen, Leith and Perth all seeming to show evidence for diversity in their trading contacts, especially in the 12th and early 13th centuries if not earlier. For example, the archaeological evidence from Perth would seem to suggest that it had a lot more contact with the South East of England. This would seem to reinforce Stevenson's view that the Thames valley area in particular may have been more important, in terms of Scottish trade, than the later percentages of English traffic and bullion exports of 1331-1333, would suggest (1996, 248-9).

It is also possible that it was the trade in fish and probably herring in particular from Scone, to the south east of England, which was instrumental in bringing what must have been fairly substantial amounts of 12th century or earlier shell and sand tempered ceramics to Perth. The importance of this trade is attested to in a later London statute of 1382, which proclaimed that due to its superior quality, 'no herring from Scone or from Jernemouth shall be taken out of the City of London for sale by retail,' (Riley

1886, 458). It may also have been herring, which led, in c.1378, to three Colchester merchants sailing with a small boat of merchandise to Scone near Perth (Cockerill and Woodford 1975). Unfortunately the two ceramic groups which illustrate best in pottery terms, the differences in trade between the ports of Perth and Leith, are 75 High Street Perth and Ronaldson's Wharf Leith, both as yet unpublished. That said the Perth High Street ceramic report is in preparation (Hall and Haggarty forthcoming 2013).

At present there is little archaeological evidence to support any serious importation or use of French pottery in Scotland in the later 14th and early 15th centuries, which, given the political, social, and economic backdrop of the period, may be no surprise. This is however in contrast to the 16th and 17th centuries, where there is good documentation for the transforming of the kitchen in European households, with the consequent changes in ceramic forms to facilitate this. A number of these new continental ceramic forms are fairly well represented in the Scottish archaeological record of the period, with chafing dishes, mainly but certainly not exclusively from the area of the Saintonge, small jugs probably from the area of the Loire, and most importantly a range of well-made vessels, dominated by large earthenware dishes and stoneware drinking bowls, from the region around Beauvais. Interestingly the two largest Scottish groups of this high quality 16th century Beauvais earthenware and stonewares both come from Franciscan friaries at Shuttle Street, Glasgow, established in 1470 (Haggarty and Hall 2013 forthcoming) and Jedburgh (Crowdy 2000, 32-42), which was returned to the Kerrs in 1564.

As yet there is no direct correlation between sites occupied by French troops in the 1540's and 1550's and the ceramics recovered. For example there was no French pottery amongst the ceramic assemblage from the limited excavations on the French phase of the Eyemouth forts.

I believe that in general my research supports what Dunning wrote in his seminal paper on the trade in medieval pottery around the North Sea: '… trade in pottery can be used to supplement the written sources, but can also be used independently for the 13th century and earlier, when the documentary evidence is scanty or unknown' (Dunning 1966, 35).

As a result of my work for this paper and other research that I have carried out on Scottish medieval and post-medieval pottery, it would seem to be an irrefutable fact, that in terms of pottery production, with the exception of the second half of the 12th and possibly early 13th century, Scotland's small scale indigenous pottery industries, perched out on the edge of Europe, were bound within a strongly conservative culture. Indeed there is some archaeological evidence (Haggarty 2004), which suggests that it outlasted, by 20 years or so, the introduction into central Scotland in c. 1750 of industrial potteries manufacturing tin glazed earthenware, white salt glazed stoneware and creamware.

In the future if we wish to get the best from our medieval and later ceramic heritage I would suggest that there is an urgent need to define our academic priorities. We must as a matter of the utmost priority set up a properly funded national ceramic fabric database and type series without which it will be almost impossible to move forward by asking the correct questions and sampling the relevant material.

It is my strongly held belief that if we tailor our ongoing chemical and geological programs, the results can reveal aspects of consumption, linked to the social and economic significance of our indigenous pottery industries. We must combine our results, and those of future scientific programmes, with analysis of distribution patterns: local, regional and national. It would for example be very useful to sample and chemically analyse, by ICP-MS, some of my French ceramic whiteware groups, linking the results into the research on French whiteware pottery recently carried out in England by Mike Hughes and the late Alan Vince, and at the same time utilise the results of the recently completed Scottish white ware project (Jones *et al.* 2006). It would also be useful in the light of their visual similarities to German Siegburg, to sample a number of the Beauvais stoneware shards.

When endeavouring to identify trade links within Scotland and examine our wider commercial networks, we must interact much more with economic historians. As a priority we must also intensify our collaborate with specialists working on other groups of archaeological material such as metal, wood, and glass, while cooperating with experts on food processing and diet etc. Indeed I would go as far as to suggest that unless we pursue this all-inclusive course we cannot hope to play a part, however small, in the elucidation of Europe's medieval ceramic traditions.

I also believe very strongly that the way in which we in Scotland presently excavate, process, retrieve data, publish and eventually store our ceramic heritage all has deficiencies and is in urgent need of review. In the main the responsibility for this lies with Historic Scotland, but there are also extremely important roles for the National Museums of Scotland, other museums holding shard collections, those producing archaeological briefs, and archaeological contractors. That said medieval and later ceramic specialists working in Scotland are not immune from blame and it is from us, through the Scottish branch of the Medieval Pottery Research Group, that the pressure for change must come.

Acknowledgments

My published survey of French pottery in Scotland (Haggarty 2006) could not have been undertaken without information and help from colleagues working on unpublished ceramic groups, and I would like to thank them all. I am also obliged to all the curators who granted me access to material held in their museums and to staff at AOC Archaeology, CFA, SUAT, GUARD and Headland Archaeology who gave of their time.

Many people in Historic Scotland, but especially Olwyn Owen, Patrick Ashmore and Noel Fojut deserve thanks for their long-term support of our research into Scotland's medieval and later ceramic industries. I am also grateful for the support of David Caldwell and George Dalgleish in the Department of Scotland and Europe, National Museums Scotland, who for a number of years have made available workrooms and meeting facilities at Customs House Leith, both to facilitate my ceramic research and support Historic Scotland's funded, Scottish ICP-MS redware project. Finally my sincere and heartfelt thanks go to Marjorie my understanding wife and to Derek Hall, who has been incredibly supportive and found time to visit a number of Scottish museums with me.

It is my intention to try and keep my catalogue on French ceramics in Scotland up to date and I intend to put it and all my other published CDs on Scottish pottery on line. I would therefore be obliged if all new imported medieval and later ceramic finds in Scotland were brought to my attention. I can be contacted at haggartyg@aol.com

George R. Haggarty asserts and gives notice of his right under section 77 of the Copyright Designs and Patent Act 1988 to be identified as the author of this paper on French pottery in Scotland.

Maps reproduced in this paper can be downloaded in colour from the National Museum of Scotland website at http://repository.nms.ac.uk/303/1/303_-_Ceramic_resource_disc_3_-_French_pottery_in_Scotland.pdf

Bibliography

Allan, J. P. and Barber, J. 1992. A seventeenth-century pottery group from Kitto Institute, Plymouth. In D. Gaimster and M. Redknap (eds), *Everyday and Exotic pottery from Europe c.650-1900. Studies in honour of John G Hurst*, 225-240. Oxford.

Barclay, K. 2001. *Scientific Analysis of Archaeological ceramics*. Oxford,

Barton, K. J. 1992. Ceramic changes in the Western European littoral at the end of the Middle Ages A personal view. In D. Gaimster and M. Redknap (eds), *Everyday and Exotic pottery from Europe c650-1900. Studies in honour of John G Hurst* (1992), 246-255. Oxford.

Bonner, E. A. 1992. Continuing the 'Auld Alliance' in the sixteenth century: Scots in France and French in Scotland. In G. G. Simpson (ed.) *The Scottish Soldier Abroad 1247-1967*, 31-46. Edinburgh.

Brown, C. 1966. *Scotland's Past in Action Feeding Scotland*. National Museums of Scotland (1966) Coventry.

Brears, P. C. D. 1971. *The English Country Potter, its History and Techniques*. Newton Abbot.

Caldwell, D. and Dean, V. 1993. The pottery industry at Throsk, Stirlingshire, in the seventeenth and early eighteenth century, *Post Medieval Archaeology* 26 (1993), 1-46.

C D S: Bain, J. 1881. *Calendar of Documents relating to Scotland*, Vol. 1, 1108-1272 Edinburgh (1881).

Chapelot, J. 1983. The Saintonge Pottery Industry in the later Middle Ages. In P. Davey and R. Hodges (eds) *Ceramics and Trade*, 49-53. Sheffield.

Chenery, S. R. N. Philips, E. and G. Haggarty 2003. An Evaluation of Geochemical Fingerprinting for Establishing the Province of Scottish Red Ware Pottery, *Medieval Ceramics* 25 (2004), 45-53.

Clark, H. 1983. The historical background to North Sea trade, c. 1200-1500. In P. Davey and R. Hodges (eds), *Ceramics and Trade* (1983), 49-53. Sheffield.

Claughton, P. *Production and economic impact: Northern Pennine (English) silver in the 12th century* www.exeter.ac.uk/-pfclaugh/contents.worn

Cockerill, C. and Woodward, D. 1975. *The Hythe: Port, Church and fisheries' Colchester Public Library*, E. COL 387.1

Cochran-Patrick, R. W. 1878. *Early Records Relating to Mining in Scotland*. Edinburgh.

Contamine, P. 1992. *Scottish Soldiers in France in the second half of the fifteenth century: mercenaries, immigrants or Frenchmen in the making*. In G. G. Simpson (ed.) *The Scottish Soldier Abroad 1247-1967*, 16-30. Edinburgh.

Cressey, M. 1995. *The Identification of Early Lead Mining: Environmental, Archaeological And Historical Perspectives From Islay, Inner Hebrides, Scotland*. Unpublished Ph.D. Thesis, Department of Archaeology, University of Edinburgh.

Crowdy, A. 2000. The Pottery. In P. Dixon, J. O'Sullivan, and I. Rogers, *Archaeological Excavations at Jedburgh Friary 1983-1992*, Edinburgh (= AOC Archaeology Group Monograph Ser, 5), 32-42.

Cruden, S. 1951. Glenluce Abbey finds recovered during excavations Part 1, *Transactions of Dumfriesshire Galloway Natural History and Antiquaries Society*, 3rd Series 29 (1950-1), 177-194.

Davey, P. and Hodges, R. 1983. Ceramic and Trade: a critique of the archaeological evidence. In P. Davey, R. Hodges (eds), *Ceramics and Trade*, (1983), 1-14. Sheffield.

Davidson, J and Grey, A. 1909. *The Scottish Staple at Veere*. London.

Deroeux, D. and Dufournier, D. 1991. Réflexions sur la diffusion de la céramique très décorée d'origine française en Europe du North-Quest XIIIè-XIVè siècles, *Archéologie Médiévale* 21 (1991), 167-77.

Deroeux, D. Dufournier, D. and Herteig, A. E. 1994. French Medieval Ceramics from The Bryggen Excavation in Bergen Norway. In *The Bryggen Papers Supplementary Series* No 5 (1994), 161-208. Bergen.

Ditchburn, D. 2001. *Scotland and Europe The Medieval Kingdom and its Contact with Christendom c1215-1545*, East Linton.

Donaldson, G. 1965. *Scotland James V- James VII The Edinburgh History of Scotland* Vol. 3. Edinburgh.

Duncan, A. A. M. 1975. *Scotland the making of the Kingdom* (=Edinburgh History of Scotland vol 1), Edinburgh.

Evans, G. 1994. The Mace of St Salvator's Collage. In J. Higgitt (ed.) Medieval Art and Architecture in the Diocese of St Andrews, *The British Archaeological Association Conference* Transactions (1986), 197-212. Leeds.

Fulford, M. G. and Huddleston, K. 1991. *The Current State of Romano-British Pottery Studies. English Heritage Occasional Paper* 1.

Gahan, A. McCutcheon, C. and Twohig, D. C. 1997. Medieval Pottery. In R. M. Cleary, M. F. Hurley, E. S. Twohig (eds.) *Skiddys Castle and Christ Church Cork Excavations 1974-77*, 108-129 (1997) Cork.

Gow, I. 1996. The Dining Room. In A. Carruthers (ed.) *The Scottish Home* (1996), 125-54, Edinburgh.

Haggarty, G. 1980. The Pottery. In G. Ewart, Excavations at Stirling Castle 1977-1978, *Post-Medieval Archaeology* 14 (1980), 36-46.

Haggarty, G. 1984. Observations on the ceramic material from Phase 1 Pits BY and AQ. In C. J. T. Tabraham, Excavation at Kelso Abbey, *Proceedings of the Society of Antiquaries of Scotland*, 114 (1984), 395-397.

Haggarty, G. 2004. *A report on the Post Medieval and later pottery from Wester Dalmeny Steading Dalmeny*. Produced for C.F.A. Archaeology Ltd.

Haggarty, G. and Forbes, S. 2004. A-Marked Porcelain Lind and Scotland, *Northern Ceramic Society Journal* 20, (2004), 1-10.

Haggarty, G. 2006. A gazetteer and summary of French pottery imported into Scotland *c*. 1150 to *c*. 1650 a ceramic contribution to Scotland's economic history. A CD Rom *in Tayside and Fife Archaeological Journal*, 12 (2006), 117-8 with a CD Rom

Haggarty, G. Hall, D. and Chenery, S. 2010. *Sourcing Scottish Redware* (=Medieval Pottery Research Group Occasional Paper 5.

Haggarty, G. and Hall, D. forthcoming 2013. The Medieval Pottery. In *Excavations at Greyfriars Friary, Shuttle St, Glasgow* http://www.sair.org.uk/

Hall, D. and Haggarty, G. forthcoming (2013), *Perth High Street; Ceramics metalwork, religious, and wooden objects*, (=Fascicule Series Vol 2).

Hodges, R. 1977. Some early medieval imported wares in the British Isles: an archaeological assessment of the French wine trade. In D. P. S. Peacock (ed.) *Pottery and early commerce characterization and trade in Roman and later ceramics* (1977), 239-255 London.

Hurst, J. G. 1977. Discussion of Pottery. In D. S. Neal, Excavations at the Palace of King's Langley, Hertfordshire 1974-6, *Medieval Archaeology* XXI (1977), 155-7.

Hurst, J. G. Neal, D. S. and van H. J. E. Beuningen 1986. Pottery produced and traded in north-west Europe 1350-1650, *Rotterdam Papers* V1 (1986) Rotterdam.

Hurst, J. G. 1988. Medieval Pottery imported into Ireland. In G. McNiocaill and P. F. Wallace (eds.), *Keimelia-Studies in Medieval Archaeology and History in memory of Tom Delaney* (1988), 229-53 Galway.

Ickowicz, P. 1993. Martincamp Ware: a problem of attribution, *Medieval Ceramics* 17, (1993) 51-60.

Jones, R. Will, D. Haggarty, G. and Hall, D. 2006. Sourcing Scottish White Gritty Ware, *Medieval Ceramics* 26-7 (2002-3), 45-83.

Laing, L. R. and Robertson, W. N. 1970. Notes on Scottish medieval pottery. *Proceeding of the Society of Antiquaries of Scotland* 102 (1969-70), 146 –54.

Laing, L. R. Laing, J. and Longley, D. 1998. The early Christian and later medieval ecclesiastical site at St Blanes, Kingarth, Bute, *Proceeding of the Society of Antiquaries of Scotland* 128 (1988), 551-565.

Lengendre, A. 1888. Documents pour Servir a l'History de la Cathédrale de Nantes, *Bulletin de la Société Archéologique de Nantes et du Département de la Loire-Inferieure*, XXVIII (1888), 35-72.

Lynch, A. 1996. Scottish trade in the seventeenth century. In P. G. B. McNeill and H. L. MacQueen (eds), *Atlas of Scottish History to 1707* (1966), 266-83, Edinburgh.

Lynch, M. and Strang, A. 1996. Overseas trade: the Middle Ages to the sixteenth century. In P. G. B. McNeill and H. L. MacQueen (eds) *Atlas of Scottish History to 1707* (1966), 250-56, Edinburgh.

Macdougall, N. 2001. *An Antidote to the English The Auld Alliance 1295-1560*. East Linton.

Marshall, D. N. 1964. Report on the excavations at Little Dunagoil, *Transactions of the Bulletin of the Natural History Society* 16 (1964), 1-69.

McEnaeaney, E. 1979. Waterford and New Ross trade Competition, c1300, *Decies* 12, 16-24 Waterford.

McKeen, C. 2003. Scotland versus France The Politics of Architecture in 16th Century Scotland, *History Scotland* 3 N. 5, (2003), 13-19.

McNamee, C. 1997. *The Wars of the Bruce*. East Linton.

Peacock, D. P. S. and Thomas, C. 1967. Class E imported post-Roman pottery: a suggested origin, *Cornish Archaeology* 6 (1967), 35-46.

Platt, C. and Coleman-Smith, R. 1975. *Excavations in Medieval Southampton 1953-1969*, Volume 2 The Finds (1975), Leicester.

Riley, H. T. 1868. *Memorials of London and London Life in the XIIIth, XIVth and XVth Centuries. Being A Serious of Extracts, Local, Social, and Political, from the Early Archives of the City of London A.D. 1276 -1419*. London.

R. R. S: *Regesta Regum Scottorum* vol 1.

Smout, T. C. 1978 (ed.). Journal of Henry Kalmater Travels in Scotland 1719-1720, *Scottish Industrial History. A Miscellany*, Scottish History Society (1978), 1-52.

Vince, A. 2002. The Use of Pottery to Chart Trade Routes in the North Sea and Baltic Sea Areas. In L. Bergen, N. Hybel and A. Landen (eds), *Cogs, Cargos, and Commerce: maritime Bulk Trade in Northern Europe, 1150-1400* (2002), 128-142. Toronto.

Warren, J .1997. *A Feast of Scotland*. London.

Wallace, P. 1983. North European pottery imported into Dublin 1200-1500. In P. Davey and R. Hodges (eds), *Ceramics and Trade, Appendix 2*, 225-30 Sheffield.

www.ingramcontent.com/pod-product-compliance
Lightning Source LLC
Chambersburg PA
CBHW041709290426
44108CB00027B/2904